QUEEN VICTORIA'S
Highland Journals

A group of gillies at Balmoral in 1858: standing, from left to right
Kennedy, Smith, Stewart, Brown, Farquharson, Morgan, Coutts;
lying down Robertson, Grant.

QUEEN VICTORIA'S
Highland Journals

Edited by

David Duff

Webb&Bower

EXETER, ENGLAND

Other books by David Duff include:

Biography:
HESSIAN TAPESTRY
MOTHER OF THE QUEEN
THE SHY PRINCESS
EDWARD OF KENT
PRINCESS LOUISE, DUCHESS OF ARGYLL
THE DUKE OF CAMBRIDGE (with E. M. Duff)
VICTORIA TRAVELS
ALBERT AND VICTORIA
WHISPER LOUISE
EUGENIE AND NAPOLEON III

Anthology:
PUNCH ON CHILDREN

Novels:
LOCH SPY
CASTLE FELL
TRAITORS' PASS

Essay:
MAN OF GOD — THE STORY OF A NORFOLK PARSON

First published 1980 by
Webb & Bower (Publishers) Limited,
9 Colleton Crescent, Exeter, Devon EX2 4BY

This paperback edition
first published 1983

Designed by Vic Giolitto

Parts of this book were originally published, in different
form, in the UK in 1968 by Frederick Muller Limited and in
the USA in 1969 by Taplinger Publishing Co., Inc., under
the title *Victoria in the Highlands*. Copyright © David Duff 1968

This new and revised edition copyright © David Duff/Webb & Bower 1980.

British Library Cataloguing in Publication Data

Victoria, *Queen of Great Britain*
    [Leaves from the journal of our life in the
    Highlands of Scotland, Selections]. Queen
    Victoria's Highland journals – New and rev. ed.
    1. Highlands of Scotland – Social life and
    customs
    I. Title   II. Queen Victoria's Highland
    journals   III. Duff, David
    941.1'5081'0924   DA880.H6

ISBN 0–906671–74–4

Filmset in Great Britain by Keyspools Ltd
Printed and bound in Hong Kong by
Mandarin Offset International Ltd

CONTENTS

INTRODUCTION

Queen Victoria kept a diary from 1832, when she was thirteen, until a few days before she died in January 1901. Her mother, the Duchess of Kent, gave her her first diary so that she might keep a record of a holiday in North Wales; and thereafter Victoria made daily entries until her life ended with the dawn of the twentieth century. The annual volumes weave an unrivalled tapestry of seventy vital years of British history, years of imperial splendour, years of dramatic change and progress in the fields of transportation, electric power, medicine and public welfare.

When the thirteen-year-old girl, then Princess Victoria of Kent, began describing the events in her daily life, King William IV was on the British throne. She wrote, then, as any girl of her age would write—of her lessons, of the people that she met, of adventures on her walks such as seeing a gypsy encampment, of a strange dog and of encounters with foreign sailors at the seaside. But because she was an only child and lonely, the detail of her entries was pronounced, for the diary was her "special friend". From the first she excelled in describing scenery and making interesting the little things of life.

In 1837 she became Queen and, understandably, the focus of the diary switched on to State affairs and meetings with ministers and the famous. Then love entered her life and her writings centred about Albert, the handsome Prince from Coburg in Germany whom she was to marry in 1840. Very soon the emphasis was on babies.

In 1842 she went to Scotland for the first time; it was to prove the most important journey of her life. She was enthralled with both the country and the people, and so, to her delight, was Albert. Now the length of her diary entries increased. No point, however small, was missed, and her enthusiasm for all things Scottish is as vivid to us today as it must have been to her.

Queen Victoria's visit to Scotland was historic because, excepting a short visit by King George IV in 1822, no reigning British monarch had travelled north of the Border since Charles I. Memories of "Bonnie Prince Charlie" were still strong in 1842, and the massacre of the Highlanders at the battle of Culloden on 16th April 1746 well remembered. The man responsible for that massacre was William Augustus, son of George II, by birth a member of the House of Hanover, as was Queen Victoria. Despite these and other difficulties which faced her, Victoria's love and understanding were to conquer the hearts of her Scottish people.

On this first visit she went to Edinburgh, Perth, Taymouth and Stirling. Everywhere she met friendliness and welcome and, as she sailed away on the morning of 15th September and watched "the fair shore of Scotland" slip below the horizon, she wrote in her diary that this had been a holiday which she would never forget.

Royal holidays were liable to interruption by the frequent arrival of babies, but Victoria and Albert were back in 1844, staying in the grandeur of Blair Atholl, and in 1847, when they toured the West Coast.

Now they felt a part of Scotland; and the winter evenings were spent in planning a home of their own there. Both the Queen and Prince Albert, young as they were, suffered from twinges of rheumatism. The royal doctor, Sir James Clark,

Queen Victoria at Balmoral:
a morning call.

a Scotsman, was consulted as to the best area to choose from the point of view of climate. He was emphatic that Deeside was the place. It was Lord Aberdeen, later to be Prime Minister, who suggested Balmoral Castle near Ballater, adding that an unexpired portion of a lease was available. It would, he said, suit them admirably. After studying sketches of the estate, Victoria and Albert took his word and the lease was transferred.

When the royal couple reached Deeside, in September 1848, it was a case of love at first sight. The Queen confided to her diary: "All seemed to breathe freedom and peace, and to make one forget the world and its sad turmoils." The tenants, staff and crofters took the pair to their hearts. As the royal party began its sad way back to England it passed under a triumphal arch on which were the words: "More beloved than ever, Haste ye back to your home of heather."

Again the winter evenings at Windsor and Osborne were spent in house planning and the floors covered with maps and drawings. The first priority of the Queen and her husband was to obtain the freehold of Balmoral so that they could build a larger house. Delightful as the old castle was, space was limited. Not only was it necessary to have accommodation for the royal household—equerries, ladies-in-waiting, secretaries, etc.—but also there must be guest rooms for visiting Ministers. Then there were the demands of the children to be considered. By 1849 Victoria and Albert had a family of six, and it was anticipated that more would arrive. The eldest, Victoria, known as "Vicky", was eight. Next came Albert

Edward, Prince of Wales, known as "Bertie", who was seven. There followed Alice, Alfred, Helena and baby Louise, who was only one. Thus room had to be found for their nurses, governesses and tutors. And so negotiations to buy the freehold of the Balmoral estate were put in hand without delay.

Prince Albert's plans were laid beyond Balmoral. He wished to include in his new retreat Abergeldie, the neighbouring estate to the east, and beyond that the 6,500 acres of Birkhall, at the head of Glen Muick. To the west, his eyes rested on the great forest of Ballochbuie, the property of the Farquharsons. Within a few weeks of his return to London, he was successful in purchasing Birkhall and partly successful in the case of Abergeldie: the Gordons, who had long been associated with the property, were unwilling to part with the freehold, but they granted a lease of forty years, with the option of further leases. The arrangement continues until this day. He failed in his negotiations to obtain the forest of Ballochbuie (the forest did not become royal property until 1878). But his chief worry was the protracted negotiations which continued over the obtaining of the freehold of Balmoral from the Fife Trustees. Prince Albert was ever a man in a hurry, as if he foresaw his early death, but he had to wait three and a half years before a price was agreed. On 22nd June 1852 the Balmoral estate passed into royal hands, 30,000 guineas being paid for the 17,400 acres.

Immediately on arrival on Deeside, in September of that year, the Queen and Prince Albert sent for architects and the work of rebuilding Balmoral Castle began. Together they decided on the new site, choosing a spot one hundred yards to the northwest of the original. This site not only had the advantage of affording finer views along the river but also allowed the existing building to be occupied without disturbance while the new castle was being built. Thereafter, each year there was the thrill of seeing how much progress had been made; in 1855 the splendid new structure—referred to by some as Prince Albert's *Schloss*— was first occupied. By the time the royal family reached Deeside the following year all traces of their former home had been cleared away and only a memorial stone gave evidence of where it had stood.

Yet, for all its new splendour, there remained one disadvantage. This was a lack of privacy. There was a right of way through the estate. From time beyond record the south Deeside road, running west from Abergeldie, had passed close by Balmoral, following there the line of the main drive of today, continuing through the Ballochbuie Forest and rejoining the north bank at the Brig of Dee at Invercauld. In former times few but local inhabitants used the track, but with the royal arrival the position changed dramatically and even in 1855 the Queen and Prince Albert had to appeal to be granted privacy while on holiday. Advantage was therefore taken of the Highway Act of 1835, which allowed of a highway being diverted if special conditions prevailed. It was considered that such conditions did apply, and in 1857 an iron bridge was erected. Travellers from the direction of Birkhall and Abergeldie were diverted across this, joining the north bank road by the spot where now stands the new Crathie Church.

Meantime there had been the interest of developing the estate and the gardens. Prince Albert had a model of the grounds made in sand, and on it he marked out new avenues, paths, plantations and banks, decided on the sites for gates and lodges, and laid out the formal gardens. These gardens were planted in the main with roses, so chosen that they would be in flower while the royal family was in residence. Old tracks and roads were repaired and new ones opened up. Waste land was drained and trenched, over a thousand acres being reclaimed and planted. New cottages were built for the outside staff, farm buildings were renewed and an ultramodern dairy was erected. The local people deeply appreciated the better living and working conditions.

Longer and longer became the visits to Deeside, and the interest of the Queen and Prince Albert was fully absorbed by their beloved new home and by family life. Three more children arrived—Arthur in 1850, Leopold in 1853 and Beatrice in 1857. That made nine in all. The Queen would dearly have liked to have made it ten, but her doctors told her that she had had enough. Then new love came to Balmoral. "Vicky", the eldest girl, became engaged to Prince Frederick William of Prussia while they rode together over the heather.

Seven autumn holidays the Queen enjoyed with her husband at the new Balmoral, every detail of their doings together being recorded in her diary. The highlights were the "Great Expeditions", when the royal family would set off on ponies to explore the countryside further afield. They would be away for several days at a time, sometimes covering nearly a hundred miles in a day, in the saddle and by carriage. For the Queen, staying in a simple inn in a remote village was a thrill indeed, for it gave her the sense of being an ordinary person, instead of for ever being the revered sovereign. There were encounters and chats with people who did not know who she and her husband were. There were strolls in the gloaming through deserted village streets. There were silent nights in sparsely furnished bedrooms which were in such violent contrast to those at Buckingham Palace and Windsor that the strangeness of it kept Victoria awake. She went again through every happening of the day, storing every minute in her memory—and, for eternity, in her diary. These were the happiest days of her life.

Always at her pony's head, on the "Great Expeditions" and on the daily rides around Balmoral, was the same man, John Brown. He was a local farmer's son and had been employed at the Castle when the Queen first went there in 1848. He was quiet, obliging and strong, and knew every track and ford for many a mile around. Prince Albert took a liking to the young man and was content to leave his wife in Brown's care when he went off shooting or on business. Soon he became what the Queen called her "particular gillie". He helped with the children, carrying them across mountain streams in spate and coping capably with every crisis that arose. He was invaluable on the royal family's "Expeditions", always knowing the right track to take, laying out the picnic lunches, serving at table at suppertime and even brushing the mud from the Queen's skirt. They were much alone together, Queen and gillie, and in those lonely Highland hours there was forged between them a link of loyalty and understanding which was to hold them close together during the tragic years of her early widowhood and to prove strong enough to resist the criticism of the world.

As Prince Albert approached forty, his health deteriorated. The fogs and damp of the English winters did not suit him, and he worked too hard and worried too much. He suffered from rheumatism, catarrh, migraine, cramp, insomnia, biliousness and upset liver. Victoria considered him to be somewhat of a hypochondriac, commenting that he was "as usual desponding as men really only are when unwell—not inclined himself ever to admit he is better". Yet it was noted

Queen Victoria and Prince Albert
enjoy the pastime of etching together.

that every year, when he reached Balmoral, his health improved, that he regained his strength and laughed again. But in 1861 the weather was inclement and the staff on Deeside noticed that he had no colour in his cheeks and that he tired easily. When plain-spoken John Brown said goodbye to the Queen at the end of the visit the gillie said that he hoped that the Family would all remain well through the winter and return safe to Scotland, and "above all, that you may have no deaths in the family". On 14th December 1861 Albert, Prince Consort, died of typhoid fever. Brown's words flashed back into the memory of Queen Victoria, and from then on she credited him with the gift of second sight.

Now, on visits to Balmoral in the deep gloom of her mourning, Queen Victoria saw the ghost of Prince Albert in every room, on every garden path and lawn and under the trees—all the work of his hands. She heard his laughter in the tumbling music of the river Dee and his voice echo in the mountains. In the evenings she would read, and reread, the pages of her diary which told of their life together in Scotland, for memories are the second happiness. Privileged guests to the Castle were allowed to share her reading and they found the pages so fresh and stimulating that they urged her to consider their publication.

On the plea of "a near and dear relative" she at last consented to the idea. Her mentor was Arthur Helps, Clerk of the Privy Council, an experienced and gifted writer. He worked with the Queen to convert the diary into book form—a task which was often difficult. In 1867 the first edition appeared, restricted to private circulation. It was entitled *Leaves from the Journal of our Life in the Highlands*, and was dedicated: "To the dear memory of him who made the life of the writer bright and happy, these simple records are lovingly and gratefully inscribed." The following year a public edition came from the presses and became an immediate bestseller.

The publication of *Leaves* changed the image of Balmoral. Firstly, it transformed it into a part of the British heritage, Queen Victoria having arranged that it should be the Scottish home of succeeding monarchs. Secondly, Deeside became a mecca for tourists, the journey by rail from England now being simple—the track reached Ballater in 1867. No longer could the Queen retire into seclusion and privacy as she had been able to do when her husband was alive. Sightseers now gathered to watch her attend Crathie Church and go out on her daily drives. Thirdly, *Leaves* drew attention to John Brown, by this time already a subject of countrywide speculation.

Loneliness was the cross which Queen Victoria carried in the years after Prince Albert's death. She had depended on him for everything and she was not a woman who gave her friendship easily. She had therefore come to rely for companionship on her two eldest daughters. Both were married, Vicky to Prince Frederick William of Prussia in 1858 and Alice to Prince Louis of Hesse and the Rhine in 1862. Both had homes in Germany, and families and duties there, and frequent visits to Britain were an inconvenience and unpopular in Germany. Both daughters noticed that the only occasions on which their mother appeared content were when John Brown was attending to her needs at Balmoral. It was therefore arranged, at the instigation of Alice, that the gillie should be in permanent attendance on the Queen. The plan worked and thereafter there were less frequent demands for the presence of Vicky and Alice in Britain. In December 1865 Brown was promoted to be an upper servant and the Queen's personal attendant. Whenever she drove out he was on the box of her carriage, and he was ever by her side, on call by night and by day.

Having spent his life on Deeside, Brown was parochially minded, Scotland forming the limits of his world. He did not approve of certain aspects of life in England and he upset many people there. Although he accompanied the Queen on her trips to the Continent, he was always ill-at-ease.

Balmoral was where the Queen and Brown were happiest and felt most at home. While rumours ran around England and the Continent about the relationship between the two, there were no problems of this nature on Deeside. When a French tourist attempted to discover the attitude towards John Brown around the Castle, he was told by a woman who worked in the dairy: "If ye want to hear cracks about her Majesty, ye maun gae somewhere else."

The Queen now sought a seclusion that even Balmoral could not provide, and in 1868 she built for herself a cottage at the western end of lonely Loch Muick. It was called the Glassalt Shiel—the lodge "of the grey burn"—but to her it was the "Widow's House". There was a shiel at the other end of the loch named Altnagiuthasach—the "Hut"—but she had spent too many happy days there with her husband and did not wish to be tortured by the memories. Yet, in selecting the Glassalt site, the Queen was once again but following her husband's thoughts, for this had been a favourite spot of his and he had often said that one day he would build there.

The Queen's first impression of the western shores of the loch, whose name she was told meant Darkness or Sorrow, had been one of fear mixed with excitement at the grandeur of the scene—the flooded Glassalt burn tumbling down from the White Mounth, the water of the Dhu Loch spilling into Muick, the sheer, 800-foot wall rising on the southern side, black waves whipped up by the wind compressed in the tunnel through the hills. But now, in her mourning, she had come to terms with the grandeur and she would retire to the Glassalt with Brown and a few servants who knew her well. For a few days she could forget that she was Queen.

She found happiness and relaxation when strolling on the strip of sand and pebbles which separates the bay by the shiel from the high hills behind. When she first went to the Glassalt, she had an overpowering feeling that she would find her husband there. Certain it is that, over a century later, one cannot visit the shiel by the lonely loch without being inwardly conscious of the presence of Queen Victoria, turning to see if her eyes are upon one.

Now that the railways made the journey more simple and comfortable, Queen Victoria visited Balmoral twice each year, making a short stay in May and June and a longer one from August to mid-November. Train journeys always excited her and details were arranged many weeks in advance, the man responsible being Mr J. J. Kanné, her Director of Continental Journeys. Seats were allocated to everyone travelling, both to staff and to guests invited to stay at the Castle.

The detailed instructions about the journey caused one guest considerable amusement—Empress Eugenie of the French. With her tongue in her cheek, she asked if ladies undressed and donned nightdresses. On being assured that this was the case, Eugenie replied that, if there was an accident, it would be somewhat embarrassing for a naked Empress to be found on the railway line.

Queen Victoria stipulated that the speed of her special train should be limited to thirty-five miles an hour by day and twenty-five by night. As she was a sufferer from the heat, a bucket of ice was placed under her bed on warm evenings.

Her royal progresses became the subject of considerable public interest, and it was noted that her train sometimes made a lengthy stop at Leamington. Strange rumours ran around as to the reason for this, one being that in the early hours she had a *rendezvous* there with an illegitimate royal relation, the identity of whom was kept secret—in fact, she had made arrangements with the buffet there that she be provided with a cup of tea! On one occasion, at a halt at a station in the north of England, the engine driver saw John Brown standing by the footplate. The gillie's message was terse: "The Queen says her carriage is shaking like the very divil."

The railways also brought about a change in the way of life at Balmoral. Without the company of Albert, and with her advancing years, the Queen no longer wished to ride out on long expeditions, picnicking and staying in lonely inns. But she had not lost her taste for excursions, and the train allowed her to move much further afield. She now saw Scotland from the Cheviot Hills in the south to Loch Maree in the northwest. And she accepted invitations to stay at the big houses, visiting the Duke of Argyll at Inveraray, the Duke of Roxburghe at Floors and the Duke of Sutherland at Dunrobin. On occasion she would stay alone in houses placed at her disposal by absent owners.

One such was Invertrossachs, the home of Lady Emily Macnaghten, overlooking Loch Vennachar; the reason was that the Queen wished to explore the Trossachs, that lovely glen extending from Loch Achray to Loch Katrine, made famous by Sir Walter Scott's *The Lady of the Lake* and *Rob Roy*. Lady Emily, who had arranged to go away during the royal visit, was in somewhat of a tizzy over the honour. Decorators and furnishers were busy about Invertrossachs for weeks before and maids scoured every room. A week before the arrival day Lady Emily received this letter from Kanné:

Victoria and Albert
entertained with Scottish songs in 1847.

I am now able to give you positive information about Her Majesty's intended visit to your country seat. The Queen will leave this (Balmoral) on Wednesday, September the first and reach Invertrossachs the same day ...
I subjoin an approximate list of her Majesty's Suite and Personnel.

	Her Majesty
5	Two Princesses (Louise and Beatrice)
	Lady Churchill
	Colonel Ponsonby
	Four Female Attendants,
6	viz. Dressers and Maid and
	one House, one Kitchen Maid
2	Two Cooks
3	Footmen
4	Stablemen
1	Her Majesty's personal Servant (Mr. Brown)
1	and myself.

Her Majesty will send one or two Carriages and four ponies. You will perhaps

The wooing of the Princess Royal, Princess Victoria,
by Crown Prince Frederick.

permit me to repeat to you Her Majesty's private observation to me. The Queen said: "She hoped you would not go to any unnecessary expense in regard to new Carpets or new furniture, etc."

It was somewhat late in the day to tell Lady Emily not to buy new carpets, for they already lay—in their untrampled glory—in every room and corridor.

As time passed Balmoral became a garden of remembrance. Cairns, memorials and plaques, marking events happy, sad or of contemporary interest, were sited in the grounds and on the skyline of the hills. Births, marriages and deaths, jubilees, victories and high-flood marks took their places as milestones through the years. Inscribed stones marked the graves of beloved dogs. All were dominated by William Theed's bronze statue of the Prince Consort, in Highland dress, his retriever at his feet, standing sentinel by the south bank road.

Queen Victoria was seven years older than John Brown and she thought that she would die before him, so she had a house built at Balmoral for him in his retirement. It was called Baile na Coille, which means "town of the wood". It was furnished, and in it were placed the many gifts and signed portraits that had come to him during his long period of royal service.

But the Queen's premonition was wrong, for it was Brown who died first. Early in 1883 he caught a chill while at Windsor. This was followed by erysipelas, a disease which causes extensive inflammation of the skin and is rarely fatal.

Nevertheless, on 27th March the seemingly indestructible Brown was dead. His coffin was sent to Balmoral and lay for the night on the dining table of Baile na Coille, the house which the Queen had built for him so that he might end his days in peace.

The Queen was prostrate with grief. She wrote: "The Queen is trying hard to occupy herself but she is utterly crushed and her life has again sustained one of those shocks like in '61 when every link has been shaken and torn and at every turn and every moment the loss of the strong arm ... is most cruelly missed."

On a spring day John Brown was buried in old Crathie churchyard, as the sun picked out the new green of the birch leaves and sparkled on the weeping patches of mountain snow. Sir Henry Ponsonby, the Queen's private secretary, wrote: "Wreaths from Princesses, Empresses, and Ladies in Waiting are lying on Brown's grave. He was the only person who could fight and make the Queen do what she did not wish ... he was undoubtedly a most excellent servant to her."

Queen Victoria's own message was inscribed in the stone: "Well done, good and faithful servant; thou hast been faithful over a few things, I will make thee ruler over many things." She strove to keep the memory of Brown fresh through the years ahead, as she had done in the case of her husband. She ordered a life-size statue of him to be executed by Boehm, and this was put up at Balmoral Castle, near the small wooden building where she had worked at her Despatch Boxes, Brown beside her.

She decided that she would pay further tribute to him by compiling for publication a second book founded on her Highland diary. To counteract her loneliness, she began work at once.

Sir Arthur Helps, who had given her editorial assistance with *Leaves*, was dead, and she now relied for guidance on a Scottish lady, Miss Macgregor. But this time she wrote the preface herself. By the end of the year the manuscript was ready. It was entitled *More Leaves from the Journal of a Life in the Highlands*, and was dedicated: "To my loyal Highlanders, and especially to the memory of my devoted Personal Attendant and faithful friend, John Brown, These records of my widowed life in Scotland are gratefully dedicated. Victoria R.I."

As Queen Victoria divided the memories of her life in Scotland into two volumes, the first dominated by Prince Albert, and the second by John Brown, so this book is presented in two Parts, covering the same periods as do the published volumes. Yet, when John Brown died, Queen Victoria had still eighteen years of life left to her, years that were integrally involved with Balmoral. Thus the happenings there in the years 1883–1900 are covered in a Conclusion.

PART ONE

The royal party on the ascent of Loch-na-Gar.

On Board the Royal George Yacht, Monday, August 29, 1842

AT FIVE O'CLOCK IN THE MORNING WE LEFT Windsor for the railroad, the Duchess of Norfolk,[1] Miss Matilda Paget,[2] General Wemyss,[3] Colonel Bouverie,[4] and Mr. Anson[5] following us. Lord Liverpool,[6] Lord Morton,[7] and Sir James Clark,[8] who also accompany us, had already gone on to Woolwich.

We reached London at a quarter to six, got into our carriages, and arrived at Woolwich before seven. Albert and I immediately stepped into our barge. There was a large crowd to see us embark. The Duke of Cambridge,[9] Lord Jersey,[10] Lord Haddington,[11] Lord Bloomfield,[12] and Sir George Cockburn[13] were present in full uniform. Sir George handed me into the barge. It was raining very hard when we got on board, and therefore we remained in our sitting-room.

I annex a list of our squadron:—
1. The ship *Pique*, 36 guns.
2. The sloop *Daphne*, 18 guns—(both of which join us at the Nore).
3. The steam-vessel *Salamander* (with the carriages on board).
4. The steam-vessel *Rhadamanthus* (Lord Liverpool and Lord Morton on board).
5. The steam-vessel *Monkey* Tender, which has towed us till nine o'clock (Mr. Anson and the equerries on board).
6. The steam-vessel *Shearwater*, which is now towing us (Sir James Clark on board).
7. The steam-vessel *Black Eagle* (which has the ladies on board, and which tows us in front of the *Shearwater*).
8. The steam-vessel *Lightning* (with the Jäger Benda, and our two dogs, "Eôs" and "Cairnach," on board) in front, which has gone to take our barge on board from the *Pique*.
9. The steam-vessel *Fearless* (for survey).

This composes our squadron, besides which the Trinity-House steamer goes with us, and, also, a packet. Innumerable little pleasure steamboats have been following us covered with people.

Tuesday, August 30

We heard, to our great distress, that we had only gone 58 miles since eight o'clock last night. How annoying and provoking this is! We remained on deck all day lying on sofas; the sea was very rough towards evening, and I was very ill. We reached Flamborough Head on the Yorkshire coast by half-past five.

Wednesday, August 31

At five o'clock in the morning we heard, to our great vexation, that we had only been going three knots an hour in the night, and were 50 miles from St. Abb's Head. We passed Coquet Island and Bramborough Castle on the Northumberland coast, which I was unfortunately unable to see; but from my cabin I saw Ferne Island, with Grace Darling's[14] lighthouse on it; also Rocky Islands and Holy Island. At half-past five I went on deck, and immediately lay down. We then came in sight of the Scotch coast, which is very beautiful, so dark, rocky, bold, and wild, totally unlike our coast. We passed St. Abb's Head at half-past six. Numbers of fishing-boats (in one of which was a piper playing) and steamers full of people came out to meet us, and on board of one large steamer they danced a reel to a band. It was a beautiful evening, calm, with a fine sunset, and the air so pure.

One cannot help noticing how much longer the days are here than they were in England. It was not really dark till past eight o'clock, and on Monday and Tuesday evening at Windsor it was nearly dark by half-past seven, quite so before eight. The men begged leave to dance, which they did to the sound of a violin played by a little sailor-boy; they also sang.

We remained on deck till twenty-five minutes to nine, and saw many bonfires on the Scotch coast—at Dunbar—Lord Haddington's place, Tyninghame, and at other points on the coast. We let off four rockets, and burned two blue lights. It is surprising to see the sailors climb on the bowsprit and up to the top of the masthead—this too at all times of the day and night. The man who carried the lantern to the main-top ran up with it in his mouth to the top. They are so handy and so well conducted.

We felt most thankful and happy that we were near our journey's end.

Thursday, September 1

At a quarter to one o'clock, we heard the anchor let down—a welcome sound. At seven we went on deck, where we breakfasted. Close on one side were Leith and the high hills towering over Edinburgh, which was in fog; and on the other side was to be seen the Isle of May (where it is said Macduff held out against Macbeth), the Bass Rock being behind us. At ten minutes past eight we arrived at Granton Pier where we were met by the Duke of Buccleuch,[15] Sir Robert Peel and others. They came on board to see us, and Sir Robert told us that the people were all in the highest good humour, though naturally a little disappointed at having waited for us yesterday. We then stepped over a gangway on to the pier, the people cheering and the Duke saying that he begged to be allowed to welcome us. Our ladies and gentlemen had landed before us, safe and well, and we two got into a barouche, the ladies and gentlemen following. The Duke, the equerries, and Mr. Anson rode.

There were, however, not nearly so many people in Edinburgh, though the crowd and crush were such that one was really continually in fear of accidents. More regularity and order would have been preserved had there not been some mistake on the part of the Provost about giving due notice of our approach. The impression Edinburgh has made upon us is very great; it is quite beautiful, totally unlike anything else I have seen; and what is even more, Albert, who has seen so much, says it is unlike anything *he* ever saw; it is so regular, everything built of massive stone, there is not a brick to be seen anywhere. The High Street, which is pretty steep, is very fine. Then the Castle, situated on that grand rock in the middle of the town, is most striking. On the other side the Calton Hill, with the National Monument, a building in the Grecian style; Nelson's Monument; Burns'

The *Royal George* at Leith in 1842

Monument; the Gaol; the National School, etc.; all magnificent buildings, and with Arthur's Seat in the background, overtopping the whole, form altogether a splendid spectacle. The enthusiasm was very great, and the people very friendly and kind. The Royal Archers Body Guard met us and walked with us the whole way through the town. It is composed entirely of noblemen and gentlemen, and they all walked close by the carriage; but were dreadfully pushed about. Amongst them were the Duke of Roxburgh and Lord Elcho on my side; and Sir J. Hope on Albert's side. Lord Elcho[16] (whom I did not know at the time) pointed out the various monuments and places to me as we came along. When we were out of the town, we went faster. Every cottage is built of stone, and so are all the walls that are used as fences.

The country and people have quite a different character from England and the English. The old women wear close caps, and all the children and girls are barefooted. I saw several handsome girls and children with long hair; indeed all the poor girls from sixteen and seventeen down to two or three years old, have loose flowing hair; a great deal of it red.

As we came along, we saw Craigmillar Castle, a ruin, where Mary, Queen of Scots, used to live. We reached Dalkeith at eleven; a large house, constructed of reddish stone, the greater part built by the Duchess of Monmouth, and the park is very fine and large. The house has three fronts, with the entrance on the left as you drive up. The Duchess of Buccleuch arrived directly after us, and we were shown

Victoria's arrival in Edinburgh, 1842.

up a very handsome staircase to our rooms, which are very comfortable. We both felt dreadfully tired and giddy.

We drove out together. The park is very extensive, with a beautiful view of Arthur's Seat and the Pentland Hills; and there is a pretty drive overhanging a deep valley. At eight we dined—a large party. Everybody was very kind and civil, and full of inquiries as to our voyage.

Dalkeith House, Friday, September 2

At breakfast I tasted the oatmeal porridge, which I think very good, and also some of the "Finnan haddies". We then walked out. The pleasure-grounds seem very extensive and beautiful, wild and hilly. We walked down along the stream (the river Esk), up a steep bank to a little cottage, and came home by the upper part of the walk. At four o'clock we drove out with the Duchess of Buccleuch and the Duchess of Norfolk—the Duke and equerries riding—the others in another carriage. We drove through Dalkeith, which was full of people, all running and cheering.

Albert says that many of the people look like Germans. The old women with that kind of cap which they call a "mutch", and the young girls and children with flowing hair, and many of them pretty, are very picturesque; you hardly see any women with bonnets.

Such a thick "Scotch mist" came on that we were obliged to drive home through the village of Lasswade, and through Lord Melville's Park, which is very fine.

The Palace of Holyrood-
house, Edinburgh, in the
late nineteenth century.

Inspecting Mons Meg at
Edinburgh Castle on
Victoria's first visit to
Scotland: this vast gun is
still to be seen today.

Edinburgh photographed
by Robert Murray from
the slopes of Castle Rock
in the late nineteenth
century.

Dalkeith Palace.

Saturday, September 3

At ten o'clock we set off—we two in the barouche—all the others following, for Edinburgh. We drove in under Arthur's Seat, where the crowd began to be very great, and here the Guard of Royal Archers met us; Lord Elcho walking near me, and the Duke of Roxburgh and Sir J. Hope on Albert's side. We passed by Holyrood Chapel, which is very old and full of interest, and Holyrood Palace,[17] a royal-looking old place. The procession moved through the Old Town up the High Street, which is a most extraordinary street from the immense height of the houses, most of them being eleven stories high, and different families living in each story. Every window was crammed full of people.

They showed us Knox's House, a curious old building, as is also the Regent Murray's House, which is in perfect preservation. In the Old Town the High Church, and St. Paul's in the New Town, are very fine buildings. At the barrier, the Provost presented us with the keys.

The girls of the Orphan Asylum, and the Trades in old costumes, were on a platform. Further on was the New Church, to which—strange to say, as the church is nearly finished—they were going to lay the foundation stone. We at length reached the Castle, to the top of which we walked.

The view from both batteries is splendid, like a panorama in extent. We saw from them Heriot's Hospital, a beautiful old building, founded, in the time of James, by a goldsmith and jeweller, whom Sir Walter Scott has made famous in his *Fortunes of Nigel*. After this, we got again into the carriages and proceeded in the same way as before, the pressure of the crowd being really quite alarming;[18] and both I and Albert were quite terrified for the Archers Guard, who had very hard work of it; but were of the greatest use. They all carry a bow in one hand, and have their arrows stuck through their belts.

Unfortunately, as soon as we were out of Edinburgh, it began to rain, and continued raining the whole afternoon without interruption. We reached Dalmeny, Lord Roseberry's,[19] at two o'clock. The park is beautiful, with the trees growing down to the sea. It commands a very fine view of the Forth, the Isle of May, the Bass Rock, and of Edinburgh; but the mist rendered it almost impossible to see anything. The grounds are very extensive, being hill and dale and wood. The house is quite modern: Lord Roseberry built it, and it is very pretty and comfortable. We lunched there. The Roseberrys were all civility and attention. We left them about half-past three, and proceeded home through Leith.

The view of Edinburgh from the road before you enter Leith is quite enchanting; it is, as Albert said, "fairy-like", and what you would only imagine as a

John Knox's House as it appeared early in this century.

Dalmeny, the seat of Lord Rosebery.

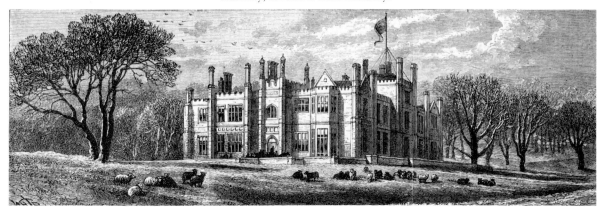

thing to dream of, or to see in a picture. There was that beautiful large town, all of stone (no mingled colours of brick to mar it), with the bold Castle on one side, and the Calton Hill on the other, with those high sharp hills of Arthur's Seat and Salisbury Crags towering above all, and making the finest, boldest background imaginable. Albert said he felt sure the Acropolis could not be finer; and I hear they sometimes call Edinburgh "the modern Athens". The Archers Guard met us again at Leith, which is not a pretty town.

The people were most enthusiastic, and the crowd very great. The Porters all mounted, with curious Scotch caps, and their horses decorated with flowers, had a very singular effect; but the fishwomen are the most striking-looking people, and are generally young and pretty women—very clean and very Dutch-looking, with their white caps and bright-coloured petticoats. They never marry out of their class.

At six we returned well tired.

Sunday, September 4

Received from Lady Lyttelton[20] good accounts of our little children. At twelve o'clock there were prayers in the house, read by Mr. Ramsay, who also preached.

At half-past four the Duchess drove me out in her own phaeton, with a very pretty pair of chestnut ponies, Albert riding with the Duke and Colonel Bouverie. We drove through parts of the park, through an old wood, and along the banks of the South Esk and the North Esk, which meet at a point from which there is such a beautiful view of the Pentland Hills. Then we drove, by a private road, to Newbattle, Lord Lothian's place.[21] The park is very fine, and the house seems large; we got out to look at a most magnificent beech-tree. The South Esk runs close before the house, by a richly wooded bank.

From thence we went to Dalhousie, Lord Dalhousie's.[22] The house is a real old Scotch castle, of reddish stone. We got out for a moment, and the Dalhousies showed us the drawing-room. From the window you see a beautiful wooded valley, and a peep of the distant hills.

Lord Dalhousie said there had been no British sovereign there since Henry IV.[23] We drove home by the same way that we came. The evening was—as the whole day had been—clear, bright, and frosty, and the Moorfoot Hills (another range) looked beautiful as we were returning. It was past seven when we got home.

Monday, September 5

I held a Drawing-room at Dalkeith to-day, in the gallery. The Ministers and Scotch Officers of State were in the room, and the Royal Archers were in attendance in the room and outside of it, like the Gentlemen at Arms in London. Before the Drawing-room I received three addresses—from the Lord Provost and Magistrates, from the Scotch Church, and from the Universities of St. Andrews, Glasgow, and Edinburgh—to which I read answers. Albert received his just after I did mine, and read his answers beautifully.

Tuesday, September 6

At nine o'clock we left Dalkeith as we came. It was a bright, clear, cold, frosty morning. As we drove along we saw the Pentlands, which looked beautiful, as did also Arthur's Seat, which we passed quite close by. The Salisbury Crags, too, are very high, bold, and sharp. Before this we saw Craigmillar. We passed through a back part of the town (which is most solidly built), close by Heriot's Hospital, and had a very fine view of the Castle.

I forgot to say that, when we visited the Castle, we saw the Regalia, which are very old and curious (they were lost for one hundred years); also the room in which James VI of Scotland and the First of England was born—such a very, very small room, with an old prayer written on the wall. We had a beautiful view of Edinburgh and the Forth. At Craigleith (only a half-way house, nine miles) we changed horses. The Duke rode with us all the way as Lord Lieutenant of the county, until we arrived at Dalmeny, where Lord Hopetoun[24] met us and rode with us. At eleven we reached the South Queensferry, where we got out of our carriage and embarked in a little steamer; the ladies and gentlemen and our carriages going in another. We went a little way up the Forth, to see Hopetoun House, Lord Hopetoun's, which is beautifully situated between Hopetoun and Dalmeny. We also saw Dundas Castle, belonging to Dundas of Dundas, and further on, beyond Hopetoun, Blackness Castle, famous in history. On the opposite side you see a square tower, close to the water, called Rosyth, where Oliver Cromwell's mother was said to have been born, and in the distance Dunfermline, where Robert Bruce is buried. We passed close by a very pretty island in the Forth, with an old castle on it, called Inchgarvie; and we could see the Forth winding beautifully, and had a distant glimpse of Edinburgh and its fine Castle. We landed safely on the other side at North Queensferry, and got into our carriages. Captain Wemyss, elder brother to General Wemyss, rode with us all the way beyond Cowdenbeath (eight miles). The first village we passed through on leaving the Queensferry, was Inverkeithing. We passed by Sir P. Durham's property.

We changed horses at Cowdenbeath. At a quarter-past one we entered Kinross-shire. Soon after, the country grew prettier, and the hills appeared again, partly wooded. We passed Loch Leven, and saw the castle on the lake from which poor Queen Mary escaped.[25] There the country is rather flat, and the hills are only on one side. We changed horses next at Kinross. Soon after this, the mountains, which are rather barren, began to appear. Then we passed the valley of Glen Farg; the hills are very high on each side, and completely wooded down to the bottom of the valley, where a small stream runs on one side of the road—it is really lovely.

On leaving this valley you come upon a beautiful view of Strathearn and Moncrieffe Hill. We were then in Perthshire. We changed horses next at the Bridge of Earn (twelve miles). At half-past three we reached Dupplin, Lord Kinnoull's.[26] All the time the views of the hills, and dales, and streams were lovely. The last part of the road very bad travelling, up and down hill. Dupplin is a very fine modern house with a very pretty view of the hills on one side, and a small waterfall close in front of the house. A battalion of the 42nd Highlanders was drawn up before the house, and the men looked very handsome in their kilts. We each received an address from the nobility and gentry of the county, read by Lord Kinnoull; and from the Provost and Magistrates of Perth. We then lunched. The Willoughbys,

The interior of the royal railway carriage which Victoria
travelled in.

Kinnairds, Ruthvens, and Lord Mansfield,[27] and one of his sisters, with others, were there. After luncheon, we walked a little way in the grounds, and then at five o'clock we set off again. We very soon came upon Perth, the situation of which is quite lovely; it is on the Tay, with wooded hills skirting it entirely on one side, and hills are seen again in the distance, the river winding beautifully.

Albert was charmed, and said it put him in mind of the situation of Basle. The town itself (which is very pretty) was immensely crowded, and the people very enthusiastic; triumphal arches had been erected in various places. The Provost[28] presented me with the keys, and Albert with the freedom of the city. Two miles beyond is Scone (Lord Mansfield's), a fine-looking house of reddish stone.

Lord Mansfield and the Dowager Lady Mansfield received us at the door, and took us to our rooms, which were very nice.

Wednesday, September 7

We walked out, and saw the mound on which the ancient Scotch kings were always crowned; also the old arch with James VI's arms, and the old cross, which is very interesting.

Before our windows stands a sycamore-tree planted by James VI. A curious old book was brought to us from Perth, in which the last signatures are those of James I (of England) and of Charles I, and we were asked to write our names in it, and we did so. Lord Mansfield told me yesterday that there were some people in the town who wore the identical dresses that had been worn in Charles I's time. At eleven o'clock we set off as before. We drove through part of Perth, and had a very fine view of Scone. A few miles on, we passed the field of battle of Luncarty, where tradition says the Danes were beaten by Lord Erroll's ancestor. We also passed Lord Lynedoch's property. We then changed horses at the "New Inn" at Auchtergaven. The Grampians came now distinctly into view; they are indeed a grand range of mountains.

To the left we saw Tullybelton, where it is said the Druids used to sacrifice to Bel; there are a few trees on the top of the mountain.

To the left, but more immediately before us, we saw Birnam, where once stood Birnam Wood, so renowned in *Macbeth*. We passed a pretty shooting place of Sir W. Stewart's, called Rohallion, nearly at the foot of Birnam. To the right we saw the Stormont and Strathtay. Albert said, as we came along between the mountains, that to the right, where they were wooded, it was very like Thüringen, and on the left more like Switzerland. Murthly, to the right, which belongs to Sir W. Stewart, is in a very fine situation, with the Tay winding under the hill. This lovely scenery continues all along to Dunkeld. Lord Mansfield rode with us the whole way.

Just outside Dunkeld, before a triumphal arch, Lord Glenlyon's Highlanders, with halberds, met us, and formed our guard—a piper playing before us. Dunkeld is beautifully situated, in a narrow valley, on the banks of the Tay. We drove in to where the Highlanders were all drawn up, in the midst of their encampments, and where a tent was prepared for us to lunch in. Poor Lord Glenlyon[29] received us; but he had suddenly become totally blind, which is dreadful for him. He was led about by his wife; it was very melancholy. His blindness was caused by over-fatigue. The Dowager Lady Glenlyon, the Mansfields, Kinnoulls, Buccleuchs, and many others were there. We walked down the ranks of the Highlanders, and then partook of luncheon, the piper played, and one of the Highlanders danced the "sword dance". (Two swords crossed are laid upon the ground, and the dancer has to dance across them without touching them.) Some of the others danced a reel.

At a quarter to four we left Dunkeld as we came, the Highland Guard marching with us till we reached the outside of the town. The drive was quite beautiful all the way to Taymouth. The two highest hills of the range on each side are (to the right, as you go on after leaving Dunkeld) Craig-y-Barns and (to the left, immediately

Scone Palace as it was in the late nineteenth century.

[27]

A nineteenth-century view of Loch Tay, showing Taymouth Castle.

above Dunkeld) Craigvinean. The Tay winds along beautifully, and the hills are richly wooded. We changed horses first at Balanagard (nine miles), to which place Captain Murray, Lord Glenlyon's brother, rode with us. The hills grew higher and higher, and Albert said it was very Swiss-looking in some parts. High ribbed mountains appeared in the distance, higher than any we have yet seen. This was near Aberfeldy (nine miles), which is charmingly situated and the mountains very lofty. At a quarter to six we reached Taymouth. At the gate a guard of Highlanders, Lord Breadalbane's men, met us. Taymouth lies in a valley surrounded by very high, wooded hills; it is most beautiful. The house is a kind of castle, built of granite. The *coup-d'œil* was indescribable. There were a number of Lord Breadalbane's Highlanders, all in the Campbell tartan, drawn up in front of the house, with Lord Breadalbane[30] himself in a Highland dress at their head, a few of Sir Neil Menzies'[31] men (in the Menzies red and white tartan), a number of pipers playing, and a company of the 92nd Highlanders, also in kilts. The firing of the guns, the cheering of the great crowd, the picturesqueness of the dresses, the beauty of the surrounding country, with its rich background of wooded hills, altogether formed one of the finest scenes imaginable. It seemed as if a great chieftain in olden feudal times was receiving his sovereign. It was princely and romantic. Lord and Lady Breadalbane took us upstairs, the hall and stairs being lined with Highlanders.

The Gothic staircase is of stone and very fine; the whole of the house is newly and exquisitely furnished. The drawing-room, especially, is splendid. Thence you go into a passage and a library, which adjoins our private apartments. They showed us two sets of apartments, and we chose those which are on the right hand of the corridor or ante-room to the library. At eight we dined. Staying in the house, besides ourselves, are the Buccleuchs and the two Ministers, the Duchess of

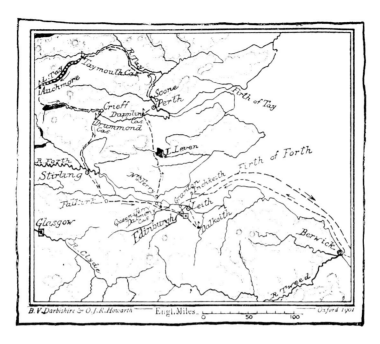

A map of the Queen's first tour of Scotland.

Sutherland and Lady Elizabeth Leveson Gower,[32] the Abercorns, Roxburghs, Kinnoulls, Lord Lauderdale, Sir Anthony Maitland, Lord Lorne,[33] the Fox Maules, Belhavens, Mr. and Mrs. William Russell, Sir J. and Lady Elizabeth, and the Misses Pringle, and two Messrs. Baillie, brothers of Lady Breadalbane. The dining-room is a fine room in Gothic style, and has never been dined in till this day. Our apartments also are inhabited for the first time.[34] After dinner the grounds were most splendidly illuminated,—a whole chain of lamps along the railings, and on the ground was written in lamps, "Welcome Victoria—Albert."

A small fort, which is up in the wood, was illuminated, and bonfires were burning on the tops of the hills. I never saw anything so fairy-like. There were some pretty fireworks, and the whole ended by the Highlanders dancing reels, which they do to perfection, to the sound of the pipes, by torchlight, in front of the house. It had a wild and very gay effect.

Taymouth,
Thursday, September 8

Albert went off at half-past nine o'clock to shoot with Lord Breadalbane. I walked out with the Duchess of Norfolk along a path overlooking the Tay, which is very clear, and ripples and foams along over the stones, the high mountains forming such a rich background. We got up to the dairy, which is a kind of Swiss cottage, built of quartz, very clean and nice.[35] From the top of it there is a very pretty view of Loch Tay.

We returned home by the way we came. It rained the whole time, and very hard for a little while. Albert returned at half-past three. He had had excellent sport, and the trophies of it were spread out before the house—nineteen roe-deer, several hares and pheasants, and three brace of grouse; there was also a capercailzie that had been wounded, and which I saw afterwards, a magnificent large bird.

Albert had been near Aberfeldy, and had to shoot and walk the whole way back, Lord Breadalbane himself beating, and three hundred Highlanders out. We went out at five, with Lady Breadalbane and the Duchess of Sutherland; we saw part of Loch Tay, and drove along the banks of the Tay under fine trees, and saw Lord Breadalbane's American buffaloes.

Saturday, September 10

We walked to the dairy and back—a fine bright morning; the weather the two preceding days had been very unfortunate. I drove a little way with Lady Breadalbane, the others walking, and then got out, and each of us planted two trees, a fir and an oak. We got in again, and drove with the whole party down to the lake, where we embarked. Lady Breadalbane, the Duchess of Sutherland and Lady Elizabeth went by land, but all the others went in boats. With us were Lord Breadalbane and the Duchess of Norfolk and Duchess of Buccleuch; and two pipers sat on the bow and played very often. I have since been reading in *The Lady of the Lake*, and this passage reminds me of our voyage:

> See the proud pipers on the bow,
> And mark the gaudy streamers flow
> From their loud chanters down, and sweep
> The furrow'd bosom of the deep,
> As, rushing through the lake amain,
> They plied the ancient Highland strain.

Our row of sixteen miles up Loch Tay to Auchmore, a cottage of Lord Breadalbane's, near the end of the lake, was the prettiest thing imaginable. We saw the splendid scenery to such great advantage on both sides: Ben Lawers, with small waterfalls descending its sides, amid other high mountains wooded here and there; with Kenmore in the distance; the view, looking back, as the loch winds, was most beautiful. The boatmen sang two Gaelic boat-songs, very wild and singular; the language so guttural and yet so soft. Captain McDougall, who steered, and who is the head of the McDougalls, showed us the real "brooch of Lorn", which was taken by his ancestor from Robert Bruce in a battle. The situation of Auchmore is exquisite; the trees growing so beautifully down from the top of the mountains, quite into the water, and the mountains all round, make it an enchanting spot. We landed and lunched in the cottage, which is a very nice little place. The day was very fine; the Highlanders were there again. We left Auchmore at twenty minutes past three, having arrived there at a quarter before three. The kindness and attention to us of Lord and of Lady Breadalbane (who is very delicate) were unbounded. We passed Killin, where there is a mountain stream running over large stones, and forming waterfalls.

Killin in the late nineteenth century.

The country we came to now was very wild, beginning at Glen Dochart, through which the Dochart flows; nothing but moors and very high rocky mountains. We came to a small lake called, I think, Laragilly,[36] amidst the wildest and finest scenery we had yet seen. Glen Ogle, which is a sort of long pass, putting one in mind of the prints of the Kyber Pass, the road going for some way down hill and up hill, through these very high mountains, and the escort in front looking like mere specks from the great height. We also saw Ben Voirlich. At Loch Earn Head we changed horses. Lord Breadalbane rode with us the whole way up to this point, and then he put his Factor (in Highland dress) up behind our carriage. It came on to rain, and rained almost the whole of the rest of the time. We passed along Loch Earn, which is a very beautiful long lake skirted by high mountains; but is not so long or so large as Loch Tay. Just as we turned and went by St. Fillans, the view of the lake was very fine. There is a large detached rock with rich verdure on it, which is very striking.

We also saw Glenartney, the mountain on which Lord Willoughby[37] has his deer forest. We passed by Sir D. Dundas's place, Dunira, before we changed horses at Comrie, for the last time, and then by Mr. Williamson's, and by Ochtertyre, Sir W. Keith Murray's.

Triumphal arches were erected in many places. We passed through Crieff, and a little past seven reached Drummond Castle, by a very steep ascent. Lord Willoughby received us at the door, and showed us to our rooms, which are small but nice.

Drummond Castle, Sunday, September 11

We walked in the garden, which is really very fine, with terraces, like an old French garden. Part of the old castle and the archway remains.

At twelve o'clock we had prayers in the drawing-room, which were read by a young clergyman, who preached a good sermon.

It poured the whole afternoon, and, after writing, I read to Albert the three first cantos of *The Lay of the Last Minstrel*, which delighted us both; and then we looked over some curious, fine old prints by Ridinger.

Drummond Castle.

Monday, September 12

Albert got up at five o'clock to go out deer-stalking. I walked out with the Duchess of Norfolk.

All the Highlanders (Lord Willoughby's people, 110 in number), were drawn up in the court, young Mr. Willoughby and Major Drummond being at their head, and I walked round with Lady Willoughby. All the arms they wore belonged to Lord Willoughby; and there was one double-hilted sword, which had been at the battle of Bannockburn. I hear that at Dunkeld there were nearly 900 Highlanders, 500 being Athole men; and, altogether with the various Highlanders who were on guard, there were 1,000 men.

At length—a little before three—to my joy, Albert returned, dreadfully sunburnt, and a good deal tired; he had shot a stag. He said the exertion and difficulty were very great. He had changed his dress at a small farm-house.

opposite above: Arrival of the royal yacht, the *Royal George*, off Granton Pier, Leith, bearing Victoria and Albert; watercolour by W. Joy, 1842.

opposite below: An encounter on the road by Loch Laggan; oil painting by Sir Edwin Landseer, 1847.

Balmoral Castle; oil painting by J. Giles, 1848.

Albert, Prince Consort, in hunting gear on the
Scottish moors.

Glenartney is ten miles from Drummond Castle; he drove there. Campbell of Monzie (pronounced "Monie"), a young gentleman who has a place near here, went with him and was, Albert said, extremely active. To give some description of this curious sport, I will copy an extract from a letter Albert has written to Charles,[38] giving a short account of it:—

> Without doubt deer-stalking is one of the most fatiguing, but it is also one of the most interesting of pursuits. There is not a tree, or a bush behind which you can hide yourself. . . . One has, therefore, to be constantly on the alert in order to circumvent them; and to keep under the hill out of their wind, crawling on hands and knees, and dressed entirely in grey.

Tuesday, September 13

We had to start early, and therefore got up soon after seven o'clock; breakfast before eight. At nine we set off. The morning was very foggy and hazy. We passed near Lord Strathallan's[39] place and stopped for a moment where old Lady Strathallan was seated. Lord Willoughby rode with us the whole way till we arrived here. Soon after this we came to a very extraordinary Roman encampment at Ardoch, called the "Lindrum". Albert got out; but I remained in the carriage, and Major Moray showed it to him. They say it is one of the most perfect in existence.

We changed horses at Greenloaning, and passed through Dunblane. At twelve o'clock we reached Stirling, where the crowd was quite fearful, and the streets so narrow, that it was most alarming; and order was not very well kept. Up to the Castle, the road or street is dreadfully steep; we had a foot procession before us the whole way, and the heat was intense. The situation of the Castle is extremely grand; but I prefer that of Edinburgh Castle. Old Sir Archibald Christie explained

Stirling Castle.

everything to us very well. We were shown the room where James II killed Douglas,[40] and the window out of which he was thrown. The ceiling is most curious. A skeleton was found in the garden only twenty-five years ago, and there appears to be little doubt it was Douglas's. From the terrace the view is very extensive; but it was so thick and hazy, that we could not see the Highland hills well. Sir A. Christie showed us the field of the battle of Bannockburn; and the "Knoll", close under the walls of the Castle, from which the ladies used to watch the tournaments; all the embankments yet remain. We also saw Knox's pulpit.

We next passed through Falkirk, and changed horses at Callander Park, Mr. Forbes's; both he and Sir Michael Bruce having ridden with us from beyond Stirling. We passed Lord Zetland[41] on the road, and shortly before reaching Linlithgow, where we changed horses,[42] Lord Hopetoun met us. Unfortunately, we did not see the Palace, which, I am told, is well worth seeing. The Duke of Buccleuch met us soon after this, and, accompanied by a large number of his tenants, rode with us on horseback to Dalkeith. We changed horses at Kirkliston, and lastly at the outskirts of Edinburgh. There were a good many people assembled at Edinburgh; but we were unable to stop. We reached Dalkeith at half-past five.

The journey was sixty-five miles, and I was very tired, and felt most happy that we had safely arrived here.

Dalkeith, Wednesday, September 14

This is our last day in Scotland[43]; it is really a delightful country, and I am very sorry to leave it. We walked out and saw the fine greenhouse the Duke has built, all in stone, in the Renaissance style. At half-past three o'clock we went out with the Duchess of Buccleuch, only Colonel Bouverie riding with us. We drove through Melville Park, and through one of the little collier villages (of which there are a great many about Dalkeith), called Loanhead, to Rosslyn.

We got out at the chapel, which is in excellent preservation; it was built in the fifteenth century, and the architecture is exceedingly rich. It is the burying place of the family of Lord Rosslyn, who keeps it in repair. Twenty Barons of Rosslyn are buried there in armour. A great crowd had collected about the chapel when we came out of it.

From Rosslyn we then drove to Hawthornden, which is also beautifully situated at a great height above the river. To our great surprise we found an immense crowd of people there, who must have run over from Rosslyn to meet us.

We got out, and went down into some of the very curious caves in the solid rock, where Sir Alexander Ramsay[44] and his brave followers concealed themselves, and held out for so long a time. The Duchess told us there were many of these caves all along the river to Rosslyn.

We came home through Bonnyrigg, another collier village, and through Dalkeith.

Thursday, September 15

We breakfasted at half-past seven o'clock, and at eight we set off. The ladies and equerries had embarked earlier. The day was very bright and fine. The arrangements in Edinburgh, through which we had to pass, were extremely well managed, and excellent order was kept. We got out of the carriage on the pier, and went at once on board the *Trident*, a large steamboat belonging to the General Steam Navigation Company. We both thanked the Duke and Duchess for their extreme kindness, attention, and hospitality to us, which really were very great—indeed we had felt ourselves quite at home at Dalkeith.

As the fair shores of Scotland receded more and more from our view, we felt quite sad that this very pleasant and interesting tour was over; but we shall never forget it.

Monday, September 9, 1844

WE GOT UP AT A QUARTER TO SIX O'CLOCK. We breakfasted. Mama[45] came to take leave of us; Alice[46] and the baby[47] were brought in, poor little things, to wish us "good-by". Then good Bertie[48] came down to see us, and Vicky[49] appeared as "voyageuse", and was all impatience to go. At seven we set off with her for the railroad, Viscountess Canning[50] and Lady Caroline Cocks[51] in our carriage. A very wet morning. We got into the carriage again at Paddington, and proceeded to Woolwich, which we reached at nine. Vicky was safely put into the boat, and then carefully carried on deck of the yacht by Renwick, the sergeant-footman, whom we took with us in the boat on purpose. Lord Liverpool, Lord Aberdeen,[52] and Sir James Clark met us on board. Sir Robert Peel was to have gone with us, but could not, in consequence of his little girl being very ill.

Blair Athole,
Wednesday, September 11

At six o'clock we inquired and heard that we were in the port of Dundee. Albert saw our other gentlemen, who had had a very bad passage. Tuesday night they had a dreadful storm. Dundee is a very large place, and the port is large and open; the situation of the town is very fine, but the town itself is not so. The Provost and people had come on board, and wanted us to land later, but we got this satisfactorily arranged. At half-past eight we got into our barge with Vicky, and our ladies and gentlemen. The sea was bright and blue; the boat danced along beautifully. We had about a quarter of a mile to row.

A staircase, covered with red cloth, was arranged for us to land upon, and there were a great many people; but everything was so well managed that all crowding was avoided, and only the Magistrates were below the platform where the people were. Albert walked up the steps with me, I holding his arm and Vicky his hand, amid the loud cheers of the people, all the way to the carriage, our dear Vicky behaving like a grown-up person—not put out, nor frightened, nor nervous. We got into our postchaise, and at the same time Renwick took Vicky up in his arms and put her in the next carriage with her governess and nurse.

There was a great crowd in Dundee, but everything was very well managed, and there would have been no crowding at all, had not, as usual, about twenty people begun to run along with the carriage, and thus forced a number of others to follow. About three miles beyond Dundee we stopped at the gate of Lord Camperdown's place: here a triumphal arch had been erected, and Lady Camperdown and Lady Duncan and her little boy, with others, were all waiting to welcome us, and were very civil and kind. The little boy, beautifully dressed in the Highland dress, was carried to Vicky, and gave her a basket with fruit and flowers. I said to Albert I could hardly believe that our child was travelling with us—it put me so in mind of myself when I was the "little Princess." Albert observed that it was always said that parents lived their lives over again in their children, which is a very pleasant feeling.

The country from here to Cupar Angus is very well cultivated, and you see hills in the distance. The harvest is only now being got in, but is very good; and everything much greener than in England. Nothing could be quieter than our journey, and the scenery is so beautiful! It is very different from England: all the houses built of stone; the people so different,—sandy hair, high cheek-bones; children with long shaggy hair and bare legs and feet; little boys in kilts. Near Dunkeld, and also as you get more into the Highlands, there are prettier faces.

At King William Dock, Dundee.

The bridge at Dunkeld.

Those jackets which the girls wear are so pretty; all the men and women, as well as the children, look very healthy.

Cupar Angus is a small place—a village—fourteen miles from Dundee. There you enter Perthshire. We crossed the river Isla, which made me think of my poor little dog "Isla". For about five or six miles we went along a very pretty but rough cross-road, with the Grampians in the distance. We saw Birnam Wood and Sir W. Stewart's place in that fine valley on the opposite side of the river. All along such

Victoria and Albert view the Pass of Killiecrankie.

splendid scenery, and Albert enjoyed it so much—rejoicing in the beauties of nature, the sight of mountains, and the pure air.

The peeps of Dunkeld, with the river Tay deep in the bottom, and the view of the bridge and cathedral, surrounded by the high wooded hills, as you approached it, were lovely in the extreme. We got out at an inn (which was small, but very clean) at Dunkeld, and stopped to let Vicky have some broth. Such a charming view from the window! Vicky stood and bowed to the people out of the window. There never was such a good traveller as she is, sleeping in the carriage at her usual times, not put out, not frightened at noise or crowds; but pleased and amused. She never heard the anchor go at night on board ship; but slept as sound as a top.

Shortly after leaving Dunkeld, which is twenty miles from Blair, and fifteen from Cupar Angus, we met Lord Glenlyon in a carriage; he jumped out and rode with us the whole way to Blair,—and a most beautiful road it is. Six miles on, in the woods to the left, we could see Kinnaird House, where the late Lady Glenlyon (Lord Glenlyon's mother, who died about two or three months ago) used to live. Then we passed the point of Logierait, where there are the remains of an ancient castle,—the old Regality Court of the Dukes of Athole. At Moulinearn we tasted some of the "Athole brose",[53] which was brought to the carriage.

We passed Pitlochrie, a small village, Faskally, a very pretty place of Mr. Butter's, to the left, and then came to the Pass of Killiecrankie, which is quite magnificent; the road winds along it, and you look down a great height, all wooded on both sides; the Garry rolling below it. I cannot describe how beautiful it is. Albert was in perfect ecstasies. Lude, Mr. McInroy's, to the right, is very pretty. Blair Athole is only four or five miles from the Killiecrankie Pass. Lord Glenlyon has had a new approach made. The house is a large plain white building, surrounded by high hills, which one can see from the windows. Lord and Lady Glenlyon, with their little boy, received us at the door, and showed us to our rooms, and then left us.

Blair Castle, Blair Athole, Thursday, September 12

We took a delightful walk of two hours. Immediately near the house the scenery is very wild, which is most enjoyable. The moment you step out of the house you see those splendid hills all around. We went to the left through some neglected pleasure-grounds, and then through the wood, along a steep winding path overhanging the rapid stream. These Scotch streams, full of stones, and clear as glass, are most beautiful; the peeps between the trees, the depth of the shadows, the mossy stones, mixed with slate, etc., which cover the banks, are lovely; at every turn you have a picture. We were up high, but could not get to the top; Albert in such delight; it is a happiness to see him, he is in such spirits. We came back by a higher drive, and then went to the Factor's house, still higher up, where Lord and Lady Glenlyon are living, having given Blair up to us. We walked on, to a corn-field where a number of women were cutting and reaping the oats ("shearing" as they call it in Scotland), with a splendid view of the hills before us, so rural and romantic, so unlike our daily Windsor walk (delightful as that is); and this change does such good: as Albert observes, it refreshes one for a long time. We then went into the kitchen-garden, and to a walk from which there is a magnificent view. This mixture of great wildness and art is perfection.

At a little before four o'clock Albert drove me out in the pony phaeton till nearly six—such a drive! Really to be able to sit in one's pony carriage, and to see such wild, beautiful scenery as we did, the farthest point being only five miles from the house, is an immense delight. We drove along Glen Tilt, through a wood overhanging the river Tilt, which joins the Garry, and as we left the wood we came upon such a lovely view,—Ben-y-Ghlo straight before us—and under these high hills the river Tilt gushing and winding over stones and slates, and the hills and mountains skirted at the bottom with beautiful trees; the whole lit up by the sun; and the air so pure and fine; but no description can at all do it justice, or give an idea of what this drive was.

Oh! what can equal the beauties of nature! What enjoyment there is in them! Albert enjoys it so much; he is in ecstasies here. He has inherited this love for nature from his dear father.

We went as far as the Marble Lodge, a keeper's cottage, and came back the same way.

Victoria talks with a reaper at Blair Castle.

The Upper Falls of Bruar in the late
nineteenth century—a photograph by
Robert Murray.

Monday, September 16

After our luncheon at half-past three, Albert drove me (Lord Glenlyon riding with us) to the Falls of the Bruar. We got out at the road, and walked to the upper falls, and down again by the path on the opposite side. It is a walk of three miles round, and a very steep ascent; at every turn the view of the rushing falls is extremely fine, and looking back on the hills, which were so clear and so beautifully lit up, with the rapid stream below, was most exquisite. We threw stones down to see the effect in the water. The trees which surrounded the falls were planted by the late Duke of Athole in compliance with Burns's *Petition*.[54]

The evening was beautiful, and we feasted our eyes on the ever-changing, splendid views of the hills and vales as we drove back. Albert said that the chief beauty of mountain scenery consisted in its frequent changes. We came home at six o'clock.

Tuesday, September 17

At a quarter to four o'clock we drove out, Albert driving me, and the ladies and Lord Glenlyon following in another carriage. We drove to the Pass of Killiecrankie, which looked in its greatest beauty and splendour, and appeared quite closed, so that one could not imagine how one was to get out of it. We drove over a bridge[55] to the right, where the view of the pass both ways, with the Garry below, is beautiful. We got out a little way beyond this and walked on a mile to the

Falls of the Tummel, the stream of which is famous for salmon; these falls, however, are not so fine, or nearly so high, as those of the Bruar. We got home at half-past six; the day was fast fading, and the lights were lovely.

We watched two stags fighting just under our window; they are in an enclosure, and roar incessantly.

Wednesday, September 18

At nine o'clock we set off on ponies, to go up one of the hills, Albert riding the dun pony and I the grey, attended only by Lord Glenlyon's excellent servant, Sandy McAra, in his Highland dress. We went out by the back way across the road, and to the left through the ford, Sandy leading my pony and Albert following closely, the water reaching up above Sandy's knees. We then went up the hill of Tulloch, first straight up a very steep cabbage-field, and then in a zigzag manner round, till we got up to the top; the ponies[56] scrambling up over stones and everything, and never making a false step; and the view all round being splendid and most beautifully lit up. We went up to the very highest top, which cannot be seen from the house or from below; and from here the view is like a panorama: you see the Falls of the Bruar, Ben-y-Chat, Ben Vrackie, Ben-y-Ghlo, the Killiecrankie Pass, and a whole range of distant hills on the other side, which one cannot at all see from below. In the direction of Taymouth you also see Dalnacardoch, the first stage from Blair. Blair itself and the houses in the village looked like little toys from the great height we were on. It was quite romantic. Here we were with only this Highlander behind us holding ponies (for we got off twice and walked about)—not a house, not a creature near us, but the pretty Highland sheep, with their horns and black faces,— up at the top of Tulloch, surrounded by beautiful mountains.

We came back the same way that we went, and stopped at the ford to let the ponies drink before we rode through. We walked from inside the gate, and came home at half-past eleven,—the most delightful, most romantic ride and walk I ever had. I had never been up such a mountain, and then the day was so fine. The hill of Tulloch is covered with grass, and is so delightfully soft to walk upon.

Blair Castle and Glen Tilt, as seen from the top of Tulloch.

Thursday, September 19

Albert set off, immediately after luncheon, deer-stalking, and I was to follow and wait below in order to see the deer driven down. At four o'clock I set off with Lady Glenlyon and Lady Canning, Mr. Oswald and Lord Charles Wellesley[57] riding, by the lower Glen Tilt drive. We stopped at the end; but were still in the wood; Sandy was looking out and watching. After waiting we were allowed to come out of the carriage, and came upon the road, where we saw some deer on the brow of the hill. We sat down on the ground, Lady Canning and I sketching, and Sandy and Mr. Oswald, both in Highland costume (the same that they all wear here, viz. a grey cloth jacket and waistcoat, with a kilt and a Highland bonnet), lying on the grass and looking through glasses. After waiting again some time, we were told in a mysterious whisper that "they were coming", and indeed a great herd *did* appear on the brow of the hill, and came running down a good way, when most provokingly two men who were walking on the road—which they had no business to have done—suddenly came in sight, and then the herd all ran back again and the sport was spoilt. After waiting some little while we observed Albert, Lord Glenlyon, and the keepers on the brow of the hill, and we got into the carriage, drove a little way, went over the bridge, where there is a shepherd's "shiel", and got out and waited for them to join us, which they did almost immediately,—looking very picturesque with their rifles. My poor Albert had not even fired one shot for fear of spoiling the whole thing, but had been running about a good deal. The group of keepers and dogs was very pretty. After talking and waiting a little while, we walked some way on, and then Albert drove home with us.

Saturday, September 21

After breakfast Albert saw Lord Glenlyon, who proposed that he should go deer-stalking and that I should follow him. At twenty minutes to eleven we drove off with Lady Canning for Glen Tilt. The day was glorious and it would have been a pity to lose it, but it was a long hard day's work, though extremely delightful and enjoyable, and unlike anything I had ever done before. I should have enjoyed it still more had I been able to be with Albert the whole time.

We drove nearly to Peter Fraser's house, which is between the Marble Lodge and Forest Lodge. Here Albert and I walked about a little, and then Lady Canning and we mounted our ponies and set off on our journey, Lord Glenlyon leading my pony the whole way, Peter Fraser, the headkeeper (a wonderfully active man) leading the way; Sandy and six other Highlanders carrying rifles and leading dogs, and the rear brought up by two ponies with our luncheon-box. Lawley, Albert's Jäger, was also there, carrying one of Albert's rifles; the other Albert slung over his right shoulder, to relieve Lawley. So we set off and wound round and round the hill, which had the most picturesque effect imaginable. Such a splendid view all round, finer and more extensive the higher we went! The day was delightful; but the sun very hot. We saw the highest point of Ben-y-Ghlo, which one cannot see from below, and the distant range of hills we had seen from Tulloch was beautifully softened by the slightest haze. We saw Loch Vach. The road was very good, and as

An etching based on a Landseer painting—"The Eagle's Nest".

we ascended we had to speak in a whisper, as indeed we did almost all day, for fear of coming upon deer unawares. The wind was, however, right, which is everything here for the deer. I wish we could have had Landseer with us to sketch our party, with the background, it was so pretty, as were also the various "halts", etc. If I only had had time to sketch them!

We stopped at the top of the Ghrianan, whence you look down an immense height. It is here that the eagles sometimes sit. Albert got off and looked about in great admiration, and walked on a little, and then remounted his pony. We then went nearly to the top of Cairn Chlamain, and here we separated, Albert going off with Peter, Lawley, and two other keepers, to get a "quiet shot" as they call it; and Lady Canning, Lord Glenlyon, and I went up quite to the top, which is deep in moss. Here we sat down and stayed some time sketching the ponies below; Lord Glenlyon and Sandy remaining near us. The view was quite beautiful, nothing but mountains all around us, and the solitude, the complete solitude, very impressive. We saw the range of Mar Forest, and the inner range to the left, receding from us, as we sat facing the hill, called Scarsach, where the counties of Perth, Aberdeen and Inverness join. My pony was brought up for me, and we then descended this highest pinnacle, and proceeded on a level to meet Albert, whom I descried coming towards us. We met him shortly after; he had had bad luck, I am sorry to say. We then sat down on the grass and had some luncheon; then I walked a little with Albert and we got on our ponies. As we went on towards home some deer were seen in Glen Chroine, which is called the "Sanctum"; where it is supposed that there are a great many. Albert went off soon after this, and we remained on Sron a Chro, for an hour, I am sure, as Lord Glenlyon said by so doing we should turn the deer to Albert, whereas if we went on we should disturb and spoil the whole thing. So we submitted. Albert looked like a little speck creeping about on an opposite hill. We saw four herds of deer, two of them close to us. It was a beautiful sight.

Meanwhile I saw the sun sinking gradually, and I got quite alarmed lest we should be benighted, and we called anxiously for Sandy, who had gone away for a moment, to give a signal to come back. We then began our descent, "squinting" the

Victoria and Albert at Blair Atholl Church.

hill, the ponies going as safely and securely as possible. As the sun went down the scenery became more and more beautiful, the sky crimson, golden-red and blue, and the hills looking purple and lilac, most exquisite, till at length it set, and the hues grew softer in the sky and the outlines of the hills sharper. I never saw anything so fine. It soon, however, grew very dark.

At length Albert met us, and he told me he had waited all the time for us, as he knew how anxious I should be. He had been very unlucky, and had lost his sport, for the rifle would not go off just when he could have shot some fine harts; yet he was as merry and cheerful as if nothing had happened to disappoint him. We got down quite safely to the bridge; our ponies going most surely, though it was quite dusk when we were at the bottom of the hill. We walked to the Marble Lodge, and then got into the pony carriage and drove home by very bright moonlight, which made everything look very lovely; but the road made one a little nervous.

We saw a flight of ptarmigan, with their white wings, on the top of Sron a Chro, also plovers, grouse and pheasants. We were safely home by a quarter to eight.

Tuesday, October 1

At a quarter-past eight o'clock we started, and were very very sorry to leave Blair and the dear Highlands! Every little trifle and every spot I had become attached to; our life of quiet and liberty, everything was so pleasant, and all the Highlanders and people who went with us I had got to like so much. Oh! the dear hills, it made me very sad to leave them behind!

Lord Glenlyon rode with us, and we went back exactly the same road we came; through Killiecrankie, Pitlochrie, saw Logierait, etc. The battle of Killiecrankie[58] was fought in a field to your left, as you come from Blair and before you come to the pass; and Lord Dundee[59] was shot in a garden immediately above the field at Urrard (formerly called Kinrory) which belongs to Mr. Stewart of Urrard; the Stewarts of Urrard used formerly to live on Craig Urrard. We reached Dunkeld at half-past

Victoria and Albert leaving the Church at Blair Atholl.

eleven. Mr. Oswald and Mr. Patrick Small Keir, with a detachment of Highlanders, were there. We drove up to the door of the cottage at Dunkeld and got out there. It is beautifully situated and the cottage is very pretty, with a good view of the river from the windows. Craig-y-Barns is a fine rocky hill to the left as you drive from Blair.

We walked to look at the beginning of the new house which the late Duke of Athole commenced, but which has been left unfinished, and also at a beautiful larch-tree, the first that was brought to Scotland. I rode back on "Arghait Bhean" for the last time, and took a sad leave of him and of faithful Sandy McAra. We walked into the ruins of the old cathedral and into that part which the late Duke fitted up for service, and where there is a fine monument of him. I should never have recognised the grounds of Dunkeld, so different did they look without the encampment. Beautiful as Dunkeld is, it does not approach the beauty and wildness of Blair.

After twelve o'clock we set off again, and to our astonishment Lord Glenlyon insisted upon riding on with us to Dundee, which is fifty miles from Blair! Captain J. Murray also rode with us from Dunkeld. It made me feel sad to see the country becoming flatter and flatter. There was a great crowd at Cupar Angus, and at Dundee a still larger one, and on the pier the crush was very great.

We took leave of Lord Glenlyon with real regret, and he seemed quite unhappy at our going. No one could be more zealous or kinder than he was.

There was a fearful swell when we went in the barge to the yacht.

Thursday, October 3

The English coast appeared terribly flat. Lord Aberdeen was quite touched when I told him I was so attached to the dear, dear Highlands and missed the fine hills so much. There is a great peculiarity about the Highlands and Highlanders; and they are such a chivalrous, fine, active people. Our stay among them was so delightful. Independently of the beautiful scenery, there was a quiet, a retirement, a wildness, a liberty, and a solitude that had such a charm for us.

On Board the Victoria and Albert, in Dartmouth Harbour, Thursday, August 12, 1847

I HAVE NOT MUCH TO RELATE. Our voyage has not been what we intended, *mais l'homme propose et Dieu dispose*; for instead of being at Falmouth we are only at Dartmouth! We started at five o'clock, and soon after felt the vessel stop, and on inquiring, heard that the fog was so thick it was impossible to proceed. At last Captain Smithett was sent out in the *Garland* to report on the state of the weather; and he soon returned, saying that all was clear enough to proceed outside The Needles (we were in Alum Bay). So we started again, and, after breakfast, we came on deck, where I remained working and talking; feeling quite well; but towards one the ground swell had increased, and we decided to run into the harbour we now are in.

In heavy seas off the Needles of the Isle of Wight.

Monday, August 16

We woke soon after four o'clock, when getting under weigh, and were surprised to feel the yacht stop not an hour after. Something had gone wrong with the paddle-wheel—just as happened last year—and it took full two hours to set it right. Then at seven we started afresh. A beautiful morning with a very smooth sea. By half-past ten we were in sight of the Isle of Man, which is a fine island with bold hills and cliffs. A little before twelve we reached the point of the bay, on which is the town of Douglas, very prettily situated, with a picturesque castle near the lighthouse, on the extreme point of the bay. We stopped off here for ten minutes or a quarter of an hour,—the rocks were covered with people. From Douglas to Ramsay Bay the hills and cliffs are high and bold; though Ramsay itself is low.

For about two hours we were out of sight of land, and I was below writing. When I came on deck at three o'clock the Scotch coast was quite close; the Mull of Galloway, and then Wigtownshire. Albert declared he saw the Irish coast, but I

An early nineteenth-century engraving of the Solway Firth . . . or "Frith", as Victoria
and many other visitors called it.

could not descry it. At five we came in sight of Loch Ryan, and saw, to the left, Ailsa
Craig rising more than 1,000 feet perpendicularly from the sea. Loch Ryan is very
fine, and the hills and glens are lovely, particularly little Glen Finnie. The loch is
very large, and the hills here are very high and wooded. The little town is called
Stranraer.

Tuesday, August 17

At six o'clock we began to move. A beautiful morning. At about eight we were
close to the Ailsa Rock or Craig, the formation of which is very curious. There were
thousands and thousands of birds,—gannets,—on the rock, and we fired a gun off
three times in order to bring them in reach of a shot—Albert and Charles tried, but
in vain. We next came in sight of the beautiful Isle of Arran. The finest point is when
you are before the Holy Island, and in sight of the Goatfell range of mountains. The
highest is about 2,800 feet; they are peculiarly fine from their bold pointed outlines.
Before them is Lamlash. After passing Holy Island we came to Brodick Bay, which
is beautiful, with high hills and a glen; in front of which, and surrounded by wood,
is the castle which Lord Douglas is building. Not long after this we came in sight of
the Isle of Bute, and entered the Clyde, the view of which from Mr. Stuart's and
Lord Bute's property is beautiful: high wooded banks, the river opening out and
widening, surrounded by the distant mountains. A small place to the right called
Largs is very prettily situated.

At half-past twelve we reached Greenock, the port of Glasgow. The shore and

Passing Ailsa Craig, off the Scottish coast.

the ships were crowded with people, there being no less (as I since learnt) than thirty-nine steamers, over-filled with people, which almost all followed us! Such a thing never was seen. Add to these steamers boats and ships of all descriptions, moving in all directions; but not getting out of the way! We, however, got safe on board the *Fairy*, and steamed up the Clyde; it was hazy, and we could not see the distance well. We passed the small town of Port Glasgow, and about one o'clock were at Dumbarton Castle. Its situation is very fine, the rock rising straight out of the river, the mountains all round, and the town of Dumbarton behind it, making it very picturesque. We landed just below the Castle, and went with Charles and the children in a carriage to the fort. There was a great crowd, but excellent order kept. We went to the battery, but had to mount many steps to get to it. Wallace was confined here; and it was one of the last castles which held out for Mary Queen of Scots. From the battery there is a very extensive view of the Clyde and Dumbarton, and we ought to have been able to see Ben Lomond; but it was in mist.

We got back to the *Fairy* by half-past two, and returned to Greenock, escorted by nineteen steamers. Steamed past Greenock, and went on towards Loch Long, passing Roseneath to the right, where the present Duke and Duchess of Argyll live. Loch Long is indeed splendid, fifteen miles in length, surrounded by grand hills, with such beautiful outlines, and very green—all so different from the eastern part of Scotland—the loch winding along most beautifully, so as to seem closed at times. Charles said it reminded him of Switzerland and the Tyrol. The finest point of Loch Long is looking towards Loch Goil. We had a very good sight of the mountain called The Cobbler; the top of which resembles a man sitting and mending his shoe! At the end of the loch we got a glimpse of Ben Lomond, and were, in fact, very near Loch Lomond.

We returned as we came. There was no sun, and once or twice a little mist; but still it was beautiful. We went on to Rothsay, which we reached at eight o'clock, and

opposte above: Loch-na-Gar; watercolour by J. Giles, 1849.
opposite below: Fort William; watercolour by J. Giles, 1851.

Completion of the Carn Elach Chuimkneachan on Craig Gowan; watercolour by W. Wyld, 1852.

immediately went on board the *Victoria and Albert*, greatly tired but much amused and interested.

The children enjoy everything extremely, and bear the novelty and excitement wonderfully. The people cheered the "Duke of Rothsay"[60] very much, and also called for a cheer for the "Princess of Great Britain". Everywhere the good Highlanders are very enthusiastic. Rothsay is a pretty little town, built round a fine bay, with hills in the distance, and a fine harbour. When we went on deck after dinner, we found the whole town brilliantly illuminated, with every window lit up, which had a very pretty effect.

Wednesday, August 18

A bright fresh morning, the hills slightly tipped with clouds. At eight o'clock we all went on board the *Fairy*, and went up the Kyles of Bute, which, as you advance, become very fine, the hills lying so curiously one behind the other, sometimes apparently closing up all outlet.

We saw Arran to the left, looking very grand in the distance. We have been turning about a good deal since yesterday, for we went by Arran and Holy Island, and then left Little and Great Cumbray to our left and went up to Dumbarton and back, and on to Loch Long, and then to Rothsay, leaving Arran to our left; then, after passing Arran, we entered Loch Fyne. I, however, had a headache, and was obliged to lie down below, and only came on deck again when we were within an hour of Inverary; where the lake widens, and the hills on either side are very green and undulating, but not very high.

The approach to Inverary is splendid; the loch is very wide; straight before you a fine range of mountains splendidly lit up,—green, pink, and lilac; to the left, the little town of Inverary; and above it, surrounded by pine woods, stands the Castle of Inverary, square, with turrets at the corners.

Our reception was in the true Highland fashion. The Duke and Duchess of Argyll[61] (dear Lady Elizabeth Leveson Gower), the Duchess of Sutherland, Lord Stafford,[62] Lady Caroline Leveson Gower, and the Blantyres received us at the landing-place, which was all ornamented with heather. The Celtic Society, including Campbell of Islay, his two sons (one grown up and the other a very pretty little boy), with a number of his men, and several other Campbells, were all drawn up near to the carriage. We got into a carriage with the two Duchesses, Charles and the Duke being on the box (we had left the children on board the *Fairy*), and took a beautiful drive amongst magnificent trees, and along a glen where we saw Ben Sheerar, etc. The weather was particularly fine, and we were much struck by the extreme beauty of Inverary—presenting as it does such a combination of magnificent timber, with high mountains, and a noble lake.

The pipers walked before the carriage, and the Highlanders on either side, as we approached the house. Outside stood the Marquis of Lorn,[63] just two years old, a dear, white, fat, fair little fellow with reddish hair, but very delicate features, like both his father and mother: he is such a merry, independent little child. He had a black velvet dress and jacket, with a "sporran", scarf, and Highland bonnet. We lunched at two with our hosts; the Highland gentlemen standing with halberds in the room. We sent for our children, who arrived during luncheon time. We left

Victoria on the Crinan Canal.

Inverary before three, and took the children with us in the carriage. The Argylls, the Duchess of Sutherland, and the others, accompanied us on board the *Fairy*, where we took leave of them.

The light on the hills was beautiful as we steamed down Loch Fyne. At five we reached Lochgilp, and all landed at Lochgilphead, a small village where there were numbers of people, and, amongst others, Sir John P. Orde, who lent his carriage and was extremely civil. We and our people drove through the little village to the Crinan Canal, where we entered a most magnificently decorated barge, drawn by three horses, ridden by postilions in scarlet. We glided along very smoothly, and the views of the hills—the range of Cruachan—were very fine indeed; but the eleven locks we had to go through—(a very curious process, first passing several by rising, and then others by going down)—were tedious, and instead of the passage lasting one hour and a half, it lasted upwards of two hours and a half, therefore it was nearly eight o'clock before we reached Loch Crinan. We instantly went on board the *Victoria and Albert*, but it was too late to proceed to Oban; we had, therefore, to lengthen our voyage by a day, and spent the night at Crinan. It is a very fine spot, hills all round, and, in the distance, those of the island of Jura. The yacht had had a good passage round the Mull of Cantire. We dined with Charles, and went on deck; and the blaze of the numerous bonfires—the half moon, the stars, and the extreme stillness of the night—had a charming effect.

Thursday, August 19

A beautiful day. At nine o'clock we left Crinan, proceeding to the right, up splendid passes, with myriads of islands, and such enchanting views, that I cannot enumerate them. We passed first up the Sound of Jura, where numbers of people met us in small boats, decorated with little flags; then up the Pass of Kerrera to Oban, one of the finest spots we have seen, with the ruins of the old Castle of Dunolly and a range of high mountains in the distance. To the left, after leaving Oban, we saw the Isle of Kerrera and to the right Dunstaffnage Castle, whence came the famous stone which supports the "Coronation Chair", in which the sovereigns are crowned at Westminster Abbey. Alexander II[64] is said to be buried here. We passed close by the flat rock, called The Lady's Rock, on which a McLean left his wife, hoping she would be washed away—she was saved however.

We then came into the Sound of Mull by Tobermory, a small place prettily situated, and from thence the views continued beautiful. At one o'clock we were in sight of the Isles of Rum, Eig and Muck (rather large islands, which Lord Salisbury[65] bought a few years ago). Next we passed the long, flat, curious islands of Coll and Tiree. The inhabitants of these islands have, unhappily, been terrible sufferers during the last winter from famine. A little further on we saw, to our right, the Treshinish Isles, very curiously-shaped rocks: one is called The Dutchman's Cap, and has the most strange shape.

At three we anchored close before Staffa, and immediately got into the barge with Charles, the children, and the rest of our people, and rowed towards the cave. As we rounded the point, the wonderful basaltic formation came in sight. The appearance it presents is most extraordinary; and when we turned the corner to go into the renowned Fingal's Cave, the effect was splendid, like a great entrance into a

The royal party visits Fingal's Cave.

Arriving at Fort William.

vaulted hall: it looked almost awful as we entered, and the barge heaved up and down on the swell of the sea. It is very high, but not longer than 227 feet, and narrower than I expected, being only forty feet wide. The sea is immensely deep in the cave. The rocks, under water, were all colours—pink, blue, and green—which had a most beautiful and varied effect. It was the first time the British standard with a Queen of Great Britain, and her husband and children, had ever entered Fingal's Cave, and the men gave three cheers, which sounded very impressive there. We backed out, and then went on a little further to look at the other cave, not of basaltic formation, and at the point called The Herdsman. The swell was beginning to get up, and perhaps an hour later we could not have gone in.

We returned to the yacht, but Albert and Charles landed again at Staffa. They returned in three quarters of an hour, and we then went on to Iona; here Albert and Charles landed, and were absent an hour. I and the ladies sketched. We saw from the yacht the ruins of the old cathedral of St. Oran. When Albert and Charles returned, they said the ruins were very curious, there had been two monasteries there, and fine old crosses and tombs of ancient kings were still to be seen. I must see it some other time. On Albert's return we went on again, and reached Tobermory at nine. The place was all illuminated.

Friday, August 20

A wet morning when we rose at half-past seven, and it was pouring with rain when we left Tobermory at half-past eight. I went down, and drew and painted. It cleared up about half-past ten, and I came on deck. The scenery in Loch Linnhe was magnificent—such beautiful mountains. From Loch Linnhe we entered Loch Eil, and passed the entrance of Loch Leven to the right, at the end of which is Glencoe, so famous for its beautiful scenery and for the horrible massacre of the Macdonald's in William III's time.[66]

A little before one we arrived at Fort William, a very small place. The afternoon was very bright, and the scenery fine. After luncheon Albert and Charles set off in the *Fairy* to see Glencoe. They returned at twenty minutes past seven, and Albert thought Glencoe was very fine, though not quite as much so as he had expected. They had driven in an extraordinary carriage, with seats for thirty. The people, who recognised Albert, were so loyal that they took the horses out and insisted on drawing the carriage.

The evening was excessively cold and showery.

I am quite sorry we shall have to leave our yacht to-morrow, in which we have been so comfortably housed, and that this delightful voyage and tour among the Western Lochs and Isles is at an end—they are so beautiful,—and so full of poetry and romance, traditions, and historical associations.

Ardverikie, Loch Laggan,
Saturday, August 21

Alas! a very wet morning. We were ready long before nine o'clock, but had to wait, as our carriages were not ready. At last we all landed at Fort William, where there was a great gathering of Highlanders, in their different tartans, with Lord Lovat[67] and Mr. Stuart Mackenzie at their head. We got into our carriage with Charles and the two children; there was a great crowd to see us off. We went by a very wild and lonely road, the latter part extremely fine, with mountains and streams that reminded us of Glen Tilt. We changed horses only once, and came at length in sight of Loch Laggan. It is a beautiful lake (small in comparison to what we have seen) surrounded by very fine mountains: the road by its side is extremely

Ardverikie Lodge, as seen from the loch.

The royal party watches the uphill race at the Laggan Games.

pretty. We saw Lord Abercorn's[68] house of Ardverikie long before we came to it. At Laggan there is only a small inn, and at the end of the lake, a ferry. Here, in spite of the pouring rain, were assembled a number of Highlanders, with Macpherson of Cluny (always called Cluny Macpherson) and three dear little boys of his, Davidson of Tulloch, and others, with Lord Abercorn, in full Highland dress. We stepped out of our carriage and stood upon the floating bridge[69] and so crossed over in two or three minutes. We then drove on, in our pony carriages, to Ardverikie,[70] and arrived there in about twenty minutes. It is quite close to the lake, and the view from the windows, as I now write, though obscured by rain, is very beautiful, and extremely wild. There is not a village, house, or cottage within four or five miles: one can only get to it by the ferry, or by rowing across the lake. The house is a comfortable shooting-lodge,[71] built of stone, with many nice rooms in it. Stags' horns are placed along the outside and in the passages; and the walls of the drawing-room and ante-room are ornamented with beautiful drawings of stags, by Landseer.[72]

There is little to say of our stay at Ardverikie; the country is very fine, but the weather was most dreadful.

On the 28th, about five o'clock, Albert drove me out across the ferry, along the Kingussie road, and from here the scenery was splendid: high bold hills, with a good deal of wood; glens with the Pattock, and a small waterfall; the meadows here and there, with people making hay, and cottages sprinkled sparingly about, reminded us much of Thüringen. We drove to the small farm, where Colonel Macpherson now lives, called Strathmashie, and back again, sixteen miles in all. We were delighted with the scenery, which is singularly beautiful, wild and romantic, — with so much fine wood about it, which greatly enhances the beauty of a landscape.

Thursday, September 16

Albert left at six this morning to go to Inverness and see the Caledonian Canal.[73]

Friday, September 17

At two o'clock I left Ardverikie with the children, and reached Fort William at half-past six, where I had the happiness of finding Albert on board the yacht. All had gone off well; but the weather had been very bad. Albert said Dochfour was beautiful; the house new and very elegant, with a fine garden, and Mr. and Lady Georgiana Baillie very pleasant people.

Albert had to go to Inverness, and to stay for a ball that was held there; and he was everywhere extremely well received. This morning he saw the Falls of Foyers, which, he tells me, are very grand indeed; and of a great height; and he says that the Caledonian Canal is a most remarkable work.

Loch Ryan, Saturday, September 18

At five o'clock we left Fort William. Rather a fine morning; but very squally, and the sea rough, even where we were. When we came on deck, we were close to the Isle of Jura, which has such a fine, bold outline. We went on to Loch Crinan, where we got into the barge: here it was very rough and pouring with rain, so unlike the beautiful evening when we were here a month ago. We landed at Crinan. Mr. Malcolm, whose castle is just opposite, received us there, and we entered the canal boat at ten. We proceeded more quickly than the last time; the people kept running along as before, and there was a piper at each lock. It rained almost the whole time. We reached Lochgilphead at twelve, in pouring rain, and embarked on board the *Black Eagle*. The yacht had again to go round the Mull of Cantire and meet us at Campbeltown. What a contrast to the weather we had when we came!

We got under weigh, and proceeded by Kilbrannan Sound and Arran. We went on deck for a little while, but were driven below by the rain; later, however, it was possible to keep on deck. We reached Campbeltown, a small and not pretty place, at the foot of Cantire, at twenty minutes to five. About half an hour after we arrived the yacht came in, with the *Garland*, *Fairy*, and *Scourge*, and we immediately went on board. They had had a very bad passage, and Captain Crispin said he was very glad that we had not been on board the *Victoria and Albert*. This rather alarmed us for the next day's voyage, the more so as the evening was squally and the sky very unpromising. There was a long consultation as to what was to be done, and at last it was decided that we should start at four in the morning, and if it were very rough, we should either run into Loch Ryan, the Mull of Galloway, the Bay of Ramsay, or into Douglas in the Isle of Man.

Loch Ryan, Sunday, September 19

We set off at four o'clock, the yacht rolling considerably; but it was quite bearable; however, at seven they came to shut down the port-holes, expecting a heavy sea, and Lord Adolphus[74] saw Albert, who had just got up, and said it would be very rough; upon which it was decided to put back a little way, and to go into Loch Ryan; we accordingly did so, and anchored there at half-past eight;—such a dreary rainy day—one could hardly recognise what was so fine when we were last in here.

Both now, and the time before when we were in Loch Ryan, Lord Orkney very civilly sent us game and all sorts of things.

At twelve o'clock Lord Adolphus read the short sea service. We then talked over our voyage, and what could be done;—the day was very wretched,—pouring with rain and blowing hard. It was at last decided to start again at three, and get this evening to the Mull of Galloway, which would only take us three hours, though it would probably be rough. As soon as we were out of the loch the yacht began to pitch, and the sea was dreadfully rough. I was very ill. Albert, however, stood it perfectly, and the children very tolerably. Presently we came in sight of the Mull of Galloway, a great rock with a lighthouse on it;—and this was our last glimpse of dear Scotland.

Balmoral,
Friday, September 8, 1848

WE ARRIVED AT BALMORAL at a quarter to three. It is a pretty little castle in the old Scottish style. There is a picturesque tower and garden in front, with a high wooded hill; at the back there is wood down to the Dee; and the hills rise all around.

There is a nice little hall, with a billiard-room; next to it is the dining-room. Upstairs (ascending by a good broad staircase) immediately to the right, and above the dining-room, is our sitting-room (formerly the drawing-room), a fine large room—next to which is our bedroom, opening into a little dressing-room which is Albert's. Opposite, down a few steps, are the children's and Miss Hildyard's three rooms. The ladies live below, and the gentlemen upstairs.

We lunched almost immediately, and at half-past four we walked out, and went up to the top of the wooded hill opposite our windows, where there is a cairn, and up which there is a pretty winding path. The view from here, looking down upon the house, is charming. To the left you look towards the beautiful hills surrounding Loch-na-Gar, and to the right, towards Ballater, to the glen (or valley) along which the Dee winds, with beautiful wooded hills, which reminded us very much of the Thüringerwald. It was so calm, and so solitary, it did one good as one gazed around; and the pure mountain air was most refreshing. All seemed to breathe freedom and peace, and to make one forget the world and its sad turmoils.

The scenery is wild, and yet not desolate; and everything looks much more prosperous and cultivated than at Laggan. Then the soil is delightfully dry. We walked beside the Dee, a beautiful, rapid stream, which is close behind the house. The view of the hills towards Invercauld is exceedingly fine.

When I came in at half-past six, Albert went out to try his luck with some stags which lay quite close in the woods, but he was unsuccessful. They come down of an evening quite near to the house.

Ballater photographed in the late nineteenth century.

G. W. Wilson's photograph of Invercauld from Craig Cluny, taken in the mid nineteenth century.

Saturday, September 16, 1848

AT HALF-PAST NINE O'CLOCK Albert and I set off in a postchaise, and drove to the bridge in the wood of Balloch Buie, about five miles from Balmoral, where our ponies and people were. Here we mounted, and were attended by a keeper of Mr. Farquharson's as guide, Macdonald[75]—who, with his shooting-jacket, and in his kilt, looked a picture—Grant[76] on a pony, with our luncheon in two baskets, and Batterbury[77] on another pony. We went through that beautiful wood for about a mile, and then turned and began to ascend gradually, the view getting finer and finer; no road, but not bad ground—moss, heather, and stones. Albert saw some deer when we had been out about three-quarters of an hour, and ran off to stalk them, while I rested; but he arrived just a minute too late. He waited for me on the other side of a stony little burn, which I crossed on my pony, after our faithful Highlanders had moved some stones and made it easier. We then went on a little way, and I got off and walked a bit, and afterwards remounted; Macdonald leading my pony. The view of Ben-na-Bhourd, and indeed of all around, was very beautiful; but as we rose higher we saw mist over Loch-na-Gar. Albert left me to go after ptarmigan, and went on with Grant, while the others remained with me, taking the greatest care of me. Macdonald is a good honest man, and was indefatigable, and poor Batterbury was very anxious also.

I saw ptarmigan get up, and Albert fire—he then disappeared from my sight, and I rode on. It became cold and misty when we were on Loch-na-Gar. In half an hour, or rather less, Albert rejoined me with two ptarmigan, having come up by a shorter way. Here it was quite soft, easy walking, and we looked down on two small lochs called Na Nian, which were very striking, being so high up in the hills. Albert was tired, and remounted his pony; I had also been walking a little way. The ascent commenced, and with it a very thick fog, and when we had nearly reached the top of Loch-na-Gar, the mist drifted in thick clouds so as to hide everything not within one hundred yards of us. Near the peak (the fine point of the mountain which is seen so well from above Grant's house) we got off and walked, and climbed up some steep stones, to a place where we found a seat in a little nook, and had some luncheon. It was just two o'clock, so we had taken four hours going up.

But, alas! nothing whatever to be seen; and it was cold, and wet, and cheerless. At about twenty minutes after two we set off on our way downwards, the wind blowing a hurricane, and the mist being like rain, and everything quite dark with it.

G. W. Wilson's photograph of the Falls of Garbhalt.

Bowman (Mr. Farquharson's keeper) and Macdonald, who preceded us, looked like ghosts. We walked some way till I was quite breathless, and remounted my pony, well wrapped up in plaids; and we came down by the same path that Albert had come up, which is shorter, but steeper; the pony went delightfully; but the mist made me feel cheerless.

Albert kept ahead a little while for ptarmigan, but he gave it up again. When we had gone on about an hour and a quarter, or an hour and a half, the fog disappeared like magic, and all was sunshine below, about one thousand feet from the top I should say. Most provoking!—and yet one felt happy to see sunshine and daylight again.

The view, as one descends, overlooking Invercauld and the wood which is called Balloch Buie, is most lovely. We saw some deer in the wood below. We rode on till after we passed the burn, and had nearly got to the wood. We came another way down, by a much rougher path; and then, from the road in the wood, we walked up to the Falls of the Garbhalt, which are beautiful. The rocks are very grand, and the view from the little bridge, and also from a seat a little lower down, is extremely pretty. We found our carriages in the road, and drove home by six o'clock.

We met Captain Gordon, and then Lord John Russell[78] and Sir James Clark. They had come to look after us, and when we got home we found the two ladies at the door waiting most anxiously for us.

September 18, 1848

A T A QUARTER-PAST TEN O'CLOCK we set off in a postchaise with Bertie, and drove beyond the house of Mr. Farquharson's keeper in the Balloch Buie. We then mounted our ponies, Bertie riding Grant's pony on the deer-saddle, and being led by a gillie, Grant walking by his side. Macdonald and several gillies were with us, and we were preceded by Bowman and old Arthur Farquharson, a deer-stalker of Invercauld's. They took us up a beautiful path winding through the trees and heather in the Balloch Buie; but when we had got about a mile or more they discovered deer. A "council of war" was held in a whisper, and we turned back and went the whole way down again, and rode along to the keeper's lodge, where we turned up the glen immediately below Craig Daign, through a beautiful part of the wood, and went on along the track, till we came to the foot of the craig, where we all dismounted.

We scrambled up an almost perpendicular place to where there was a little box, made of hurdles and interwoven with branches of fir and heather, about five feet in height. There we seated ourselves with Bertie, Macdonald lying in the heather near us, watching and quite concealed; some had gone round to beat, and others again were at a little distance. We sat quite still, and sketched a little; I doing the landscape and some trees, Albert drawing Macdonald as he lay there. This lasted for nearly an hour, when Albert fancied he heard a distant sound, and, in a few minutes, Macdonald whispered that he saw stags, and that Albert should wait and take a steady aim. We then heard them coming past. Albert did not look over the box, but

A successful shoot by Albert; Victoria looks at the stag.

through it, and fired through the branches, and then again over the box. The deer retreated; but Albert felt certain he had hit a stag. He ran up to the keepers, and at that moment they called from below that they "had got him", and Albert ran on to see. I waited for a bit; but soon scrambled on with Bertie and Macdonald's help; and Albert joined me directly, and we all went down and saw a magnificent stag, "a royal", which had dropped, soon after Albert had hit him, at one of the men's feet. The sport was successful, and every one was delighted,—Macdonald and the keepers in particular;—the former saying, "that it was her Majesty's coming out that had brought the good luck". I was supposed to have "a lucky foot", of which the Highlanders "think a great deal". We walked down to the place we last came up, got into the carriage, and were home by half-past two o'clock.

Monday, August 13, 1849

WE STARTED AT FOUR O'CLOCK in the morning, and the yacht rolled a little, but the motion was an easy one. We were in the Clyde by breakfast-time, but the day was very bad, constant squalls hiding the scenery. We left Greenock to our left, and proceeded a little way up Loch Goil, which opens into Loch Long, and is very fine; it seems extraordinary to have such deep water in a narrow loch and so immediately below the mountains, which are very rocky. We turned back and went up Loch Long, which I remembered so well, and which is so beautiful. We let go the anchor at Arrochar, the head of the lake intending to land and proceed to Loch

Lomond, where a steamer was waiting for us; but it poured with rain most hopelessly. We waited an hour in vain, and decided on stopping till after luncheon and making the attempt at three o'clock. We lunched and stepped into the boat, as it had cleared a little; but just then it began pouring again more violently than before, and we put back much disappointed, but Albert persevered, and he went off with Mr. Anson, Sir James Clark, and Captain Robinson almost directly afterwards. Just then it cleared and I felt so vexed that we had not gone; but there have been some terrible showers since. We left Arrochar a little before four, Loch Long looking beautiful as we returned.

Perth,
Tuesday, August 14

We anchored yesterday in Roseneath Bay, close to Roseneath—a very pretty spot—and looking towards the mountains which you see in Loch Goil. One of them is called "The Duke of Argyll's Bowling-green". Albert only returned soon after eight o'clock, having been able to see a good deal of Loch Lomond, and even Rob Roy's Cave, in spite of heavy showers. Captain Beechey (who was with us during the whole voyage in '47, and again the whole of this one to pilot us), Captain Crispin, and Captain Robinson (who met us this morning and piloted Albert in Loch Lomond, and did the same for us in '47), dined with us also, and we had much interesting conversation about the formation of glaciers, etc., in all of which Captain Beechey (who is a very intelligent man, and has been all over the world) took part. He was with Sir Edward Parry[79] at the North Pole, and told us that they

The port of Greenock.

The Clyde near Kilpatrick, with Dumbarton Rock in the distance.

had not seen daylight for four months. They heaped up snow over the ship and covered it in with boards to keep the cold off.

Balmoral,
Wednesday, August 15

It seems like a dream to be here in our dear Highland home again; it certainly does not seem as if it were a year since we were here! Now I must describe the doings of yesterday. We embarked on board the *Fairy* at a quarter to nine o'clock, and proceeded up the Clyde in pouring rain and high wind, and it was very stormy till after we had passed Greenock. We steamed past Port Glasgow, then came Dumbarton and Erskine. The river narrows and winds extraordinarily here, and you do not see Glasgow until you are quite close upon it. As we approached, the banks were lined with people, either on estrades or on the sea-shore, and it was amusing to see all those on the shore take flight, often too late, as the water bounded up from the swell caused by the steamer.

The weather, which had been dreadful, cleared up, just as we reached Glasgow, about eleven, and continued fine for the remainder of the day. Several addresses were presented on board, first by the Lord Provost, who was knighted, (Colonel Gordon's sword being used), then one from the county, the clergy (Established Church and Free Kirk), and from the Houses of Commerce. We landed immediately after this; the landing-place was very handsomely decorated. We then entered our carriage with the two eldest children, the two others following. Mr. Alison[80] (the celebrated historian, who is the Sheriff) rode on one side of the carriage, and General Riddell (the Commander of the Forces in Scotland) on the other. The crowds assembled were quite enormous, but excellent order was kept and they were very enthusiastic. Mr. Alison said that there were 500,000 people out. The town is a handsome one with fine streets built in stone, and many fine buildings and churches. We passed over a bridge commanding an extensive view down two quays, which

Victoria and the crowds at Glasgow's Broomielaw.

Albert said was very like Paris. There are many large shops and warehouses, and the shipping is immense.

We went up to the old cathedral, where Principal MacFarlane, a very old man, received us, and directed our attention, as we walked through the church gates, to an immensely high chimney, the highest I believe in existence, which belongs to one of the manufactories. The cathedral is a very fine one, the choir of which is fitted up as a Presbyterian church. We were shown the crypt and former burial-place of the bishops, which is in a very high state of preservation. The architecture is beautiful. It is in this crypt that the famous scene in *Rob Roy* is laid, where Rob Roy gives Frank Osbaldistone warning that he is in danger. There is an old monument of St. Kentigern, commonly called St. Mungo, the founder of the cathedral. We re-entered our carriages and went to the University, an ancient building, and which has produced many great and learned men. Here we got out and received an address. We only stopped a few minutes, and then went on again towards the Exchange, in front of which is Marochetti's equestrian statue of the Duke of Wellington, very like and beautifully executed. We got out at the railway station and started almost immediately.

We passed Stirling in the distance, and a little before four we reached Perth, where the people were very friendly. We took the four children in our carriage and drove straight to the "George Inn", where we had the same rooms that we had last time.

Albert went out immediately to see the prison, and at six we drove together along the London Road (as they rather strangely call it), towards Moncrieffe. The view was perfectly beautiful, and is the finest of Perth and the grand bridge over the Tay.

Wednesday, August 15

At a quarter to eight o'clock we started. The two boys and Vicky were in the carriage with us, Alice followed with the ladies. It was a long journey, but through very beautiful scenery. We saw the Grampians as we left Perth. We first changed horses at Blairgowrie, fifteen miles. Then came a very long stage of twenty miles, to the Spittal of Glenshee. We first passed the house of a Lieut-Colonel Clark Rattray, called Craig Hall, overhanging a valley or glen above which we drove, and after this we came into completely wild Highland scenery, with barren rocky hills, through which the road winds to the Spittal of Glenshee, which can scarcely be called a village, for it consists of only an inn and two or three cottages. We got out at the inn, where we found Mr. Farquharson and his son, and some of his men. Here we had some luncheon, and then set off again. The next stage of fifteen miles to Castleton is over a very bad, and at night, positively dangerous road, through wild, grand scenery, with very abrupt turns and steep ascents. One sharp turn is called The Devil's Elbow. The Farquharson men joined us again here, some having gone on before, and others having followed from the inn, skipping over stones and rocks with the rapidity and lightness peculiar to Highlanders. They remained with us till we were able to trot on again.

We drove through a very fine pass called Cairn Wall and were overtaken by a heavy shower. When we reached Castleton the day had cleared, and we were able to open the carriage again. Here we were met by Sir Alexander Duff and the Duke of Leeds[81] at the head of their men. Lady Duff, Mr[82] and Lady Agnes Duff, Miss Farquharson, and several of the children, and the Duchess of Leeds, came up to the carriage. The drive from Castleton to Balmoral, particularly the beautiful part from the Balloch Buie, was well known to us; and it was a great pleasure to see it all again in its beauty. Grant had met us at the Spittal of Glenshee, and ridden the whole way with us. At the door at Balmoral were Mackay, who was playing, and Macdonald in full dress. It was about four when we arrived.

August 30, 1849

AFTER WRITING OUR LETTERS, we set off on our ponies, with Miss Dawson,[83] Macdonald, Grant, Batterbury, and Hamis Coutts; Hamis is Gaelic for James, and is pronounced "Hamish". The road has been improved since last year, and though it is still very rough, there are no fords to pass, nor real difficulties any longer. We rode the whole way, and Albert only walked the last two miles. He took a Gaelic lesson during our ride, asking Macdonald, who speaks it with great purity, many words, and making him talk to Jemmie Coutts. Albert has already picked up many words: but it is a very difficult language, for it is pronounced in a totally different way from that in which it is written.

We arrived at our little "bothie" at two o'clock, and were amazed at the transformation. There are two huts, and to the one in which we live a wooden addition has been made. We have a charming little dining-room, sitting-room, bedroom, and dressing-room, all *en suite*; and there is a little room where Caroline Dawson (the Maid of Honour) sleeps, one for her maid, and a little pantry. In the other house, which is only a few yards distant, is the kitchen, where the people

The pony Jock Wemyss with the luncheon, escorted by Gow.

Alt-na-Guithasach as it was in the nineteenth century.

generally sit, a small room where the servants dine, and another, which is a sort of store-room, and a loft above in which the men sleep. Margaret French (my maid), Caroline's maid, Löhlein (Albert's valet), a cook, Shackle (a footman), and Macdonald, are the only people with us in the house, old John Gordon and his wife excepted. Our rooms are delightfully papered, the ceilings as well as walls, and very nicely furnished. We lunched as soon as we arrived, and at three walked down (about twenty minutes' walk) to the loch called "Muich"; which some say means "darkness" or "sorrow". Here we found a large boat, into which we all got, and Macdonald, Duncan, Grant, and Coutts rowed; old John Gordon and two others going in another boat with the net. They rowed up to the head of the loch, to where the Muich runs down out of the Dhu Loch, which is on the other side.

The scenery is beautiful here, so wild and grand—real severe Highland scenery, with trees in the hollow. We had various scrambles in and out of the boat and along the shore, and saw three hawks, and caught seventy trout. I wish an artist could have been there to sketch the scene; it was so picturesque—the boat, the net, and the people in their kilts in the water, and on the shore. In going back, Albert rowed and Macdonald steered; and the lights were beautiful.

We came home at a quarter-past seven. At eight we dined. Löhlein, Macdonald, and Shackle waiting on us. After dinner we played with Caroline Dawson at whist with dummy, and afterwards walked round the little garden. The silence and solitude, only interrupted by the waving of the fir-trees, were very solemn and striking.

September 11, 1849

THE MORNING WAS VERY FINE. I heard the children repeat some poetry in German, and then at ten o'clock we set off with Lady Douro[84] in our carriage, and drove on beyond Inch Bobbard, changing horses near Birkhall, and stopping for a moment at the Linn of Muich; here we found the ponies, which we mounted, forded the river, and were almost immediately at the hut. We stopped there only for an instant, and remounted our ponies directly; Grant, Macdonald (who led my pony the whole time, and was extremely useful and attentive), Jemmie Coutts (leading Lady Douro's pony), Charlie Coutts, and John Brown going with us: old John Gordon leading the way. It was half-past twelve when we began ascending the hill immediately behind the house, and proceeded along over the hills, to a great height, whence the view was very fine, quite overhanging the loch, and commanding an extensive view of Glen Muich beyond on the opposite side. The road got worse and worse. It was particularly bad when we had to pass the Burn of the Glassalt, which falls into the loch, and was very full. There had been so much rain, that the burns and rivers were very full, and the ground quite soft. We rode over the Strone Hill, the wind blowing dreadfully hard when we came to the top. Albert walked almost from the first, and shot a hare and a grouse; he put up a good many of them. We walked to a little hollow immediately above the Dhu Loch, and at half-past three seated ourselves there, and had some very welcome luncheon. The loch is only a mile in length, and very wild; the hills, which are very rocky and precipitous, rising perpendicularly from it.

In about half an hour we began our journey homewards. We came straight down beside the Muich, which falls in the most beautiful way over the rocks and stones in the glen. We rode down, and only had to get off to cross the Glassalt, which was an awkward ford to scramble over. The road was rough, but certainly far less soft and disagreeable than the one we came by. I rode "Lochnagar" at first, but changed him for Colonel Gordon's pony, as I thought he took fright at the bogs; but Colonel Gordon's was broken-winded, and struggled very much in the soft ground, which was very disagreeable.

We were only an hour coming down to the boat. The evening was very fine, but it blew very hard on the lake and the men could not pull, and I got so alarmed that I begged to land, and Lady Douro was of my opinion that it was much better to get out. We accordingly landed, and rode home along a sort of sheep-path on the side of the lake, which took us three-quarters of an hour. It was very rough and very narrow, for the hill rises abruptly from the lake; we had seven hundred feet above us, and I suppose one hundred feet below. However, we arrived at the hut quite safely at twenty minutes to seven, thankful to have got through all our difficulties and adventures, which are always very pleasant to look back upon.

We dined a little before eight with Lady Douro, and played two rubbers of whist with her.

Old John Gordon amused Albert by saying, in speaking of the bad road we had gone, "It's something steep and something rough", and "this is the only best", meaning that it was very bad,—which was a characteristic reply.

September 6, 1850

AT HALF-PAST TEN O'CLOCK we set off with Lady Douro and Ernest Leiningen[85] and drove to Invercauld, about three-quarters of a mile beyond the house, where we found our people and ponies, together with Arthur Farquharson, Shewin, and others. We then walked a little way, after which we mounted our ponies and began the ascent towards Ben-na-Bhourd; Macdonald leading my pony, good little "Lochnagar", and James Coutts Lady Douro's. There is an excellent path, almost a narrow road, made up to within the last two miles and a half, which are very steep and rocky. The scenery is beautiful. We first rode up a glen (where a stone of the house in which Finla, the first of the Farquharsons, was born, is still shown), through which the Glassalt runs. Further on comes a very narrow, rocky, and precipitous glen, called the Sluggan, said to mean the "swallow", or "swallowing". Some little distance after this the country opens widely before you, with Ben-na-Bhourd rising towards the left; and then you enter the Forest of Mar, which the Duke of Leeds rents from Lord Fife. There is a very pretty little shooting-box, called Sluggan Cottage, which is half way from Invercauld to the top of Ben-na-Bhourd. Below this is the Quoich, which we forded. The last bit of the real road is a long steep ascent on the brow of a hill, the name of which means the "Tooth's craig". (Macdonald translated all the names for us.) The ascent, after the path ceases, is very stony; in fact, nothing but bare granite. Albert had walked a great deal, and we ladies got off after it became more uneven, and when we were no longer very far from the top. We came upon a number of "cairngorms", which we all began picking up, and found some very pretty ones. At the top, which is perfectly flat, the ground is entirely composed of stones or wet swampy moss, and the granite seems to have stopped just a few feet below. We sat down at a cairn, and had our luncheon. The wind was extremely cold, but whenever we got out of it, the air was very hot. The view from the top was magnificent and most extensive: Ben-na-Bhourd is 3,940 feet high. We saw Ben-y-Ghlo very clear, Cairngorm and Ben Muich Dhui quite close but in another direction; the Moray Firth, and, through the glass, ships even could be seen; and on the other side rose Loch-na-Gar, still the jewel of all the mountains here.

After luncheon we began our downward progress, and walked the whole of the steep part till we reached the path; we came down very quickly, my pony making great haste, though he had half a mind to kick. Albert found some beautiful little rock crystals in the Sluggan, and walked the remainder of the way; we ladies left our horses about a quarter of a mile before we met the carriage. The whole distance from Invercauld to the top of Ben-na-Bhourd is nine miles, so we must have been at least eighteen miles riding and walking. It has been a delightful expedition. It was six o'clock when we reached the carriage, and we were home at a little past seven.

September 12, 1850

WE LUNCHED EARLY, and then went at half-past two o'clock, with the children and all our party, except Lady Douro, to the Gathering[86] at the Castle of Braemar, as we did last year. The Duffs, Farquharsons, the Leeds's, and those staying with them, and Captain Forbes[87] and forty of his men who had come over from Strath Don, were there. Some of our people were there also. There were the usual games of "putting the stone", "throwing the hammer" and "caber", and racing up the hill of Craig Cheunnich, which was accomplished in less than six minutes and a half; and we were all much pleased to see our gillie Duncan, who is an active, good-looking young man, win. He was far before the others the whole way. It is a fearful exertion. Mr. Farquharson brought him up to me afterwards. Eighteen or nineteen started, and it looked very pretty to see them run off in their different coloured kilts, with their white shirts (the jackets or doublets they take off for all the games), and scramble up through the wood, emerging gradually at the edge of it, and climbing the hill.[88]

After this we went into the castle, and saw some dancing; the prettiest was a reel by Mr. Farquharson's children and some other children, and the "Ghillie Callum" beautifully danced by John Athole Farquharson, the fourth son. The twelve children were all there, including the baby, who is two years old.

Mama, Charles, and Ernest joined us at Braemar. Mama enjoys it all very much; it is her first visit to Scotland. We left after the dancing.

September 13, 1850

WE WALKED WITH CHARLES, the boys, and Vicky to the river side above the bridge, where all our tenants were assembled with poles and spears, or rather "leisters", for catching salmon. They all went into the river, walking up it, and then back again, poking about under all the stones to bring fish up to where the men stood with the net. It had a very pretty effect; about one hundred men wading through the river, some in kilts with poles and spears, all very much excited. Not succeeding the first time, we went higher up, and moved to three or four different places, but did not get any salmon; one or two escaping. Albert stood on a stone, and Colonel Gordon and Lord James Murray waded about the whole time. Duncan, in spite of all his exertions yesterday, and having besides walked to and from the Gathering, was the whole time in the water. Not far from the laundry there was another trial, and here we had a great fright. In one place there was a very deep pool, into which two men very foolishly went, and one could not swim; we suddenly saw them sink, and in one moment they seemed drowning, though surrounded by people. There was a cry for help, and a general rush, including Albert, towards the spot, which frightened me so much, that I grasped Lord Carlisle's arm in great agony. However, Dr. Robertson[89] swam in and pulled the man out, and all was safely over; but it was a horrid moment.

A salmon was speared here by one of the men; after which we walked to the ford, or quarry, where we were very successful, seven salmon being caught, some in the net, and some speared. Though Albert stood in the water some time he caught nothing: but the scene at this beautiful spot was exciting and picturesque in the extreme. I wished for Landseer's pencil. The sun was intensely hot. We did not get back till after three o'clock, and then took luncheon. The Duchess of Gordon came to see us afterwards; and while she was still with us, Captain Forbes (who had asked permission to do so) marched through the grounds with his men, the pipers going in front. They stopped, and cheered three-times-three, throwing up their bonnets. They then marched off; and we listened with pleasure to the distant shouts and the sound of the pibroch.

We heard afterwards that our men had carried all Captain Forbes's men on their backs through the river. They saw the fishing going on, and came to the water's edge on the opposite side; and on being greeted by our people, said they would come over, on which ours went across in one moment and carried them over—Macdonald at their head carrying Captain Forbes on his back. This was very courteous, and worthy of chivalrous times.

September 16, 1850

WE REACHED THE HUT AT THREE O'CLOCK. At half-past four we walked down to the loch, and got into the boat with our people: Duncan, J. Brown,[90] P. Coutts, and Leys rowing. They rowed mostly towards the opposite side, which is very fine indeed, and deeply furrowed by the torrents, which form glens and corries

John Brown in 1860.

where birch and alder trees grow close to the water's edge. We landed on a sandy spot below a fine glen, through which flows the Black Burn. It was very dry here; but still very picturesque, with alder-trees and mountain-ash in full fruit overhanging it. We afterwards landed at our usual place at the head of the loch, which is magnificent; and rode back. A new road has been made, and an excellent one it is, winding along above the lake.

The moon rose, and was beautifully reflected on the lake, which, with its steep green hills, looked lovely. To add to the beauty, poetry, and wildness of the scene, Coutts played in the boat; the men, who row very quickly and well now, giving an occasional shout when he played a reel. It reminded me of Sir Walter Scott's lines in *The Lady of the Lake*:

> Ever, as on they bore, more loud
> And louder rung the pibroch proud.
> At first the sound, by distance tame,
> Mellow'd along the waters came,
> And, lingering long by cape and bay,
> Wail'd every harsher note away.

We were home at a little past seven; and it was so still and pretty as we entered the wood, and saw the light flickering from our humble little abode.

September 10, 1852

WE DINED AT A QUARTER-PAST SIX O'CLOCK in morning gowns, (not ordinary ones, but such as are worn at a "breakfast",) and at seven started for Corriemulzie,[91] for a *torch-light ball* in the open air. I wore a white bonnet, a grey water silk, and (according to Highland fashion) my plaid scarf over my shoulder; and Albert his Highland dress which he wears every evening. We drove in the postchaise; the two ladies, Lord Derby [92] and Colonel Gordon following in the other carriage.

It was a mild though threatening evening, but fortunately it kept fine. We arrived there at half-past eight, by which time, of course, it was quite dark. Mr. and Lady Agnes Duff [93] received us at the door, and then took us at once through the house to the open space where the ball was, which was hid from our view till the curtains were drawn asunder. It was really a beautiful and most unusual sight. All the company were assembled there. A space about one hundred feet in length and sixty feet in width was boarded, and entirely surrounded by Highlanders bearing torches, which were placed in sockets, and constantly replenished. There were seven pipers playing together, Mackay [94] leading—and they received us with the usual salute and three cheers, and "Nis! nis! nis!" (pronounced: "Neesh! neesh! neesh!" the Highland "Hip! hip! hip!") and again cheers; after which came a most animated reel. There were above sixty people, exclusive of the Highlanders, of whom there were also sixty; all the Highland gentlemen, and any who were at all Scotch, were in kilts, the ladies in evening dresses. The company and the

Albert in Highland dress at Balmoral.

The Falls of Corriemulzie in the late nineteenth century.

Highlanders danced pretty nearly alternately. There were two or three sword dances. We were upon a *haut pas*, over which there was a canopy. The whole thing was admirably done, and very well worth seeing. Albert was delighted with it. I must not omit to mention a reel danced by eight Highlanders holding torches in their hands.

We left at half-past nine o'clock, and were home by a little past eleven. A long way certainly (fourteen miles I believe).

Monday, October 11, 1852

T HIS DAY HAS BEEN A VERY HAPPY, lucky, and memorable one—our last! A fine morning.

Albert had to see Mr. Walpole, and therefore it was nearly eleven o'clock before we could go up to the top of Craig Gowan, to see the cairn built, which was to commemorate our taking possession of this dear place; the old cairn having been pulled down. We set off with all the children, ladies, gentlemen, and a few of the servants, including Macdonald and Grant, who had not already gone up; and at the Moss House, which is half way, Mackay met us, and preceded us, playing, Duncan and Donald Stewart[95] going before him, to the highest point of Craig Gowan; where were assembled all the servants and tenants, with their wives and children and old relations. All our little friends were there: Mary Symons and Lizzie Stewart, the four Grants, and several others.

I then placed the first stone, after which Albert laid one, then the children, according to their ages. All the ladies and gentlemen placed one; and then every one came forward at once, each person carrying a stone and placing it on the cairn. Mr. and Mrs. Anderson[96] were there; Mackay played; and whisky was given to all. It took, I am sure, an hour building; and whilst it was going on, some merry reels were danced on a stone opposite. All the old people (even the gardener's wife from Corbie Hall, near Abergeldie,) danced; and many of the children, Mary Symons and Lizzie Stewart especially, danced so nicely; the latter with her hair all hanging down. Poor dear old "Monk", Sir Robert Gordon's faithful old dog, was sitting there amongst us all. At last, when the cairn, which is, I think, seven or eight feet high, was nearly completed, Albert climbed up to the top of it, and placed the last stone; after which three cheers were given. It was a gay, pretty, and touching sight; and I felt almost inclined to cry. The view was so beautiful over the dear hills; the day so fine; the whole so *gemüthlich*. May God bless this place, and allow us yet to see it and enjoy it many a long year!

After luncheon, Albert decided to walk through the wood for the last time, to have a last chance, and allowed Vicky[97] and me to go with him. At half-past three o'clock we started, got out at Grant's, and walked up part of Carrop, intending to go along the upper path, when a stag was heard to roar, and we all turned into the wood. We crept along, and got into the middle path. Albert soon left us to go lower, and we sat down to wait for him; presently we heard a shot—then complete silence—and, after another pause of some little time, three more shots. This was again succeeded by complete silence. We sent some one to look, who shortly after

A nineteenth-century engraving by A. F. Lydon of part of the River Dee.

returned, saying the stag had been twice hit and they were after him. Macdonald next went, and in about five minutes we heard "Solomon" give tongue, and knew he had the stag at bay. We listened a little while, and then began moving down hoping to arrive in time; but the barking had ceased, and Albert had already killed the stag; and on the road he lay, a little way beyond Invergelder—the beauty that we had admired yesterday evening. He was a magnificent animal, and I sat down and scratched a little sketch of him on a bit of paper that Macdonald had in his pocket, which I put on a stone—while Albert and Vicky, with the others, built a little cairn to mark the spot. We heard, after I had finished my little scrawl, and the carriage had joined us, that another stag had been seen near the road; and we had not gone as far as the "Irons",[98] before we saw one below the road, looking so handsome. Albert jumped out and fired—the animal fell, but rose again, and went on a little way, and Albert followed. Very shortly after, however, we heard a cry, and ran down and found Grant and Donald Stewart pulling up a stag with a very pretty head. Albert had gone on, Grant went after him, and I and Vicky remained with Donald Stewart, the stag, and the dogs. I sat down to sketch, and poor Vicky, unfortunately, seated herself on a wasp's nest, and was much stung. Donald Stewart rescued her, for I could not, being myself too much alarmed. Albert joined us in twenty minutes, unaware of having killed the stag. What a delightful day!

September 28, 1853

A FINE MORNING EARLY, but when we walked out at half-past ten o'clock it began raining, and soon poured down without ceasing. Most fortunately it cleared up before two, and the sun shone brightly for the ceremony of laying the foundation stone of the new house. Mama and all her party arrived from Abergeldie a little before three. I annex the Programme of the Ceremony, which was strictly adhered to, and was really very interesting:—

PROGRAMME.

The stone being prepared and suspended over that upon which it is to rest, (in which will be a cavity for the bottle containing the parchment and the coins):

The workmen will be placed in a semicircle at a little distance from the stone, and the women and home servants in an inner semicircle.

Her Majesty the Queen, and His Royal Highness the Prince, accompanied by the Royal Children, Her Royal Highness the Duchess of Kent, and attended by Her Majesty's guests and suite, will proceed from the house.

Her Majesty, the Prince, and the Royal Family, will stand on the South side of the stone, the suite being behind and on each side of the Royal party.

The Rev. Mr. Anderson will then pray for a blessing on the work. Her Majesty will affix her signature to the parchment, recording the day upon which the foundation stone was laid. Her Majesty's signature will be followed by that of the Prince and the Royal Children, the Duchess of Kent, and any others that her Majesty may command, and the parchment will be placed in the bottle.

One of each of the current coins of the present reign will also be placed in the bottle, and the bottle having been sealed up, will be placed in the cavity. The trowel will then be delivered to Her Majesty by Mr. Smith of Aberdeen, the architect, and the mortar having been spread, the stone will be lowered.

The level and square will then be applied, and their correctness having been ascertained, the mallet will be delivered to Her Majesty by Mr. Stuart (the clerk of the works), when Her Majesty will strike the stone and declare it to be laid. The cornucopia will be placed upon the stone, and the oil and wine poured out by Her Majesty.

The pipes will play, and Her Majesty, with the Royal Family, will retire.

As soon after as it can be got ready, the workmen will proceed to their dinner. After dinner, the following toasts will be given by Mr. Smith:—

"The Queen."

"The Prince and the Royal Family."

"Prosperity to the house, and happiness to the inmates of Balmoral."

The workmen will then leave the dinner-room, and amuse themselves upon the green with Highland games till seven o'clock, when a dance will take place in the ball-room.

We walked round to the spot, preceded by Mackay. Mr. Anderson made a very appropriate prayer. The wind was very high; but else everything went off as well as could possibly be desired.

The workmen and people all gave a cheer when the whole was concluded. In about three-quarters of an hour's time we went in to see the people at their dinner; and after this walked over to Craig Gowan for Albert to get a chance for black game.

We dressed early, and went for twenty minutes before dinner to see the people dancing in the ballroom, which they did with the greatest spirit.

Dr Norman Macleod.

October 29, 1854

WE WENT TO KIRK, as usual, at twelve o'clock. The service was performed by the Rev. Norman McLeod[99] of Glasgow, son of Dr. McLeod, and anything finer I never heard. The sermon, entirely extempore, was quite admirable; so simple, and yet so eloquent, and so beautifully argued and put. The text was from the account of the coming of Nicodemus to Christ by night; St. John, chapter 3. Mr. McLeod showed in the sermon how we *all* tried to please *self*, and live for *that*, and in so doing found no rest. Christ had come not only to die for us, but to show how we were to live. The second prayer was very touching; his allusions to us were so simple, saying, after his mention of us, "bless their children." It gave me a lump in my throat, as also when he prayed for "the dying, the wounded, the widow, and the orphans". Every one came back delighted; and how satisfactory it is to come back from church with such feelings! The servants and the Highlanders—*all*—were equally delighted.

Some of the model cottages built at Crathie by order of Victoria and Albert.

September 7, 1855

AT A QUARTER-PAST SEVEN O'CLOCK we arrived at dear Balmoral. Strange, very strange, it seemed to me to drive past, indeed *through*, the old house; the connecting part between it and the offices being broken through. The new house looks beautiful. The tower and the rooms in the connecting part are, however, only half finished, and the offices are still unbuilt: therefore the gentlemen (except the Minister[100]) live in the old house, and so do most of the servants; there is a long wooden passage which connects the new house with the offices. An old shoe was thrown after us into the house, for good luck, when we entered the hall. The house is charming; the rooms delightful; the furniture, papers, everything perfection.

William Ross, the Queen's Piper.

September 29, 1855

OUR DEAR VICTORIA WAS THIS DAY engaged to Prince Frederick William of Prussia,[101] who had been on a visit to us since the 14th. He had already spoken to us, on the 20th, of his wishes; but we were uncertain, on account of her extreme youth, whether he should speak to her himself, or wait till he came back again. However, we felt it was better he should do so; and during our ride up Craigna-Ban this afternoon, he picked a piece of white heather (the emblem of "good luck"), which he gave to her; and this enabled him to make an allusion to his hopes and wishes, as they rode down Glen Girnoch, which led to this happy conclusion.

October 14, 1855

To KIRK AT TWELVE O'CLOCK. The Rev. J. Caird, one of the most celebrated preachers in Scotland, performed the service, and electrified all present by a most admirable and beautiful sermon, which lasted nearly an hour, but which kept one's attention riveted. The text was from the twelfth chapter of Romans, and the eleventh verse: *"Not slothful in business; fervent in spirit; serving the Lord."* He explained, in the most beautiful and simple manner, what real religion is; how it ought to pervade every action of our lives; not a thing only for Sundays, or for our closet; not a thing to drive us from the world; not "a perpetual moping over 'good' books", but "being and doing good"; "letting everything be done in a Christian spirit". It was as fine as Mr. McLeod's sermon last year, and sent us home much edified.

Victoria's bedroom at Balmoral.

The dining room at Balmoral.

Albert's room at Balmoral.

August 30, 1856

O

N ARRIVING AT BALMORAL at seven o'clock in the evening, we found the tower finished as well as the offices, and the poor old house gone! The effect of the whole is very fine.

August 31, 1856

W

E WALKED ALONG THE RIVER and outside the house. The new offices and the yard are excellent; and the little garden on the west side, with the eagle fountain which the King of Prussia gave me, and which used to be in the greenhouse at Windsor, is extremely pretty; as are also the flower-beds under the walls of the side which faces the Dee. There are sculptured arms on the different shields, gilt, which has a very good effect and a bas-relief under our windows—not gilt—representing St. Hubert, with St. Andrew on one side and St. George on the other side: all done by Mr. Thomas.

September 8, 1857

A

T HALF-PAST ONE O'CLOCK we started in "highland state",—Albert in a royal Stewart plaid, and I and the girls in skirts of the same,—with the ladies (who had only returned at five in the morning from the ball at Mar Lodge) and gentlemen, for the Linn of Dee, to open the new bridge there. The valley looked

G. W. Wilson's mid nineteenth-century photograph of the Linn of Dee.

beautiful. A triumphal arch was erected, at which Lord Fife and Mr. Brooke received us, and walked near the carriage, pipers playing—the road lined with Duff men. On the bridge Lady Fife received us, and we all drank in whisky "prosperity to the bridge". The view of the linn is very fine from it.

Saturday, September 26, 1857

ALBERT WENT OUT WITH ALFRED for the day, and I walked with the two girls and Lady Churchill,[102] stopped at the shop and made some purchases for poor people and others; drove a little way, got out and walked up the hill to Balnacroft, Mrs. P. Farquharson's, and she walked round with us to some of the cottages to show me where the poor people lived, and to tell them who I was. Before we went into any we met an old woman, who, Mrs. Farquharson said, was very poor, eighty-eight years old, and mother to the former distiller. I gave her a warm petticoat, and the tears rolled down her old cheeks, and she shook my hands, and prayed God to bless me: it was very touching.

I went into a small cabin of old Kitty Kear's, who is eighty-six years old—quite erect, and who welcomed us with a great air of dignity. She sat down and spun. I gave her, also, a warm petticoat; she said, "May the Lord ever attend ye and yours, here and hereafter; and may the Lord be a guide to ye, and keep ye from all harm." She was quite surprised at Vicky's height; great interest is taken in her. We went on to a cottage (formerly Jean Gordon's), to visit old widow Symons, who is "past

Jane, Lady Churchill,
at Balmoral in October 1857.

Willie Blair, the fiddler.

four-score", with a nice rosy face, but was bent quite double; she was most friendly, shaking hands with us all, asking which was I, and repeating many kind blessings: "May the Lord attend ye with mirth and with joy; may He ever be with ye in this world, and when ye leave it." To Vicky, when told she was going to be married, she said, "May the Lord be a guide to ye in your future, and may every happiness attend ye." She was very talkative; and when I said I hoped to see her again, she expressed an expectation that "she should be called any day", and so did Kitty Kear.

We went into three other cottages: to Mrs. Symons's (daughter-in-law to the old widow living next door), who had an "unwell boy"; then across a little burn to another old woman's; and afterwards peeped into Blair the fiddler's.[103] We drove back, and got out again to visit old Mrs. Grant (Grant's mother), who is so tidy and clean, and to whom I gave a dress and handkerchief, and she said, "You're too kind to me, you're over kind to me, ye give me more every year, and I get older every year." After talking some time with her, she said, "I am happy to see ye looking so nice." She had tears in her eyes, and speaking of Vicky's going, said, "I'm very sorry, and I think she is sorry hersel'"; and, having said she feared she would not see her (the Princess) again, said: "I am very sorry I said that, but I meant no harm; I always say just what I think, not what is fut" (fit). Dear old lady; she is such a pleasant person.

Really the affection of these good people, who are so hearty and so happy to see you, taking interest in everything, is very touching and gratifying.

Spearing salmon in the River Dee; watercolour by Carl Haag, 1853.

Bringing the stags home to Balmoral
after a day's hunting; oil painting by Carl Haag, 1854

Watercolour by Victoria of Glen Shiel.

September 18, 1858

Alas! the last day! When we got up the weather seemed very hopeless. Everything was white with snow, which lay, at least, an inch on the ground, and it continued snowing heavily, as it had done since five this morning. I wished we might be snowed up, and unable to move. How happy I should have been could it have been so! It continued snowing till half-past ten or eleven, and then it began to clear up. The hills appeared quite white; the sun came out, and it became splendidly bright. Albert was going to have the woods driven—which are not properly called Carrop Woods, but Garmaddie Woods—but had first to ride round Craig Gowan with Dr. Robertson to see Robrech, the place where Duncan's new house is to be built, which is above the village, opposite Craig Luraghain, with a most splendid view; and at Grant's house I was to meet him.

At one o'clock I left with Alice and Lenchen[104] for Grant's, where we met Albert, who joined us in the carriage: the day was truly splendid. We got out at the river, and were going down to Nelly's Bush, when a stag was heard roaring very near; so we had to stop, and, with our plaids and cloaks to sit upon, really avoided getting very wet. We waited till Albert was near to the stag, saw it move, heard Albert fire twice, and the stag turn, stop, and then disappear. Albert fired again, but the stag had crossed the Dee; so we turned up on to the road, and went into the dear old Corrie Buie; Albert turning off to see if there were any deer near, while we waited for him. We then came to a place which is always wet, but which was particularly bad after the late rain and snow. There was no pony for me to get on; and as I wished not to get my feet wet by walking through the long grass, Albert proposed I should be carried over in a plaid; and Lenchen was first carried over; but it was held too low, and her feet dangled; so Albert suggested the plaid should be put round the men's shoulders, and that I should sit upon it; Brown and Duncan, the two strongest and handiest, were the two who undertook it, and I sat safely enough with an arm on each man's shoulder, and was carried successfully over. All the Highlanders are so amusing, and really pleasant and instructive to talk to—women as well as men—and the latter so gentlemanlike.

September 22, 1859

The morning dawned brightly. Suddenly a very high wind arose which alarmed us, but yet it looked bright, and we hoped the wind would keep off the rain; but after breakfast, while watching the preparations, showers began, and from half-past eleven a fearful down-pour, with that white curtain-like appearance which is so alarming; and this lasted till half-past twelve. I was in despair; but at length it began to clear, just as the neighbours with their families, and some of the farmers opposite (the Herrons, Duncans, Brown's father and brothers) arrived, and then came the huge omnibuses and carriages laden with "philosophers".[105] At two o'clock we were all ready. Albert and the boys were in their kilts, and I and the girls in royal Stewart skirts and shawls over black velvet bodies.

It was a beautiful sight in spite of the frequent slight showers which at first tormented us, and the very high cold wind. There were gleams of sunshine, which, with the Highlanders in their brilliant and picturesque dresses, the wild notes of the pipes, the band, and the beautiful background of mountains, rendered the scene wild and striking in the extreme. The Farquharson's men headed by Colonel Farquharson, the Duff's by Lord Fife, and the Forbes's men by Sir Charles Forbes, had all marched on the ground before we came out, and were drawn up just opposite to us, and the spectators (the people of the country) behind them. We stood on the terrace, the company near us, and the "savants", also, on either side of us, and along the slopes, on the grounds. The games began about three o'clock:

1. "Throwing the Hammer."
2. "Tossing the Caber."
3. "Putting the Stone."

We gave prizes to the three best in each of the games. We walked along the terrace to the large marquee, talking to the people, to where the men were "putting the stone". After this returned to the upper terrace, to see the race, a pretty wild sight; but the men looked very cold, with nothing but their shirts and kilts on; they ran beautifully. They wrapped plaids round themselves, and then came to receive the prizes from me. Last of all came the dancing—reels and "Ghillie Callum". The latter the judges could not make up their minds about; it was danced over and over again; and at last they left out the best dancer of all! They said he danced "too well"! The dancing over, we left amid the loud cheers of the people. It was then about half-past five. We watched from the window the Highlanders marching away, the different people walking off, and four weighty omnibuses filling with the scientific men.

Friday, October 7, 1859

Breakfast at half-past eight. At ten minutes to nine we started, in the sociable, with Bertie and Alice and our usual attendants. Drove along the opposite side of the river. The day very mild and promising to be fine, though a little heavy over the hills, which we anxiously watched. At Castleton we took four post-horses, and drove to the Shiel of the Derry, that beautiful spot where we were last year—which Albert had never seen—and arrived there just before eleven. Our ponies were there with Kennedy, Robertson, and Jemmie Smith. One pony carried the luncheon-baskets. After all the cloaks, etc. had been placed on the ponies, or carried by the men, we mounted and began our "journey". I was on "Victoria", Alice on "Dobbins". George McHardy, an elderly man who knew the country (and acts as a guide, carrying luggage for people across the hills "on beasts" which he keeps for that purpose), led the way. We rode (my pony being led by Brown most of the time both going up and down) at least four miles up Glen Derry, which is very fine, with the remnants of a splendid forest, Cairn Derry being to the right, and the

Derry Water running below. The track was very bad and stony, and broken up by cattle coming down for the "Tryst". At the end of the glen we crossed a ford, passed some softish ground, and turned up to the left by a very rough, steep, but yet gradual ascent to Corrie Etchan, which is in a very wild rugged spot, with magnificent precipices, a high mountain to the right called Ben Main, while to the left was Cairngorm of Derry. When we reached the top of this very steep ascent (we had been rising, though almost imperceptibly, from the Derry Shiel), we came upon a loch of the same name, which reminded us of Loch-na-Gar and of Loch-na-Nian. You look from here on to other wild hills and corries—on Ben A'an, etc. We ascended very gradually, but became so enveloped in mist that we could see nothing—hardly those just before us! Albert had walked a good deal; and it was very cold. The mist got worse; and as we rode along the stony, but almost flat ridge of Ben Muich Dhui, we hardly knew whether we were on level ground or the top of the mountain. However, I and Alice rode to the very top, which we reached a few minutes past two; and here, at a cairn of stones, we lunched, in a piercing cold wind.

Just as we sat down, a gust of wind came and dispersed the mist, which had a most wonderful effect, like a dissolving view—and exhibited the grandest, wildest scenery imaginable. We sat on a ridge of the cairn to take our luncheon,—our good people being grouped with the ponies near us. Luncheon over, Albert ran off with Alice to the ridge to look at the splendid view, and sent for me to follow. I did so; but not without Grant's help, for there were quantities of large loose stones heaped up together to walk upon. The wind was fearfully high, but the view was well worth seeing. I cannot describe all, but we saw where the Dee rises between the mountains called the Well of Dee—Ben-y-Ghlo—and the adjacent mountains, Ben Vrackie—then Ben-na-Bhourd—Ben A'an, etc.—and such magnificent wild rocks, precipices, and corries. It had a sublime and solemn effect; so wild, so solitary—no one but ourselves and our little party there.

Albert went on further with the children, but I returned with Grant to my seat on the cairn, as I could not scramble about well. Soon after, we all began walking and looking for "cairngorms", and found some small ones. The mist had entirely cleared away below, so that we saw all the beautiful views. Ben Muich Dhui is 4,297 feet high, one of the highest mountains in Scotland. I and Alice rode part of the way, walking wherever it was very steep. Albert and Bertie walked the whole time. I had a little whisky and water as the people declared pure water would be too chilling. We then rode on without getting off again, Albert talking so gaily with Grant. Upon which Brown observed to me in simple Highland phrase, "It's very pleasant to walk with a person who is always 'content'." Yesterday, in speaking of dearest Albert's sport, when I observed he never was cross after bad luck, Brown said, "Every one on the estate says there never was so kind a master; I am sure our only wish is to give satisfaction." I said, they certainly did.

By a quarter-past six o'clock we got down to the Shiel of the Derry, where we found some tea, which we took in the "shiel",[106] and started again by moonlight at about half-past six. We reached Castleton at half-past seven—and after this it became cloudy. At a quarter-past eight precisely we were at Balmoral, much delighted and not at all tired; everything had been so well arranged, and so quietly, without any fuss. *Never* shall I forget this day, or the impression this very grand scene made upon me; truly sublime and impressive; such solitude!

Hotel Grantown,
Tuesday, September 4, 1860

ARRIVED THIS EVENING after a most interesting tour; I will recount the events of the day. Breakfasted at Balmoral in our own room at half-past seven o'clock, and started at eight or a little past, with Lady Churchill and General Grey,[107] in the sociable (Grant and Brown on the box as usual) for Castleton, where we changed horses. We went on five miles beyond the Linn of Dee, to the Shepherd's Shiel of Geldie, or, properly speaking, Giuly, where we found our ponies and a guide, Charlie Stewart. We mounted at once, and rode up along the Geldie, which we had to ford frequently to avoid the bogs, and rode on for two hours up Glen Geldie, over a moor which, was so soft and boggy in places, that we had to get off several times. The hills were wild, but not very high, bare of trees, and even of heather to a great extent, and not picturesque till we approached the Fishie, and turned to the right up to the glen which we could see in the distance. The Fishie and Geldie rise almost on a level, with very little distance between them. The Fishie is a fine rapid stream, full of stones. As you approach the glen, which is very narrow, the scenery becomes very fine—particularly after fording the Etchart, a very deep ford. Grant, on his pony, led me through: our men on foot took off their shoes and stockings to get across. From this point the narrow path winds along the base of the hills of Craig-na-Go'ar—the rocks of the "Goat Craig";—Craig-na-Caillach; and Strong-na-Barin—"the nose of the queen". The rapid river is overhung by rocks, with trees, birch and fir; the hills, as you advance, rise very steeply on both sides, with rich rocks and corries, and occasional streamlets falling from very high—while the path winds along, rising gradually higher and higher. It is quite magnificent!

We stopped when we came to a level spot amongst the trees. The native firs are particularly fine; and the whole is grand in the extreme. We lunched here—a charming spot—at two o'clock; and then pursued our journey. We walked on a little way to where the valley and glen widen out, and where there is what they call here a green "hard". We got on our ponies again and crossed the Fishie (a stream we forded many times in the course of the day) to a place where the finest fir-trees are, amidst some of the most beautiful scenery possible.

Then we came upon a most lovely spot—the scene of all Landseer's glory—and where there is a little encampment of wooden and turf huts, built by the late Duchess of Bedford;[108] now no longer belonging to the family, and, alas! all falling into decay—among splendid fir-trees, the mountains rising abruptly from the sides of the valley. We were quite enchanted with the beauty of the view. This place is about seven miles from the mouth of the Fishie. Emerging from the wood we came upon a good road, with low hills, beautifully heather-coloured, to the left; those to the right, high and wooded, with noble corries and waterfalls.

We met Lord and Lady Alexander Russell at a small farmhouse, just as we rode out of the wood, and had some talk with them. They feel deeply the ruin of the place where they formerly lived, as it no longer belongs to them. We rode on for a good long distance, twelve miles, till we came to the ferry of the Spey. Deer were being

Late nineteenth-century photograph of the river Spey from Grantown.

driven in the woods, and we heard several shots. We saw fine ranges of hills on the Spey-side, or Strathspey, and opening to our left, those near Loch Laggan. We came to a wood of larch; from that, upon cultivated land, with Kinrara towards our right, where the monument to the late Duke of Gordon is conspicuously seen on a hill, which was perfectly crimson with heather.

Before entering the larch wood, Lord Alexander Russell caught us up again in a little pony carriage, having to go the same way, and he was so good as to explain everything to us. He showed us "The Duke of Argyll's Stone"—a cairn on the top of a hill to our right, celebrated, as seems most probable, from the Marquis of Argyll having halted there with his army. We came to another larch wood, when I and Lady Churchill got off our ponies, as we were very stiff from riding so long; and at the end of this wood we came upon Loch Inch, which is lovely, and of which I should have liked exceedingly to have taken a sketch, but we were pressed for time and hurried. The light was lovely; and some cattle were crossing a narrow strip of grass across the end of the loch nearest to us, which really made a charming picture. It is not a wild lake, quite the contrary; no high rocks, but woods and blue hills as a background. About a mile from this was the ferry. There we parted from our ponies, only Grant and Brown coming on with us. Walker, the police inspector, met us, but did not keep with us. He had been sent to order everything in a quiet way, without letting people suspect who we were: in this he entirely succeeded. The ferry was a very rude affair; it was like a boat or coble, but we could only stand on it, and it was moved at one end by two long oars, plied by the ferryman and Brown, and at the other end by a long sort of beam, which Grant took in hand. A few seconds brought us over to the road, where there were two shabby vehicles, one a kind of barouche, into which Albert and I got, Lady Churchill and General Grey into the other—a break; each with a pair of small and rather miserable horses, driven by a man from the box. Grant was on our carriage, and Brown on the other. We had gone so far forty miles, at least twenty on horseback. We had decided to call ourselves *Lord and Lady Churchill and party*, Lady Churchill passing as *Miss Spencer*, and General Grey as *Dr. Grey!* Brown once forgot this, and called me "Your Majesty" as I was getting into the carriage; and Grant on the box once called Albert "Your Royal Highness"; which set us off laughing, but no one observed it.

We had a long three hours' drive; it was six o'clock when we got into the carriage. We were soon out of the wood, and came upon the Badenoch road— passing close by Kinrara, but unfortunately not through it, which we ought to have done. It was very beautiful—fine wooded hills—the high Cairngorm range, and Ben Muich Dhui, unfortunately much obscured by the mist on the top—and the broad Spey flowing in the valley, with cultivated fields and fine trees below. Most striking, however, on our whole long journey was the utter, and to me very refreshing, solitude. Hardly a habitation! and hardly meeting a soul! It gradually grew dark. We stopped at a small half-way house for the horses to take some water; and the few people about stared vacantly at the two simple vehicles.

The mountains gradually disappeared,—the evening was mild, with a few drops of rain. On and on we went, till at length we saw lights, and drove through a long and straggling "toun", and turned down a small court to the door of the inn. Here we got out quickly—Lady Churchill and General Grey not waiting for us. We went up a small staircase, and were shown to our bedroom at the top of it—very small, but clean—with a large four-post bed which nearly filled the whole room. Opposite was the drawing and dining-room in one—very tidy and well-sized. Then came the room where Albert dressed, which was very small. The two maids (Jane Shackle was with me) had driven over by another road in the waggonette, Stewart driving them. Made ourselves "clean and tidy", and then sat down to our dinner. Grant and Brown were to have waited on us, but were "bashful" and did not. A ringletted woman did everything; and, when dinner was over, removed the cloth and placed the bottle of wine (our own which we had brought) on the table with the glasses, which was the old English fashion. The dinner was very fair, and all very clean: soup, "hodge-podge", mutton-broth with vegetables, which I did not much relish, fowl with white sauce, good roast lamb, very good potatoes, besides one or two other dishes, which I did not taste, ending with a good tart of cranberries. After dinner I tried to write part of this account (but the talking round me confused me), while Albert played at "patience". Then went away, to begin undressing, and it was about half-past eleven, when we got to bed.

opposite: Tomintoul.

Wednesday, September 5

A misty, rainy morning. Had not slept very soundly. We got up rather early, and sat working and reading in the drawing-room till the breakfast was ready, for which we had to wait some little time. Good tea and bread and butter, and some excellent porridge. Jane Shackle (who was very useful and attentive) said that they had all supped together, namely, the two maids, and Grant, Brown, Stewart, and Walker (who was still there), and were very merry in the "commercial room". The people were very amusing about us. The woman came in while they were at their dinner, and said to Grant, "Dr. Grey wants you", which nearly upset the gravity of all the others: then they told Jane, "Your lady gives no trouble"; and Grant in the morning called up to Jane, "Does his lordship want me?" One could look on the street, which is a very long wide one, with detached houses, from our window. It was perfectly quiet, no one stirring, except here and there a man driving a cart, or a boy going along on his errand. General Grey bought himself a watch in a shop for 2*l*.!

At length, at about ten minutes to ten o'clock, we started in the same carriages and the same way as yesterday, and drove up to Castle Grant, Lord Seafield's place—a fine (not Highland-looking) park, with a very plain-looking house, like a factory, about two miles from the town. It was drizzling almost the whole time. We did not get out, but drove back, having to pass through Grantown again; where evidently "the murder was out", for all the people were in the street, and the landlady waved her pocket-handkerchief, and the ringletted maid (who had curl-papers in the morning) waved a flag from the window. Our coachman evidently did not observe or guess anything. As we drove out of the town, turning to our right

through a wood, we met many people coming into the town, which the coachman said was for a funeral. We passed over the Spey, by the Bridge of Spey. It continued provokingly rainy, the mist hanging very low on the hills, which, however, did not seem to be very high, but were pink with heather. We stopped to have the cover of leather put over our carriage, which is the fashion of all the flys here. It keeps out the rain, however, very well.

The first striking feature in this country is the Pass of Dal Dhu, above which the road winds—a steep corrie, with green hills. We stopped at a small inn, with only one other house near it; and here the poor wretchedly-jaded horses got a little water, and waited for about ten minutes. Further on we came to a very steep hill, also to a sort of pass, called Glen Bruin, with green hills, evidently of slate formation. Here we got out, and walked down the hill, and over the Bridge of Bruin, and partly up another hill, the road winding amazingly after this—up and down hill. We then came in sight of the Avon, winding below the hills; and again got out at a little wood, before the Bridge of Avon; the river is fine and clear here. We re-entered our carriages (Lady Churchill and I for this short time together), and drove about a mile further up a hill to Tomintoul; our poor horses being hardly able to drag themselves any longer, the man whipping them and whistling to them to go on, which they could not, and I thought every instant the they would stop in the village. We took four hours to drive these fourteen for it was two o'clock when we were outside the town, and got out to mount our ponies. Tomintoul is the most tumble-down, poor-looking place I ever saw—a long street with three inns, miserable dirty-looking houses and people, and a sad look of wretchedness about it. Grant told me that it was the dirtiest, poorest village in the whole of the Highlands.

We mounted our ponies a short way out of the town, but only rode for a few minutes as it was past two o'clock. We came upon a beautiful view, looking down upon the Avon and up a fine glen. There we rested and took luncheon. While Brown was unpacking and arranging our things, I spoke to him and to Grant, who was helping, about not having waited on us, as they ought to have done, at dinner last night and at breakfast, as we had wished; and Brown answered, he was afraid he should not do it rightly; I replied we did not wish to have a stranger in the room, and they must do so another time.

Luncheon (provisions for which we had taken with us from home yesterday) finished, we started again, walked a little way, till we were overtaken by the men and ponies, and then rode along Avonside, the road winding at the bottom of the glen, which is in part tolerably wide; but narrows as it turns, and winds round towards Inchrory, where it is called Glen Avon. The hills, sloping down to the river side, are beautifully green. It was very muggy—quite oppressive, and the greater part of the road deep and sloppy, till we came upon the granite formation again. In order to get on, as it was late, and we had eight miles to ride, our men—at least Brown and two of the others—walked before us at a fearful pace, so that we had to trot to keep up at all. Grant rode frequently on the deer pony; the others seemed, however, a good deal tired with the two long days' journey, and were glad to get on Albert's or the General's pony to give themselves a lift; but their willingness, readiness, cheerfulness, indefatigableness, are very admirable, and make them most delightful servants. As for Grant and Brown they are perfect—discreet, careful, intelligent, attentive, ever ready to do what is wanted; and the latter, particularly, is handy and willing to do everything and anything, and to overcome every difficulty, which

Mr and Mrs John Grant with their seven children.

makes him one of my best servants anywhere.

We passed by Inchrory—seeing, as we approached, two eagles towering splendidly above, and alighting on the top of the hills. From Inchrory we rode to Loch Bulig, which was beautifully lit up by the setting sun. From Tomintoul we escaped all real rain, having only a slight sprinkling every now and then. At Loch Bulig we found our carriage and four ponies, and drove back just as we left yesterday morning, reaching Balmoral safely at half-past seven.

What a delightful, successful expedition! Dear Lady Churchill was, as usual, thoroughly amiable, cheerful, and ready to do everything. Both she and the General seemed entirely to enjoy it, and enter into it, and so I am sure did our people. To my dear Albert do we owe it, for he always thought it would be delightful, having gone on many similar expeditions in former days himself. He enjoyed it very much. We heard since that the secret came out through a man recognising Albert in the street yesterday morning; then the crown on the dog-cart made them think that it was some one from Balmoral, though they never suspected that it could be ourselves! "The lady must be terrible rich", the woman observed, as I had so many gold rings on my fingers!—I told Lady Churchill she had on many more than I had. When they heard who it was, they were ready to drop with astonishment and fright. I fear I have but poorly recounted this very amusing and never to be forgotten expedition, which will always be remembered with delight.

I must pay a tribute to our ponies. Dear "Fyvie" is perfection, and Albert's equally excellent.

Victoria on "Fyvie", attended by Brown and Grant.

Friday, September 20, 1861

LOOKED ANXIOUSLY AT THE WEATHER at seven o'clock—there had been a little rain, there was still mist on the hills, and it looked doubtful. However, Albert said it would be best to keep to the original arrangements, and so we got up early, and by eight the sun shone, and the mist began to lift everywhere. We breakfasted at half-past eight, and at half-past nine we started in two sociables—Alice and Louis[109] with us in the first, and Grant on the box; Lady Churchill and General Grey in the second, and Brown on the box. We drove to the Bridge of Muich, where we found our six ponies, and five gillies, (J. Smith, J. Morgan, Kennedy, C. Stewart, and S. Campbell). We rode up the peat-road over the hill of Polach and down it again for about four miles, and then came to a very soft bit; but still with careful management we avoided getting into any of the bogs, and I remained on my pony all the time. Albert and Louis had to get off and walk for about two hundred yards. The hills of Loch-na-Gar were very hazy, but Mount Keen was in great beauty before us, and as we come down to the Glen of Corrie Vruach, and looked down Glen Tanar, the scenery was grand and wild. Mount Keen is a curious conical-shaped hill, with a deep corrie in it. It is nearly 3,200 feet high, and we had a very steep rough ascent over the shoulder, after crossing the Tanar Water. It was six and a half miles from the Bridge of Muich to Corrie Vruach.

When we were on the level ground again, where it was hard and dry, we all got off and walked on over the shoulder of the hill. We had not gone far when we descried Lord Dalhousie[110] (whom General Grey had in confdence informed of our coming) on a pony. He welcomed us on the border of his "March", got off his pony and walked with us. After walking some little time Alice and I remounted our ponies, (Albert riding some part of the time), and turned to the left, when we came in sight of a new country, and looked down a very fine glen—Glen Mark. We descended by a very steep but winding path, called The Ladder, very grand and wild: the water running through it is called The Ladder Burn. It is very fine indeed, and very striking. There is a small forester's lodge at the very foot of it. The pass is quite a narrow one; you wind along a very steep and rough path, but still it was quite easy to ride on it, as it zigzags along. We crossed the burn at the bottom, where a picturesque group of "shearers" were seated, chiefly women, the older ones smoking. They were returning from the south to the north, whence they came. We rode up to the little cottage; and in a little room of a regular Highland cabin, with its usual "press bed", we had luncheon. This place is called Invermark, and is four and a half miles from Corrie Vruach. After luncheon I sketched the fine view. The steep hill we came down immediately opposite the keeper's lodge is called Craig Boestock, and a very fine isolated craggy hill which rises to the left—over-topping a small and wild glen—is called the Hill of Doun.

We mounted our ponies a little after three, and rode down Glen Mark, stopping to drink some water out of a very pure well, called The White Well; and crossing the Mark several times. As we approached the Manse of Loch Lee, the glen widened, and the old Castle of Invermark came out extremely well; and, surrounded by woods and corn-fields, in which the people where "shearing", looked most picturesque. We turned to the right, and rode up to the old ruined castle, which is half covered with ivy. We then rode up to Lord Dalhousie's shooting-lodge, where we dismounted. It is a new and very pretty house, built of

Glen Mark — a mid nineteenth-century photograph.

The inside of a Highland cottage, from a painting by Landseer.

The kitchen of one of the cottages on the Balmoral estate.

The inn at Fettercairn.

granite, in a very fine position overlooking the glen, with wild hills at the back. Miss Maule (now Lady C. Maule) was there. We passed through the drawing-room, and went on a few yards to the end of a walk whence you see Loch Lee, a wild, but not large, lake closed in by mountains—with a farmhouse and a few cottages at its edge. The hall and dining-room are very prettily fitted up with trophies of sport, and the walls panelled with light wood. We had a few of the very short showers which hung about the hills. We then got into our carriages. The carriage we were in was a sort of double dog-cart which could carry eight—but was very narrow inside. We drove along the glen—down by the Northesk (the Ey and Mark meeting become the Northesk), passing to the right another very pretty glen—Glen Effach, much wooded, and the whole landscape beautifully lit up. Before us all was light and bright, and behind the mist and rain seemed to come down heavily over the mountains.

Further on, we passed Poul Skeinnie Bridge and Tarf Bridge, both regular steep Highland bridges. To the right of the latter there is a new Free Kirk—further on Captain Wemyss's Retreat, a strange-looking place—to the left Mill Dane—and, on a small eminence, the Castle of Auch Mill, which now resembles an old farm-house, but has traces of a terrace garden remaining. The hills round it and near the road to the left were like small mounds. A little further on again we came to a wood, where we got out and walked along The Burn, Major McInroy's. The path winds along through the wood just above this most curious narrow gorge, which is unlike any of the other lynns; the rocks are very peculiar, and the burn very narrow, with deep pools completely overhung by wood. It extends some way. The woods and grounds might be in Wales, or even in Hawthornden. We walked through the wood and a little way along the road, till the carriages overtook us. We had three miles further to drive to Fettercairn, in all forty miles from Balmoral. We came upon a flat country, evidently much cultivated, but it was too dark to see anything.

At a quarter-past seven o'clock we reached the small quiet town, or rather village, of Fettercairn, for it was very small—not a creature stirring, and we got out at the quiet little inn, "Ramsay Arms", quite unobserved, and went at once upstairs. There was a very nice drawing-room, and next to it, a dining-room, both very clean and tidy—then to the left our bedroom, which was excessively small, but also very clean and neat, and much better furnished than at Grantown. Alice had a nice room, the same size as ours; then came a mere morsel of one, (with a "press bed"), in which Albert dressed; and then came Lady Churchill's bedroom just beyond. Louis and General Grey had rooms in an hotel, called "The Temperance Hotel", opposite. We dined at eight, a very nice, clean, good dinner. Grant and Brown waited. They were rather nervous, but General Grey and Lady Churchill carved, and they had only to change the plates, which Brown soon got into the way of doing. A little girl of the house came in to help—but Grant turned her round to prevent her looking at us! The landlord and landlady knew who we were, but no one else except the coachman, and they kept the secret admirably.

The evening being bright and moonlight and very still, we all went out, and walked through the whole village, where not a creature moved—through the principal little square, in the middle of which was a sort of pillar or Town Cross[111] on steps, and Louis read, by the light of the moon, a proclamation for collections of charities which was stuck on it. We walked on along a lane a short way, hearing nothing whatever—not a leaf moving—but the distant barking of a dog! Suddenly we heard a drum and fifes! We were greatly alarmed, fearing we had been recognised; but Louis and General Grey, who went back, saw nothing whatever. Still, as we walked slowly back, we heard the noise from time to time—and when we reached the inn door we stopped, and saw six men march up with fifes and a drum (not a creature taking any notice of them), go down the street, and back again. Grant and Brown were out; but had no idea what it could be. Albert asked the little maid, and the answer was, "It's just a band", and that it walked about in this way twice a week. How odd! It went on playing some time after we got home. We sat till half-past ten working, and Albert reading,—and then retired to rest.

Saturday, September 21

Got to sleep after two or three o'clock. The morning was dull and close, and misty with a little rain; hardly any one stirring; but a few people at their work. A traveller had arrived at night, and wanted to come up into the dining-room, which is the "commercial travellers' room"; and they had difficulty in telling him he could *not* stop there. He joined Grant and Brown at their tea, and on his asking, "What's the matter here?" Grant answered, "It's a wedding party from Aberdeen." At "The Temperance Hotel" they were very anxious to know whom they had got. All, except General Grey, breakfasted a little before nine. Brown acted as my servant, brushing my skirt and boots, and taking any message, and Grant as Albert's valet.

At a quarter to ten we started the same way as before, except that we were in the carriage which Lady Churchill and the General had yesterday. It was unfortunately misty, and we could see no distance. The people had just discovered who we were, and a few cheered us as we went along. We passed close to Fettercairn, Sir J.

Forbes's house; then further on to the left, Fasque, belonging to Sir T. Gladstone,[112] who has evidently done a great deal for the country, having built many good cottages. We then came to a very long hill, at least four miles in length, called the Cairnie Month, whence there is a very fine view; but which was entirely obscured by a heavy driving mist. We walked up part of it, and then for a little while Alice and I sat alone in the carriage. We next came to the Spittal Bridge, a curious high bridge with the Dye Water to the left, and the Spittal Burn to the right. Sir T. Gladstone's place is close to the Bridge of Dye—where we changed carriages again, re-entering the double dog-cart—Albert and I inside, and Louis sitting behind. We went up a hill again and saw Mount Battock to the north-west, close to Sir T. Gladstone's shooting-lodge. You then come to an open country, with an extensive view towards Aberdeen, and to a very deep, rough ford, where you pass the Feugh, at a place called White Stones. It is very pretty and a fine glen with wood. About two miles further to the north-west, on the left, is Finzean; and, a little beyond, is "King Durdun's Stone", as they call it, by the roadside—a large, heavy, ancient stone—the history of which, however, we have not yet discovered. Then we passed Mary's Well, to the left of which is Ballogie House, a fine property belonging to Mr. Dyce Nicol. The harvest and everything seemed prosperous, and the country was very pretty. We got out at a very small village (where the horses had some water, for it was a terribly long stage), and walked a little way along the road. Alice, Lady Churchill, and I, went into the house of a tailor, which was very tidy, and the woman in it most friendly, asking us to rest there; but not dreaming who we were.

We drove on again, watching ominous-looking clouds, which, however, cleared off afterwards. We saw the woods of Lord Huntly's forest, and the hills which one sees from the road to Aboyne. Instead of going on to Aboyne we turned to the left, leaving the Bridge of Aboyne (which we had not seen before) to the right. A little beyond this, out of sight of all habitations, we found the postmaster, with another carriage for us. This was twenty-two miles from Fettercairn. We crossed the Tanar Water, and drove to the left up Glen Tanar—a really beautiful and richly-wooded glen, between high hills—part of Lord Huntly's forest. We drove on about six miles, and then stopped, as it was past two, to get our luncheon. The day kept quite fair in spite of threatening clouds and gathering mist. The spot where we lunched was very pretty. This over, we walked on a little, and then got into the carriages again, and drove to the end of the glen—out of the trees to Eatnoch, on to a keeper's house in the glen—a very lonely place, where our ponies were. It was about four when we arrived. A wretched idiot girl was here by herself, as tall as Lady Churchill; but a good deal bent, and dressed like a child, with a pinafore and short-cut hair. She sat on the ground with her hands round her knees, rocking to and fro and laughing; she then got up and walked towards us. General Grey put himself before me, and she went up to him, and began taking hold of his coat, and putting her hand into his pockets, which set us all off laughing, sad as it was. An old man walked up hastily soon after, and on Lady Churchill asking him if he knew that poor girl, he said, "Yes, she belongs to me, she has a weakness in her mind"; and led her off hurriedly.

We walked on a few hundred yards, and then mounted our ponies a little higher up, and then proceeded across the other shoulder of the hill we had come down yesterday—crossed the boggy part, and came over the Polach just as in going. The mist on the distant hills, Mount Keen, etc., made it feel chilly. Coming down the

Victoria's mother, Victoria-Mary-Louisa,
Duchess of Kent, in youth.

peat-road to the Bridge of Muich, the view of the valleys of Muich, Gairn, and Ballater was beautiful. As we went along I talked frequently with good Grant.

We found my dearest Mother's[113] sociable, a fine large one, which she has left to Albert, waiting to take us back. It made me very sad, and filled my eyes with tears. Oh, in the midst of cheerfulness, I feel so sad! But being out a great deal here—and seeing new and fine scenery, does me good.

We got back to Balmoral, much pleased with our expedition, at seven o'clock. We had gone forty-two miles to-day, and forty yesterday, in all eighty-two.

Tuesday, October 8, 1861

THE MORNING WAS DULL and rather overcast; however, we decided to go. General Grey had gone on before. We three ladies drove in the sociable: Albert and Louis[114] in a carriage from Castleton. The clouds looked heavy and dark, though not like mist hanging on the mountains. Down came a heavy shower; but before we reached Castleton it cleared; blue sky appeared; and, as there was much wind, Grant thought all would be well, and the day very fine. Changed horses at Castleton, and drove beyond the Linn of Dee to the Giuly or Geldie Water—just where last year we mounted our ponies, eighteen miles from Balmoral. Here we found our ponies—"Inchrory" for me, and a new pony for Alice—a tall grey one,

The gillies' ball at Balmoral, 1859.

The drawing-room at Balmoral; watercolour by J. Roberts.

ugly but safe. The others rode their usual ones. The same guide, Charlie Stewart, was there, and a pony for the luncheon panniers, and a spare one for Grant and others to ride in turn.

We started about ten minutes past eleven, and proceeded exactly as last year, fording the Geldie at first very frequently. The ground was wet, but not worse than last year. We had gone on very well for about an hour, when the mist thickened all round, and down came heavy, or at least beating, rain with wind. With the help of an umbrella, and waterproofs and a plaid, I kept quite dry. Dearest Albert, who walked from the time the ground became boggy, got very wet, but was none the worse for it, and we got through it much better than before; we ladies never having to get off our ponies. At length at two o'clock, just as we were entering that beautiful Glen Fishie, which at its commencement reminds one of McInroy's Burn, it cleared, and became quite fine and very mild. Brown waded through the Etchart leading my pony; and then two of the others, who were riding together on another pony, dropped the whole bundle of cloaks into the water!

The falls of the Stron-na-Barin, with that narrow steep glen, which you ride up, crossing at the bottom, were in great beauty. We stopped before we entered the wood, and lunched on the bank overhanging the river, where General Grey joined us, and gave us an account of his arrangements. We lunched rather hurriedly, remounted our ponies and rode a short way—till we came near to a very steep place, not very pleasant to ride. So fine! numberless little burns running down in cascades. We walked a short way, and then remounted our ponies; but as we were to keep on the other side of the river, not by the Invereshie huts, we had to get off for a few hundred yards, the path being so narrow as to make it utterly unsafe to ride. Alice's pony already began to slip. The huts, surrounded by magnificent fir-trees, and by quantities of juniper-bushes, looked lovelier than ever; and we gazed with sorrow at their utter ruin. I felt what a delightful little encampment it must have been, and how enchanting to live in such a spot as this beautiful solitary wood in a glen surrounded by the high hills. We got off, and went into one of the huts to look at a fresco of stags of Landseer's, over a chimney-piece. Grant, on a pony, led me through the Fishie (all the fords are deep) at the foot of the farmhouses, where we met Lord and Lady Alexander Russell last year—and where we this time found two carriages. We dismounted and entered them, and were off at five o'clock—we were to have started at four.

We four drove together by the same way as we rode last year (and nothing could be rougher for driving), quite to the second wood, which led us past Loch Inch; but we turned short of the loch to the left along the high road. Unfortunately by this time it was nearly dark, and we therefore lost a great deal of the fine scenery. We had ridden fifteen miles. We drove along the road over several bridges—the Bridge of Carr, close below the ruined Castle of Ruthven, which we could just descry in the dusk—and on a long wooden bridge over the Spey to an inn at Kingussie, a very straggling place with very few cottages. Already, before we arrived there, we were struck by people standing at their cottage doors, and evidently looking out, which made us believe we were expected. At Kingussie there was a small, curious, chattering crowd of people—who, however, did not really make us out, but evidently suspected who we were. Grant and Brown kept them off the carriages, and gave them evasive answers, directing them to the wrong carriage, which was most amusing. One old gentleman, with a high wide-awake,[115] was especially inquisitive.

George, Duke of Atholl.

We started again, and went on and on, passing through the village of Newtonmoore. Here the Spey is crossed at its junction with the Calder, and then the road ascends for ten miles more to Dalwhinnie. It became cold and windy with occasional rain. At length, and not till a quarter to nine, we reached the inn of Dalwhinnie—twenty-nine miles from where we had left our ponies—which stands by itself, away from any village. Here, again, there were a few people assembled, and I thought they knew us; but it seems they did not, and it was only when we arrived that one of the maids recognised me. She had seen me at Aberdeen and Edinburgh. We went upstairs: the inn was much larger than at Fettercairn, but not nearly so nice and cheerful; there was a drawing-room and a dining-room; and we had a very good-sized bedroom. Albert had a dressing-room of equal size. Mary Andrews (who was very useful and efficient) and Lady Churchill's maid had a room together, every one being in the house; but unfortunately there was hardly anything to eat, and there was only tea, and two miserable starved Highland chickens, without any potatoes! No pudding, and no *fun*; no little maid (the two there not wishing to come in), nor our two people—who were wet and drying our and their things—to wait on us! It was not a nice supper; and the evening was wet. As it was late we soon retired to rest. Mary and Maxted (Lady Churchill's maid) had been dining below with Grant, Brown, and Stewart (who came, the same as last time, with the maids) in the "commercial room" at the foot of the stairs. They had only the remnants of our two starved chickens!

Wednesday, October 9

A bright morning, which was very charming. Albert found, on getting up, that Cluny Macpherson, with his piper and two ladies, had arrived quite early in the morning; and, while we were dressing, we heard a drum and fife—and discovered that the newly-formed volunteers had arrived—all indicating that we were discovered. However, there was scarcely any population, and it did not signify. The fat old landlady had put on a black satin dress, with white ribbons and orange flowers! We had breakfast at a quarter to nine o'clock; at half-past nine we started. Cluny was at the door with his wife and daughters with nosegays, and the volunteers were drawn up in front of the inn. They had all assembled since Saturday afternoon!

We drove as we did yesterday. Fine and very wild scenery, high wild hills, and no habitations. We went by the Pass of Drumouchter, with fine hills on both sides and in front of us; passed between two, the one on our left called The Boar of Badenoch, and that on the right, The Athole Sow. The Pass of Drumouchter separates Perthshire from Inverness-shire.

Again, a little farther on, we came to Loch Garry, which is very beautiful—but the mist covered the furthest hills, and the extreme distance was clouded. There is a small shooting-lodge, or farm, charmingly situated, looking up the glen on both sides, and with the loch in front; we did not hear to whom it belonged. We passed many drovers, without their herds and flocks, returning, Grant told us, from Falkirk. We had one very heavy shower after Loch Garry and before we came to Dalnacardoch Inn, thirteen miles from Dalwhinnie. The road goes beside the Garry. The country for a time became flatter; but was a good deal cultivated. At Dalnacardoch Inn there was a suspicion and expectation of our arrival. Four horses with smart postilions were in waiting; but, on General Grey's saying that this was *not* the party, but the one for whom only two horses had been ordered, a shabby pair of horses were put in; a shabby driver driving from the box (as throughout this journey), and off we started.

The Garry is very fine, rolling along over large stones—like the Quoich and the Fishie, and forming perpetual falls, with birch and mountain-ash growing down to the water's edge. We had some more heavy showers. A few miles from Dalnacardoch the Duke of Athole (in his kilt and shooting-jacket, as usual) met us on a pretty little chestnut pony, and rode the whole time near the carriage. He said, there were vague suspicions and rumours of our coming, but he had told no one anything. There was again a shower, but it cleared when we came in sight of Ben-y-Ghlo, and the splendid Pass of Killiekrankie, which, with the birch all golden—not, as on Deeside, bereft of leaves—looked very beautiful.

We passed by the Bruar, and the road to the Falls of the Bruar, but could not stop. The Duke took us through a new approach, which is extremely pretty; but near which, I cannot help regretting, the railroad will come, as well as along the road by which we drove through the Pass of Drumouchter. The Duke has made great improvements, and the path looked beautiful, surrounded as it is by hills; and the foliage still full, though in all its autumn tints—the whole being lit up with bright sunshine. We drove through an avenue, and in a few minutes more were at the door of the old castle. A thousand recollections of seventeen years ago crowded upon me—all seemed so familiar again! No one there except the dear Duchess, who

Viscountess Canning.

stood at the door, and whom I warmly embraced; and Miss MacGregor. How well I recognised the hall with all the sporting trophies; and the staircase, which we went up at once. The Duchess took us to a room which I recognised immediately as the one where Lady Canning[116] lived. There we took off our things—then went to look at the old and really very handsome rooms in which we had lived—the one in which Vicky had slept in two chairs, then not four years old! In the dining-room we took some coffee, which was most welcome; and then we looked at all the stags' horns put up in one of the corridors below; saw the Duke's pet dog, a smooth-haired black terrier, very fat; and then got into the carriage, a very peculiar one, viz., a *boat*—a mere boat (which is very light), put on four wheels, drawn by a pair of horses with a postilion. Into this we four got, with the Duke and Duchess and the dog—Lady Churchill, General Grey, and Miss MacGregor going in another carriage; with our two servants on the box, to whom all this was quite new and a great treat. The morning was beautiful. It was half-past twelve—we drove up by the avenue and about a favourite walk of ours in '44, passed through the gate, and came on to Glen Tilt—which is most striking, the road winding along, first on one side of the Tilt, and then on the other; the fine high hills rising very abruptly from each side of the rapid, rocky, stony river Tilt—the trees, chiefly birch and alder, overhanging the water.

We passed the Marble Lodge, in which one of the keepers lives, and came to Forest Lodge, where the road for carriages ends, and the glen widens. There were our ponies, which had passed the night at the Bainoch or Beynoch (a shooting "shiel" of Lord Fife's). They came over this morning; but, poor beasts, without having had any corn! Forest Lodge is eight miles from Blair. There we took leave of the dear Duchess; and saw old Peter Frazer, the former head-keeper there, now walking with the aid of two sticks! The Duke's keepers were there, his pipers, and a gentleman staying on a visit with him.

It was barely two o'clock when we started. We on our ponies, the Duke and his men (twelve altogether) on foot—Sandy MacAra, now head-keeper, grown old and grey, and two pipers, preceded us; the two latter playing alternately the whole time, which had a most cheerful effect. The wild strains sounded so softly amid those noble hills; and our caravan winding along—our people and the Duke's all in kilts, and the ponies, made altogether a most picturesque scene.

One of the Duke's keepers, Donald Macbeath, is a guardsman, and was in the Crimea. He is a celebrated marksman, and a fine-looking man, as all the Duke's men are. For some little time it was easy riding, but soon we came to a rougher path, more on the "brae" of the hill, where the pony required to be led, which I always have done, either when it is at all rough or bad, or when the pony has to be got on faster.

The Duke walked near me the greater part of the time; amusingly saying, in reference to former times, that he did not offer to lead me, as he knew I had no confidence in him. I replied, laughingly, "Oh, no, only I like best being led by the person I am accustomed to."

At length, at about three, we stopped, and lunched at a place called Dalcronachie, looking up a glen towards Loch Loch—a high bank overhanging the Tilt. Looking back the view was very fine; so, while the things were being unpacked for lunch, we sketched. We brought our own luncheon, and the remainder was as usual given to the men, but this time there were a great many to feed. After luncheon, we set off again. I walked a few paces; but as it was very wet, and the road very rough, by Albert's desire I got on again. A very few minutes brought us to the celebrated ford of the Tarff (Poll Tarff it is called), which is very deep—and after heavy rain almost impassable. The Duke offered to lead the pony on one side, and talked of Sandy for the other side, but I asked for Brown (whom I have far the most confidence in) to lead the pony, the Duke taking hold of it (as he did frequently) on the other side. Sandy MacAra, the guide, and the two pipers went first, playing all the time. To all appearance the ford of the Tarff[117] was not deeper than the other fords, but once in it the men were above their knees—and suddenly in the middle, where the current, from the fine, high, full falls, is very strong, it was nearly up to the men's waists. Here Sandy returned, and I said to the Duke (which he afterwards joked with Sandy about) that I thought he (Sandy) had better take the Duke's place; he did so, and we came very well through, all the others following, the men chiefly wading—Albert (close behind me) and the others riding through—and some of our people coming over double on the ponies. General Grey had little Peter Robertson up behind him.

The road after this became almost precipitous, and indeed made riding very unpleasant; but being wet, and difficult to walk, we ladies rode, Albert walking the greater part of the time. Only once, for a very few steps, I had to get off, as the pony could hardly keep its footing. As it was, Brown constantly could not walk next to the pony, but had to scramble below, or pull it after him. The Duke was indefatigable.

The Tilt become narrower and narrower, till its first source is almost invisible. The Tarff flows into the Tilt, about two miles or more beyond the falls. We emerged from the pass upon an open valley—with less high hills and with the hills of Braemar before us. We crossed the Bainoch or Bynack, quite a small stream, and when we came to the "County March"—where Perth and Aberdeen join—we halted. The Duke gave Albert and me some whisky to drink, out of an old silver flask of his own, and then made a short speech proposing my health, expressing the pleasure with which he and all had received me at Blair, and hoping that I would return as often as I liked, and that I should have a safe return home; ending by the true Highland "Nis! nis! nis! Sit air a-nis! A-ris! a-ris! a-ris!" (pronounced: "Neesh! neesh! neesh! Sheet eir, a-neesh! A-rees! a-rees! a-rees!") which means: "Now! now! now! That to him, now! Again! again! again!" which was responded to by cheering from all. Grant then proposed "three cheers for the Duke of Athole", which was also very warmly responded to—my pony (good "Inchrory"), which went admirably, rather resenting the vehemence of Brown's cheering.

We then went on again for about three miles to the Bainoch, which we reached at ten minutes to six, when it was already nearly dark. As we approached the "shiel", the pipers struck up, and played. The ponies went so well with the pipes, and altogether it was very pleasant to ride and walk with them. They played "the Athole Highlanders" when we started, and again in coming in.

Lady Fife had very kindly come down to the Bainoch herself, where she gave us tea, which was very welcome. We then got into our carriages, wishing the good Duke of Athole good-bye. He was going back the whole way—which was certainly rather a hazardous proceeding, at least an adventurous one, considering the night, and that there was no moon—and what the road was! We got home safely at a quarter-past eight. The night was quite warm, though slightly showery—but became very clear and starlight later.

We had travelled sixty-nine miles to-day, and sixty yesterday. This was the pleasantest and most enjoyable expedition I *ever* made; and the recollection of it will always be most agreeable to me, and increase my wish to make more! Was so glad dear Louis (who is a charming companion) was with us. Have enjoyed nothing as much, or indeed felt so much cheered by anything, since my great sorrow.[118] Did not feel tired. We ladies did not dress, and dined *en famille*; looking at maps of the Highlands after dinner.

Wednesday, October 16, 1861

To OUR GREAT SATISFACTION it was a most beautiful morning. Not a cloud was on the bright blue sky, and it was perfectly calm. There had been a sharp frost which lay on parts of the grass, and the mountains were beautifully lit up, with those very blue shades upon them, like the bloom on a plum. Up early, and breakfasted with Alice, Louis, and Lenchen,[119] in our room. At twenty minutes to nine o'clock we started, with Alice, Lenchen, and Louis. The morning was beyond everything splendid, and the country in such beauty, though the poor trees are nearly leafless.

Near Castleton, and indeed all along the road, in the shade, the frost still lay, and the air was very sharp. We took post-horses at Castleton, and proceeded up Glen Clunie to Glen Callater, which looked lovely, and which Albert admired much. In a

Loch Callater.

Castleton of Braemar in the mid nineteenth century.

little more than two hours we were at Loch Callater—the road was very bad indeed as we approached the loch, where our ponies were waiting for us. After walking a few paces we remounted them, I on my good "Fyvie", and Alice on "Inchrory".

The day was glorious—and the whole expedition delightful, and very easily performed. We ascended Little Cairn Turc, on the north side of Loch Callater, up a sort of footpath very easy and even, upon ground that was almost flat, rising very gradually, but imperceptibly; and the view became wonderfully extensive. The top of Cairn Turc is quite flat—with moss and grass—so that you could drive upon it. It is very high, for you see the high table-land behind the highest point of Loch-na-Gar. On that side you have no view; but from the other it is wonderfully extensive. It was so clear and bright, and so still there, reminding us of the day on Ben Muich Dhui last year.

There rose immediately behind us Ben Muich Dhui, which you hardly ever see, and the shape of which is not fine, with its surrounding mountains of Cairngorm, Brae Riach, Ben Avon or A'an, Ben-na-Bhourd, etc. We saw Ben-y-Ghlo quite clearly, and all that range of hills; then, further west, Shichallion, near Loch Tay; the mountains which are near the Black Mount and, quite on the horizon, we could discern Ben Nevis, which is above Fort William.

Going up Cairn Turc we looked down upon Loch Canter, a small loch above Loch Callater, very wild and dark. We proceeded to Cairn Glaishie, at the extreme point of which a cairn has been erected. We got off to take a look at the wonderful panorama which lay stretched out before us. We looked on Fifeshire, and the country between Perth and Stirling, the Lomond Hills, etc. It was beautifully clear, and really it was most interesting to look over such an immense extent of the Highlands. I give a very poor description of it; but here follows a rough account of the places we saw:

To the North—Ben Muich Dhui, Brae Riach, Cairngorm, Ben Avon, Ben-na-Bhourd.

To the East—Loch-na-Gar, etc.

To the South-West—Ben-y-Ghlo or Ben-y-Gloe, and the surrounding hills beyond Shichallion, and the mountains between Dunkeld and the Black Mount.

Quite in the extreme West—Ben Nevis.

To the South—the Lomond Hills; Perth in the middle distance.

We walked on a little way, and then I got upon my pony. Another half hour's riding again over such singular flat tableland, brought us on to the edge of the valley of Cairn Lochan, which is indeed "a bonnie place". It reminded me and Louis of Clova; only there one did not see the immense extent of mountains behind. Cairn Lochan is a narrow valley, the river Isla winding through it like a silver ribbon, with trees at the bottom. The hills are green and steep, but towards the head of the valley there are fine precipices. We had then to take a somewhat circuitous route in order to avoid some bogs, and to come to a spot where we looked right up the valley for an immense distance; to the left, or rather more to the south, was Glen Isla, another glen, but wider, and not with the same high mountains as Cairn Lochan. Beyond Glen Isla were seen the Lomond Hills behind Kinross, at the foot of which is Loch Leven.

We sat on a very precipitous place, which made one dread any one's moving backwards; and here, at a little before two o'clock, we lunched. The lights were charmingly soft, and, as I said before, like the bloom on a plum. The luncheon was

Luncheon at Cairn Lochan.

very acceptable, for the air was extremely keen, and we found ice thicker than a shilling on the top of Cairn Turc, which did not melt when Brown took it and kept it in his hand.

Helena was so delighted, for this was *the only really great* expedition in which she had accompanied us.

Duncan and the keeper at Loch Callater (R. Stewart) went with us as guides.

I made some hasty sketches; and then Albert wrote on a bit of paper that we had lunched here, put it into the Selters-water bottle, and buried it there, or rather stuck it into the ground. Grant had done the same when we visited Ben Muich Dhui the first time. This over, we walked part of the way back which we had ridden to avoid the bogs,—we ladies walking only a short way, and then riding. We altered our course, and left Cairn Glaishie to our right, and went in the direction of the Cairn Wall. Looking back on the distant hills above Glen Isla and Cairn Lochan (Lord Airlie's "Country"), it was even more beautiful; for, as the day advanced, the mountains became clearer and clearer, of a lovely blue, while the valleys were in shadow. Shichallion, and those further ranges, were also most perfectly to be seen, and gave me such a longing for further Highland expeditions! We went over Garbchory, looking down on the road to the Spittal; and on the lower mountains, which are most curiously connected one with another, and which from the height we were, we could look down upon.

Here follows the account of our route, with all the names as written down by Duncan. I cannot "mind" the names, as they say here.

From Balmoral to—

    Loch Callater, four miles,

    Left Loch Callater at 11 o'clock, A.M.,

    Little Cairn Turc,

    Big Cairn Turc,

    Loch Canter,

    Cairn Glaishie,

    Cairn Lochan,

    Ca-Ness, six miles.

Returning route:—

    Cairn Lochan,

    Cairn Glaishie,

    Garb Chory,

    Month Eigie Road,

    Glass Meall,

    Fian Chory,

    Aron Ghey,

    Shean Spittal Bridge, 4.30 P.M.

    Shean Spittal Bridge to Balmoral, sixteen miles.

This gave one a very good idea of the geography of the country, which delighted dear Albert, as this expedition was quite in a different direction from any that we had ever made before. But my head is so very ungeographical, that I cannot describe it. We came down by the Month Eigie, a steep hill covered with grass—down part of which I rode, walking where it was steepest; but it was so wet and slippery that I had two falls. We got down to the road to the Spittal Bridge, about fifteen miles from Castleton, at nearly half-past four, and then down along the new road, at least that part of it which is finished, and which is to extend to the Cairn Wall. We went back on our side of the river; and if we had been a little earlier, Albert might have got a stag—but it was too late. The moon rose and shone most beautifully, and we returned at twenty minutes to seven o'clock, much pleased and interested with this delightful expedition. Alas! I fear our *last* great one!

(IT WAS OUR LAST ONE![120])

Albert shortly before his death: his last official portrait photograph.

PART TWO

August 26th, 1868: drinking to the memory of Albert at the obelisk erected in his memory at Balmoral. "Bertie" stands to the left of the obelisk.

Balmoral, August 26, 1862

I WENT OUT AT TWELVE WITH THE TWO GIRLS[1] on ponies (I in the little carriage), Bertie on foot. We went to see the obelisk building to His dear memory: Bertie left us there, and we went on round by the village, up Craig-Gowan, in the little carriage, over the heather till we reached near to the old cairn of 1852. Grant said: "I thought you would like to be here to-day, on His birthday!"—so entirely was he of opinion that this beloved day, and even the 14th of December, must not be looked upon as a day of mourning, "That's not the light to look at it". There is so much true and strong faith in these good simple people.

Wednesday, October 7, 1863

A HAZY MORNING. I decided by Alice's[2] advice, with a heavy heart, to make the attempt to go to Clova. At half-past twelve drove with Alice and Lenchen to Altnagiuthasach, where we lunched, having warmed some broth and boiled some potatoes, and then rode up and over the Capel Month in frequent slight snow-showers. All the high hills white with snow; and the view of the green Clova hills covered with snow at the tops, with gleams of sunshine between the showers, was very fine, but it took us a long time, and I was very tired towards the end, and felt very sad and lonely. Loch Muich looked beautiful in the setting sun as we came down, and reminded me of many former happy days I spent there. We stopped to take tea at Altnagiuthasach. Grant was not with us, having gone with Vicky.[3] We started at about twenty minutes to seven from Altnagiuthasach, Brown on the box next Smith,[4] who was driving, little Willem (Alice's black serving boy) behind. It was quite dark when we left, but all the lamps were lit as usual; from the first, however, Smith seemed to be quite confused (and indeed has been much altered of late), and got off the road several times, once in a very dangerous place, when Alice called out and Brown got off the box to show him the way. After that, however, though going very slowly, we seemed to be all right, but Alice was not at all reassured, and thought Brown's holding up the lantern all the time on the box indicated that Smith could not see where he was going, though the road was as broad and plain as possible. Suddenly, about two miles from Altnagiuthasach, and about twenty minutes after we had started, the carriage began to turn up on one side; we called out: "What's the matter?" There was an awful pause, during which Alice said: "We are upsetting." In another moment—during which I had time to reflect whether we should be killed or not, and thought there were still things I had not settled and wanted to do—the carriage turned over on its side, and we were all precipitated to the ground! I came down very hard, with my face upon the ground, near the carriage, the horses both on the ground, and Brown calling out in despair, "The Lord Almighty have mercy on us! Who did ever see the like of this before! I thought you were all killed." Alice was soon helped up by means of tearing all her clothes to disentangle her; but Lenchen, who had also got caught in her dress,

The Prince and Princess Louis of Hesse at Balmoral in 1863.

called out very piteously, which frightened me a good deal; but she was also got out with Brown's assistance, and neither she nor Alice was at all hurt. I reassured them that I was not hurt, and urged that we should make the best of it, as it was an inevitable misfortune. Smith, utterly confused and bewildered, at length came up to ask if I was hurt. Meantime the horses were lying on the ground as if dead, and it was absolutely necessary to get them up again. Alice, whose calmness and coolness were admirable, held one of the lamps while Brown cut the traces, to the horror of Smith, and the horses were speedily released and got up unhurt. There was now no means of getting home except by sending back Smith with the two horses to get another carriage. All this took some time, about half an hour, before we got them off. By this time I felt that my face was a good deal bruised and swollen, and, above all, my right thumb was excessively painful and much swollen; indeed I thought at first it was broken, till we began to move it. Alice advised then that we should sit down in the carriage—that is, with the bottom of the carriage as a back—which we did, covered with plaids, little Willem sitting in front, with the hood of his "bournous" over his head, holding a lantern, Brown holding another, and being indefatigable in his attention and care. He had hurt his knee a good deal in jumping off the carriage. A little claret was all we could get either to drink or wash my face and hand. Almost directly after the accident happened, I said to Alice it was terrible not to be able to tell it to my dearest Albert, to which she answered: "But he knows it all, and I am sure he watched over us." I am thankful that it was by no imprudence of mine, or the slightest deviation from what my beloved one and I had always been in the habit of doing, and what he sanctioned and approved.

After the accident on the Alt-na-Guithasach road. This drawing by Princess Louise from a sketch by Princess Alice shows, from left to right, Victoria, Alice, Willem, Helena and John Brown.

The thought of having to sit here in the road ever so long was, of course, not very agreeable, but it was not cold, and I remembered from the first what my beloved one had always said to me, namely, to make the best of what could not be altered. We had a faint hope, at one moment, that our ponies might overtake us; but then Brown recollected that they had started before us. We did nothing but talk of the accident, and how it could have happened, and how merciful the escape was, and we all agreed that Smith was quite unfit to drive me again in the dark. We had been sitting here about half an hour when we heard the sound of voices and of horses' hoofs, which came nearer and nearer. To our relief we found it was our ponies. Kennedy (whom dear Albert liked, and who always went out with him, and now generally goes with us) had become fearful of an accident, as we were so long coming; he heard Smith going back with the ponies, and then, seeing lights moving about, he felt convinced something must have happened, and therefore rode back to look for us, which was very thoughtful of him, for else we might have sat there till ten o'clock. We mounted our ponies at once and proceeded home, Brown leading Alice's and my pony, which he would not let go for fear of another accident. Lenchen and Willem followed, led by Alick Grant. Kennedy carried the lantern in front. It was quite light enough to see the road without a lantern. At the hill where the gate of the deer-fence is, above the distillery, we met the other carriage, again driven by Smith, and a number of stable-people come to raise the first carriage, and a pair of horses to bring it home. We preferred, however, riding home, which we reached at about twenty minutes to ten o'clock. No one knew what had happened till we told them. Fritz and Louis were at the door. People were foolishly alarmed when we got upstairs, and made a great fuss.[5] Took only a little soup and fish in my room, and had my head bandaged.

I saw the others only for a moment, and got to bed rather late.

Monday, October 9, 1865

A THICK, MISTY, VERY THREATENING MORNING! There was no help for it, but it was sadly provoking. It was the same once or twice in former happy days, and my dear Albert always said we could not alter it, but must leave it as it was, and make the best of it. Our three little ones breakfasted with me. I was grieved to leave my precious Baby[6] and poor Leopold[7] behind. At ten started with Lenchen and Janie Ely[8] (the same attendants on the box). General Grey had gone on an hour and a half before. We took post-horses at Castleton. It rained more or less the whole time. Then came the long well-known stage to the Spital of Glenshee, which seemed to me longer than ever. The mist hung very thick over the hills. We changed horses there, and about a quarter of an hour after we had left it, we stopped to lunch in the carriage. After some delay we went on and turned into Strathardle, and then, leaving the Blairgowrie road, down to the farm of Pitcarmich, shortly before coming to which Mr. Small Keir of Kindrogan met us and rode before us to this farm. Here we found General Grey and our ponies, and here the dear Duchess of Athole and Miss MacGregor met us, and we got out and went for a short while into the farmhouse, where we took some wine and biscuit. Then we mounted our ponies (I on dear Fyvie, Lenchen on Brechin), and started on our course across the hill. There was much mist. This obscured all the view, which otherwise would have been very fine. At first there was a rough road, but soon there was nothing but a sheep-track, and hardly that, through heather and stones up a pretty steep hill. Mr. Keir could not keep up with the immense pace of Brown and Fyvie, which distanced every one; so he had to drop behind, and his keeper acted as guide. There was by this time heavy driving rain, with a thick mist. About a little more than an hour took us to the "March",[9] where two of the Dunkeld men met us. John McGregor, the Duke's head wood-forester, and Gregor McGregor, the Duchess's gamekeeper; and the former acted as a guide. The Duchess and Miss MacGregor were riding with us. We went from here through larch woods, the rain pouring at times violently. We passed (after crossing the Dunkeld March) Little Loch Oishne, and Loch Oishne, before coming to Loch Ordie. Here dripping wet we arrived at about a quarter-past six, having left Pitcarmich at twenty minutes to four. It was dark already from the very bad weather. We went into a lodge here, and had tea and whisky, and Lenchen had to get herself dried, as she was so wet. About seven we drove off from Loch Ordie. There was no outrider, so we sent on first the other carriage with Lenchen, Lady Ely, and Miss MacGregor, and General Grey on the box, and I went with the Duchess in a phaeton which had a hood—Brown and Grant going behind. It was pitch-dark, and we had to go through a wood, and I must own I was somewhat nervous.

We had not gone very far when we perceived that we were on a very rough road, and I became much alarmed, though I would say nothing. A branch took off Grant's cap, and we had to stop for Brown to go back and look for it with one of the carriage-lamps. This stoppage was most fortunate, for he then discovered we were on a completely wrong road. Grant and Brown had both been saying, "This is no carriage-road; it is full of holes and stones." Miss MacGregor came to us in great distress, saying she did not know what to do, for that the coachman, blinded by the driving rain, had mistaken the road, and that we were in a track for carting wood. What was to be done, no one at this moment seemed to know—whether to try and turn the carriage (which proved impossible) or to take a horse out and send the postilion back to Loch Ordie to get assistance. At length we heard from General Grey that we could go on, though where we should get out, no one could exactly tell. Grant took a lamp out of the carriage and walked before the horses, while Brown led them; and this reassured me. But the road was very rough, and we had to go through some deep holes full of water. At length, in about twenty minutes, we saw a light and passed a lodge, where we stopped and inquired where we were, for we had already come upon a good road. Our relief was great when we were told we were all right. Grant and Brown got up behind, and we trotted along the high road fast enough. Just before we came to the lodge, General Grey called out to ask which way the Duchess thought we should go, and Brown answered in her name, "The Duchess don't know at all where we are", as it was so dark she could not recognise familiar places. At length at a quarter to nine we arrived quite safely at Dunkeld, at the Duchess's nice, snug little cottage, which is just outside the town, surrounded by fine large grounds. Two servants in kilts, and the steward, received us at the door. You come at once on the middle landing of the staircase, the cottage being built on sloping ground. The Duchess took me to my room, a nice little room, next to which was one for my wardrobe maid, Mary Andrews. Lenchen was upstairs near Miss MacGregor on one side of the drawing-room, which was given up to me as my sitting-room, and the Duchess's room on the other. Brown, the only other servant in the house, below, Grant in the adjoining buildings to the house. The General and Lady Ely were at the hotel. We dined at half-past nine in a small dining-room below, only Lenchen, the Duchess, Miss MacGregor, and I. Everything so nice and quiet. The Duchess and Miss MacGregor carving, her three servants waiting. They were so kind, and we talked over the day's adventures. Lenchen and every one, except the Duchess and myself, had been drenched. The Duchess and her cousin stayed a short while, and then left us, and I wrote a little. Strange to say, it was four years to-day that we paid our visit to Blair and rode up Glen Tilt. How different!

Tuesday, October 10

A hopelessly wet morning. I had slept well, but felt sad on awaking. Breakfasted alone with Lenchen downstairs, each day waited on by Brown. A dreadful morning, pouring rain. Sat upstairs in the drawing-room, and wrote a good deal, being perfectly quiet and undisturbed.

Lenchen and I lunched with the Duchess and Miss MacGregor, and at four we drove up to the Duchess's very find model farm of St. Colme's, about four miles from Dunkeld; the Duchess and I in the phaeton, Lenchen, Janie Ely, and Miss

MacGregor going in the other carriage. We went all over the farm in detail, which is very like ours at Osborne and Windsor, much having been adopted from our farms there; and my dearest Husband had given the Duchess so much advice about it, that we both felt so sad *he* should not see it.

We took tea in the farmhouse, where the Duchess has kept one side quite for herself, and where she intends to live sometimes with Miss MacGregor, and almost by themselves. From here we drove back and stopped at the "Byres", close by the stables, which were lit up with gas, and where we saw all the cows being milked. Very fine Ayrshire cows, and nice dairymaids. It is all kept up just as the late Duke[10] wished it. We came home at past seven. It never ceased raining. The Cathedral[11] bell began quite unexpectedly to ring, or almost toll, at eight o'clock, which the Duchess told us was a very old custom—in fact, the curfew-bell. It sounds very melancholy.

Dinner just as yesterday.

Wednesday, October 11

Another wretchedly wet morning. Was much distressed at breakfast to find that poor Brown's legs had been dreadfully cut by the edge of his wet kilt on Monday, just at the back of the knee, and he said nothing about it; but to-day one became so inflamed, and swelled so much, that he could hardly move. The doctor said he must keep it up as much as possible, and walk very little, but did not forbid his going out with the carriage, which he wished to do. I did not go out in the morning, and decided to remain till Friday, to give the weather a chance. It cleared just before luncheon, and we agreed to take a drive, which we were able to do almost without any rain. At half-past three we drove out just as yesterday. There was no mist, so that, though there was no sunshine, we could see and admire the country, the scenery of which is beautiful. We drove a mile along the Blair Road to Polney Loch, where we entered the woods, and, skirting the loch, drove at the foot of Craig y Barns on grass drives—which were very deep and rough, owing to the wet weather, but extremely pretty—on to the Loch Ordie road. After ascending this for a little way we left it, driving all round Cally Loch (there are innumerable lochs) through Cally Gardens along another fine but equally rough wood drive, which comes out on the Blairgowrie high road. After this we drove round the three Lochs of the Lowes—viz. Craig Lush, Butterstone, and the Loch of the Lowes itself (which is the largest). They are surrounded by trees and woods, of which there is no end, and are very pretty. We came back by the Blairgowrie road and drove through Dunkeld (the people had been so discreet and quiet, I said I would do this), crossing over the bridge (where twenty-two years ago we were met by twenty of the Athole Highlanders, who conducted us to the entrance of the grounds), and proceeded by the upper road to the Rumbling Bridge, which is Sir William Stewart[12] of Grandtully's property. We got out here and walked to the bridge, under which the Braan flowed over the rocks most splendidly; and, swollen by the rain, it came down in an immense volume of water with a deafening noise. Returning thence we drove through the village of Inver to the Hermitage on the banks of the Braan, which is Dunkeld property. This is a little house full of looking-glasses, with painted walls, looking on another fall of the Braan, where we took tea almost in the

Sketch by Victoria of travelling on a "coble".

dark. It was built by James, the second Duke of Athole, in the last century. We drove back through Dunkeld again, the people cheering. Quite fair. We came home at half-past six o'clock. Lady Ely and General Grey dined with us. After dinner only the Duchess came to the drawing-room, and read to us again. Then I wrote, and Grant waited instead of Brown, who was to keep quiet on account of his leg.

Thursday, October 12

A fair day, with no rain, but, alas! no sunshine. Brown's leg was much better, and the doctor thought he could walk over the hill to-morrow.

Excellent breakfasts, such splendid cream and butter! The Duchess has a very good cook, a Scotchwoman, and I thought how dear Albert would have liked it all. He always said things tasted better in smaller houses. There were several Scotch dishes, two soups, and the celebrated "haggis", which I tried last night, and really liked very much. The Duchess was delighted at my taking it.

At a quarter past twelve Lenchen and I walked with the Duchess in the grounds and saw the Cathedral, part of which is converted into a parish church, and the other part is a most picturesque ruin. We saw the tomb of the Wolf of Badenoch, son of King Robert the Second. There are also other monuments, but in a very dilapidated state. The burying-ground is inside and south of the Cathedral. We walked along the side of the river Tay, into which the river Braan flows, under very fine trees, as far as the American garden, and then round by the terrace overlooking the park, on which the tents were pitched at the time of the great déjeuner that the Duke, then Lord Glenlyon, gave us in 1842, which was our first acquaintance with the Highlanders and Highland customs; and it was such a fine sight! Oh! and here we were together—both widows!

We came back through the kitchen-garden by half-past one o'clock. After the usual luncheon, drove with Lenchen, the Duchess, and Miss MacGregor, at twenty minutes to four, in her sociable to Loch Ordie, by the lakes of Rotmell and Dowally through the wood, being the road by which we ought to have come the first night when we lost our way. It was cold, but the sky was quite bright, and it was a fine evening; and the lake, wooded to the water's edge and skirted by distant hills, looked extremely pretty. We took a short row on it in a "coble" rowed by the head keeper, Gregor M'Gregor. We took tea under the trees. The evening was very cold, and it was getting rapidly dark. We came back safely by the road the Duchess had wished to come the other night, but which her coachman did not think safe on account of the precipices!

Friday, October 13

Quite a fine morning, with bright gleams of sunshine lighting up everything. The piper played each morning in the garden during breakfast. Just before we left at ten, I planted a tree, and spoke to an old acquaintance, Willie Duff, the Duchess's fisherman, who had formerly a very long black beard and hair, which are now quite grey. Mr. Carrington, who has been Secretary in the Athole family for four generations, was presented. General Grey, Lady Ely, and Miss MacGregor had gone on a little while before us. Lenchen and I, with the Duchess, went in the sociable with four horses (Brown and Grant on the box). The weather was splendid, and the view, as we drove along the Inverness Road—which is the road to Blair— with all the mountains rising in the distance, was beautiful.

We passed through the village of Ballinluig, where there is a railway station, and a quarter of a mile below which the Tay and the Tummel unite, at a place called Logierait. All these names were familiar to me from our stay in 1844. We saw the place where the monument to the Duke is to be raised, on an eminence above Logierait. About eleven miles from Dunkeld, just below Croftinloan (Captain Jack Murray's), we took post-horses. You could see Pitlochry in the distance to the left. We then left the Inverness Road, and turned to the right, up a very steep hill past Dunavourd (Mr. Napier's, son of the historian),[13] past Edradour (the Duke's property), over a wild moor, reminding one very much of Aberarder (near Balmoral), whence, looking back, you have a beautiful view of the hills Schiehallion, Ben Lomond, and Ben Lawers. This glen is called Glen Brearichan, the little river of that name uniting with the Fernate, and receiving afterwards the name of the Ardle. On the left hand a shoulder of Ben-y-Gloe is seen.

We lunched in the carriage at ten minutes past twelve, only a quarter of a mile from the West Lodge of Kindrogan (Mr. Keir's). Here were our ponies, and General Grey, Lady Ely, and Miss MacGregor. We halted a short while to let General Grey get ahead, and then started on our ponies, Mr. Keir walking with us. We passed Mr. Keir's house of Kindrogan, out at the East Lodge, by the little village of Enoch Dhu, up the rather steep ascent and approach of Dirnanean, Mr. Small's place; passing his house as we went. Mr. Small was absent, but two of his people, fine, tall-looking men, led the way; two of Mr. Keir's were also with us. We turned over the hill from here, through a wild, heathery glen, and then up a grassy hill called the Larich, just above the Spital. Looking back the view was splendid, one range of hills behind the other, of different shades of blue. After we had passed the summit, we stopped for our tea, about twenty minutes to four, and seated ourselves on the grass, but had to wait for some time till a kettle arrived which had been forgotten, and had to be sent for from the Spital. This caused some delay. At length, when tea was over, we walked down a little way, and then rode. It was really most distressing to me to see what pain poor Brown suffered, especially in going up and down the hill. He could not go fast, and walked lame, but would not give in. His endurance on this occasion showed a brave heart indeed, for he resisted all attempts at being relieved, and would not relinquish his charge.

We took leave of the dear kind Duchess and Miss MacGregor, who were going back to Kindrogan, and got into the carriage. We were able to ascend the Devil's Elbow before it was really dark, and got to Castleton at half-past seven, where we found our own horses, and reached Balmoral at half-past eight.

Hallowe'en, October 31, 1866–67

WHILE WE WERE AT MRS. GRANT's we saw the commencement of the keeping of Halloween. All the children came out with burning torches, shouting and jumping. The Protestants generally keep Halloween on the old day, November 12, and the Catholics on this day; but hearing I had wished to see it two years ago, they all decided to keep it to-day. When we drove home we saw all the gillies coming along with burning torches, and torches and bonfires appeared also on the opposite side of the water. We went upstairs to look at it from the windows, from whence it had a very pretty effect.

One of the Hallowe'en parties at Balmoral.

On the same day in the following year, viz., Thursday, October 31, 1867, we had an opportunity of again seeing the celebration of Halloween, and even of taking part in it. We had been out driving, but we hurried back to be in time for the celebration. Close to Donald Stewart's house we were met by two gillies bearing torches. Louise[14] got out and took one, walking by the side of the carriage, and looking like one of the witches in *Macbeth*. As we approached Balmoral, the keepers and their wives and children, the gillies and other people met us, all with torches; Brown also carrying one. We got out at the house, where Leopold joined us, and a

Victoria in a Hallowe'en procession at Balmoral.

torch was given to him. We walked round the whole house, preceded by Ross playing the pipes, going down the steps of the terrace. Louise and Leopold went first, then came Janie Ely and I, followed by every one carrying torches, which had a very pretty effect. After this a bonfire was made of all the torches, close to the house, and they danced reels whilst Ross played the pipes.

Wednesday, August 21, 1867

THE RAILWAY CARRIAGE SWUNG A GOOD DEAL, and it was very hot, so that I did not get much sleep. At half-past seven I was woke up to dress and hurry out at Carlisle, which we did at a quarter to eight. Here in the station we had some breakfast, and waited an hour till our carriage was taken off and another put on (which they have since found out was quite unnecessary!) The morning, which had been gloomy, cleared and became very fine, and we went on along such a pretty line through a very pretty country, through Eskdale and past Netherby, as far as Riddings, and then leaving the Esk entered Liddesdale, the railway running along the Liddel Water to Riccarton station, where we stopped for a moment. We next came along the Slitrig Water to Hawick, where we went slowly which the people

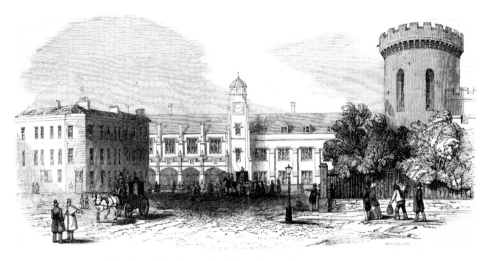

The Central Station at Carlisle in the mid nineteenth century.

had begged us to do, and where were great crowds. Here we entered Teviotdale and descended it, entering the valley of the Tweed at St. Boswell's. Between St. Boswell's and Kelso at Roxburgh station, we crossed the Teviot again. We passed close under the Eildon Hills, [15] three high points rising from the background. The country is extremely picturesque, valleys with fine trees and streams, intermingled with great cultivation. Only after half-past eleven did we reach Kelso station which was very prettily decorated, and where were standing the Duke and Duchess of Roxburghe, Lord Bowmont, the Duke of Buccleuch, and Lord C. Ker, as well as General Hamilton, commanding the forces in Scotland. We got out at once. I embraced the dear Duchess, and shook hands with the two Dukes, and then at once entered the carriage (mine) with Lenchen, Louise, and the Duchess; Beatrice, Leopold, and Christian going in the second, and the others following in other carriages.

The morning beautiful and very mild. We drove through the small suburb of Maxwell Heugh, down into the town of Kelso, and over the bridge which commands a beautiful view of the broad stream of the Tweed and of the Park of Floors, with the fine house itself. Everywhere decorations, and great and most enthusiastic crowds. The little town of Kelso is very picturesque, and there were triumphal arches, and no end of pretty mottoes, and every house was decorated with flowers and flags. Fifty ladies dressed in white strewed flowers as we passed. Volunteers were out and bands playing. At the Market Place the carriage stopped; an address was presented, not read; and a little girl was held up to give me an enormous bouquet. Immense and most enthusiastic cheering. We then drove on, amidst continued crowds and hearty cheers, up to the very park gates, where the old Sheriff, eighty-five years old, was presented. The park is remarkably fine, with the approach under splendid beech, sycamore, and oak trees. The house very handsome, built originally by Sir John Vanbrugh in 1718, but much improved by the present Duke. You drive under a large porch, and then go up a flight of steps to the hall. The Duke's band was stationed outside. Mr. and Lady Charlotte Russell, Mr. Suttie, and Lady Charles Ker were in the hall. The Duchess took us into the

The Duke of Roxburghe.

At Floors Castle: on the right, Alice, Princess Louis of Hesse, and on the left the Duchess of Roxburghe.

library, where the Duke of Buccleuch joined us, and, after waiting a little while, we had breakfast (ourselves alone) in the really splendid dining-room adjoining, at ten minutes past twelve. This over, the Duchess showed us to our rooms upstairs. I had three that were very comfortable, opening one in to the other: a sitting-room, dressing-room, and the largest of the three, the bedroom, simple, with pretty chintz, but very elegant, nice and comfortable. The children were close at hand. But the feeling of loneliness when I saw no room for my darling, and felt I was indeed alone and a widow, overcame me very sadly! It was the first time I had gone in this way on a visit (like as in former times), and I thought so much of all dearest Albert would have done and said, and how he would have wandered about everywhere, admired everything, looked at everything—and now! Oh! must it ever, ever be so?

At half-past two lunched (as at home) in the fine dining-room. A lovely day. The view from the windows beautiful. The distant Cheviot range with a great deal of wood, Kelso embosomed in rich woods, with the bridge, and the Tweed flowing beneath natural grass terraces which go down to it. Very fine. It reminded me a little of the view from the Phoenix Park near Dublin.

At half-past five walked out with Lenchen and the kind Duchess to a spot where I planted a tree,[16] and then we walked on to the flower-garden, where there are a number of very fine hot-houses, and took tea in a pretty little room adjoining them, which is entirely tiled. After this we took a pleasant drive in the fine park which is full of splendid timber, along the Tweed, and below the ruins of the celebrated old

Kelso Abbey in the mid nineteenth century.

Castle of Roxburgh, of which there is very little remaining. It is on a high eminence; the Tweed and Teviot are on either side of it, so that the position is remarkably strong. It stood many a siege and was frequently taken by the English and retaken by the Scotch. Scotch and even English kings, amongst them Edward II, held their Court there.

We came home at eight. The Duke and Duchess dined with us, and after dinner we watched the illuminations and many bonfires from the library, and afterwards went for a moment into the drawing-room to see the ladies and gentlemen, after which I went up to my room, where I sat and rested, feeling tired and only able to read the newspapers.

Thursday, August 22

A fine morning, though rather hazy. The night and moonlight had been beautiful. Breakfasted with our family in the breakfast-room. At twenty minutes to eleven went and sat out under some trees on the lawn near the house writing, where I was quite quiet and undisturbed, and remained till half-past twelve, resting, reading, etc. Immediately after luncheon started in two carriages, the Duchess and our two daughters with me; Christian, the Duke, Lady Charlotte Russell, and Lord Charles Fitz-Roy in the second carriage (with post-horses). We had the Duke's horses as far as Ravenswood. We drove through Kelso, which was full of people, crossed the Tweed and Teviot (where the waters join), and passed below the old Castle of Roxburgh. The country is very pretty, hilly, wooded, and cultivated. Not long after we started, the second carriage disappeared, and we waited for it. It seems that, at the first hill they came to, the wheelers would not hold up. So we stopped (and this delayed us some time), the leaders replaced the wheelers, and they came on with a pair. Then we drove up to St. Boswell's Green, with the three fine Eildon hills before us—which are said to have been divided by Michael Scott, the wizard— seeing Mertoun, my excellent Lord Polwarth's[17] place, on the other side of the road. Alas! he died only last Friday from a second stroke, the first of which seized him in February; and now, when he had intended to be at the head of the volunteers who received me at Kelso, he is lying dead at his house which we passed so near! It lies low, and quite in among the trees. I lament him deeply and sincerely, having liked him very much, as did my dearest Albert also, ever since we knew him in 1858.

We changed horses at Ravenswood, or old Melrose (where I had my own), having caught a glimpse of where Dryburgh Abbey is, though the railway almost hides it. The Duke of Buccleuch met us there, and rode the whole way. Everywhere, wherever there were dwellings, there was the kindest welcome, and triumphal arches were erected. We went by the side of the Eildon Hills, past an immense railway viaduct, and nothing could be prettier than the road. The position of Melrose is most picturesque, surrounded by woods and hills. The little village, or rather town, of Newstead, which we passed through just before coming to Melrose, is very narrow and steep. We drove straight up to the Abbey through the grounds of the Duke of Buccleuch's agent, and got out and walked about the ruins, which are indeed very fine, and some of the architecture and carving in beautiful preservation. David I, who is described as a "sair Saint", originally built it, but the Abbey, the ruins of which are now standing, was built in the fifteenth century. We

The library at Sir Walter Scott's Abbotsford.

saw where, under the high altar, Robert Bruce's heart is supposed to be buried; also the tomb of Alexander II, and of the celebrated wizard, Michael Scott.[18] Reference is made to the former in some lines of Sir Walter Scott's in the *Lay of the Last Minstrel*, which describes this Border country:

> They sat them down on a marble stone;
> A Scottish monarch slept below.

And then when Deloraine takes the book from the dead wizard's hand, it says—

> He thought, as he took it, the dead man frowned.

Most truly does Walter Scott say—

> If thou wouldst view fair Melrose aright,
> Go visit it by the pale moonlight.

It looks very ghostlike, and reminds me a little of Holyrood Chapel. We walked in the churchyard to look at the exterior of the Abbey, and then re-entered our carriages and drove through the densely crowded streets. Great enthusiasm and hearty affectionate loyalty. Many decorations. A number of people from Galashiels, and even from the North of England, had come into the town and swelled the crowd; many also had spread themselves along the outskirts. We took the other side of the valley returning, and saw Galashiels, very prettily situated, a flourishing town famous for its tweeds and shawls; the men are called the "braw lads of Gala Water".

Another twenty minutes or half-hour brought us to Abbotsford, the well-known residence of Sir Walter Scott. It lies low and looks rather gloomy. Mr. Hope Scott and Lady Victoria (my god-daughter and sister to the present Duke of Norfolk) with their children, the young Duke of Norfolk, and some other relations, received us. Mr. Hope Scott married first Miss Lockhart, the last surviving grandchild of Sir Walter Scott, and she died leaving only one daughter, a pretty girl of eleven, to whom this place will go, and who is the only surviving descendant of Sir Walter. They showed us the part of the house in which Sir Walter lived, and all his rooms—his drawing-room with the same furniture and carpet, the library where we saw his MS. of *Ivanhoe*, and several others of his novels and poems in a beautiful handwriting with hardly any erasures, and other relics which Sir Walter had himself collected. Then his study, a small dark room, with a little turret in which is a bust in bronze, done from a cast taken after death,[19] of Sir Walter. In the study we saw his journal, in which Mr. Hope Scott asked me to write my name (which I felt it to be a presumption in me to do), as also the others.

We went through some passages into two or three rooms where were collected fine specimens of old armour, etc., and where in a glass case are Sir Walter's last clothes. We ended by going into the dining-room, in which Sir Walter Scott died, where we took tea. . . .

We left at twenty minutes to seven—very late. It rained a little, but soon ceased. We recrossed the Tweed, and went by Gattonside to Leaderfoot Bridge. Here we were met by the Berwickshire Volunteers, commanded by Lord Binning (Lord Haddington's son), who as Deputy Lieutenant rode a long way with us. Here was a steep hill, and the road surrounded by trees. We passed soon after through Gladswood, the property of Mr. Meiklam, at whose house-door we stopped, and he and Mrs. Meiklam were presented, and their daughter gave me a nosegay. Just after this we entered Berwickshire. Changing horses and leaving this place, going over Gatehcugh, we came upon a splendid view, overlooking a great extent of country, with a glen deep below the road, richly wooded, the river at the bottom, and hills in the distance; but unfortunately the "gloaming" was already commencing—at least, the sun was gone down, and the evening was grey and dull, though very mild. We passed Bemersyde, which is eventually to belong to Alfred's Equerry, Mr. Haig, and through the village of Mertoun, behind the park; and it was striking to see the good feeling shown by the people, who neither displayed any decorations nor cheered, though they were out and bowed, as their excellent master, Lord Polwarth, was lying dead in his house.

It was nearly dark by this time, but we got well and safely home by ten minutes to nine. The Duke of Buccleuch rode with us some way beyond Gladswood. We did not come through Kelso on our way back. In passing Mertoun we left the old tower of Smailholm to the left, the scene of the "Eve of St. John". We only sat down to dinner at half-past nine, and I own I was very tired. The Duke of Buccleuch was only able to come when dinner was half over. Besides him the Duke and Duchess of

Roxburghe, Lord Bowmont,[20] Lady Charles Ker, and Mr. Suttie made the party at dinner. Lady Susan[21] was prevented by indisposition from being there. Nobody could be kinder, or more discreet, or more anxious that I should be undisturbed when at home, than the Duke and Duchess. I only stopped a few minutes downstairs after dinner, and then went up to my room, but it was then nearly eleven. The others went into the drawing-room to meet some of the neighbours.

Friday, August 23

A dull morning, very close, with a little inclination to rain, though only for a short time. Breakfast as yesterday. At twenty minutes to eleven we started: I with our daughters and the Duchess; Christian with dear Beatrice, the Duke of Marlborough (the Minister in attendance), and Lady Susan Melville, in the second carriage; and the Duke of Roxburghe, Lord Charles Fitz-Roy, Sir Thomas Biddulph, in the third, with Colonel Gordon and Dr. Jenner on the box. We proceeded through Kelso, which was very full, and the people most loyal; by the village of Heiton, prettily decorated with an arch (two young girls dressed in white threw nosegays), and up the rivers Teviot and Jed, which flow through charming valleys. The town of Jedburgh is very prettily situated, and is about the same size as Kelso, only without its large shops. It is, however, the capital of the county. It was very crowded, and very prettily decorated. The town is full of historical recollections. King Malcolm IV died there; William the Lion and Alexander II resided there; Alexander III married his second wife, Joletta, daughter of the Comte de Dreux, there; and Queen Mary was the last sovereign who came to

Melrose Abbey in the early decades of the nineteenth century.

administer severe justice. The Duchess pointed out to me a house up a side street in the town where Queen Mary had lived and been ill with fever. In the square an address was presented, just as at Kelso, and then we went on down a steep hill, having a very good view of the old Abbey, as curious in its way as Melrose, and also founded by David I. There is a very fine ruined abbey in Kelso also.

There were four pretty triumphal arches; one with two very well chosen inscriptions, viz., on one side "Freedom makes all men to have lyking", and on the other side "The love of all thy people comfort thee".

We went on through a beautiful wooded valley up the Jed, in the bank of which, in the red stone, are caves in which the Covenanters were hid. We passed Lord Cranstoun's place, Crailing, and then turned, and close before the town we turned into Jed Forest—up an interminable hill, which was very trying to the horses and the postilions—and returned through the grounds of Hartrigge, the late Lord Campbell's, now occupied by a Mr. Gordon.

We then returned by the same road we came, passing Lord Minto's place, and Kirkbank, belonging to the Duke of Buccleuch, where his late brother, Lord John Scott, used to live. Here the horses were watered. We stopped for a few minutes, and the Duke of Buccleuch, who had ridden with us the greater part of the way, into Jedburgh and back to this place, took leave.

We only got home near three o'clock. We lunched at once, and then I rested. Only at half-past six did I go out with Lenchen and the good Duchess, and walked with them to the flower-garden, where, as it began to rain, we took tea in the small room there. Lenchen walked back with the Duchess, who returned to me, and I sat out a little while with her, and then walked back to the house. It was a very oppressive evening.

At half-past eight we dined. The Duke and Duchess, Mr. and Lady Charlotte Russell and Lord Charles Ker dined. Went upstairs and wrote. At ten minutes to eleven we left Floors, where I had been most kindly received, and had been very comfortable and enjoyed all I saw, and felt much all the kindness of high and low. The carriages were open, and the night very warm and starlight. There were lamps all along the drive in the Park; the bridge was illuminated, and so was the whole town, through which we went at a foot's pace. It was densely crowded, the square especially, and the people very enthusiastic. The dear Duchess went with us to the station, whither the Duke and his sons had preceded us with the others. It was a very pretty sight. The Free Kirk, a pretty building was lit up with red light, which almost gave it the appearance of being on fire. We took leave of the dear Duchess and the Duke, got into our railway carriage, and started at once.

Saturday, August 24

We passed through Edinburgh. At eight A.M. we were at Ballater. Some coffee and tea were handed in to us before we left the train and got into our carriages.

A fine and very mild morning, the heather hardly out, but all very green; and at ten minutes to nine we were at our dear Balmoral.

Highland cattle with a drover and his dog.

Tuesday, September 24, 1867

A BRIGHT MORNING, BUT A FEARFUL GALE BLOWING. The maids, Emilie and Annie and Lady Churchill's maid, with Ross and the luggage, started at a little past seven.

Breakfasted at a quarter past nine; and at ten, taking leave of Lenchen, darling Beatrice, and the boys, and Christian, started with Louise and Jane Churchill—Brown, as usual, on the box. Sir Thomas Biddulph had gone on at eight. We drove up by Alt Craichie on to Gairnshiel, and anything like the wind I cannot describe. It blew through everything. Just beyond Gairnshiel we took another change of my own horses, which took us up that very steep hill called Glaschoil. Here we met the luggage with Blake, which had stuck completely, but was going on with the help of four cart or farm horses, and then we went on by Tornahoish and Cock Brigg, where we crossed the Don. At the small inn at the foot of the hill, called Bridge End, we found the maids' carriage halting. They were waiting for the luggage, but we sent them on. Our postilions next took a wrong road, and we had to get out to enable them to turn. Then came a very steep hill, the beginning of very wild and really grand scenery. Louise and Jane Churchill walked up to the top of this hill, and then we went down another very steep one, seeing a fearfully long ascent before us. We changed horses, and took a pair of post-horses here. Steep green hills with a deep ravine on our left as we went up, and then down again, this fearful hill—surely three miles in length—called Lecht. At the bottom we entered a glen, or rather pass, very wild, and the road extremely bad, with rapid turnings. Near this there are iron mines belonging to the Duke of Richmond. Here we met a drove of very fine Highland cattle grazing. Turning out of this glen we came into much more cultivated land with farms and trees, skirted by hills in the distance—all very clear,

as the views had been all along. By half-past one we came close by Tomintoul, which lies very prettily amongst the trees, hills, and fields; then leaving it to our left, we went on about a mile and a half beyond the town; and here by the roadside, on some grass below a heathery bank, at about a quarter-past two, we took our luncheon, and walked a little. The Duke of Richmond's keeper, Lindsay by name, joined us here and rode before us. We changed horses (again a pair) and drove on, entering Glen Livet through the small village of Knockandhu—Blairfindy Castle on the left, just behind the celebrated Glenlivet Distillery. We drove on six miles; pretty country all along, distant high hills and richly cultivated land, with houses and cottages dotted about. At Tomnavoulin, a farm, not far from a bridge, we met Sir Thomas Biddulph (who had driven on in a dogcart) and our ponies. Though the wind had gone down a good deal, there was quite enough to make it disagreeable and fatiguing, and so we decided to drive, and Sir Thomas said he would ride across with the ponies and meet the Duke,[22] while his head keeper was to come on the box with Brown and show us the way (Grant did not go with us this time). We drove on for an hour and more, having entered Glen Rinnes shortly after Tomnavoulin, with the hills of Ben Rinnes on the left. There were fine large fields of turnips, pretty hills and dales, with wood, and distant high hills, but nothing grand. The day became duller, and the mist hung over the hills; and just as we sat down by the roadside on a heathery bank, where there is a very pretty view of Glenlivet, to take our tea, it began to rain, and continued doing so for the remainder of the evening. Lindsay, the head keeper, fetched a kettle with boiling water from a neighbouring farmhouse. About two miles beyond this we came through Dufftown—a small place with a long steep street, very like Grantown—and then turned abruptly to the right past Auchindoun, leaving a pretty glen to the left. Three miles more brought us to a lodge and gate, which was the entrance of Glenfiddich.[23] Here you go quite into the hills. The glen is very narrow, with the Fiddich flowing below, green hills rising on either side with birch trees growing on them, much like at Inchrory, only narrower. We saw deer on the tops of the hills close by. The carriage-road—a very good one—winds along for nearly three miles, when you come suddenly upon the lodge, the position of which reminds me very much of Corn Davon,[24] only that the glen is narrower and the hills just round it steeper. It is a long shooting lodge, covering a good deal of ground, but only one story high. We reached it at half-past six, and it was nearly dark. Sir Thomas received us, but he had missed the Duke! A message had, however, at once been sent after him. On entering the house there is one long, low passage, at the end of which, with three windows, taking in the whole of each side and looking three different ways, is the drawing-room, where tea was prepared. We went along the passage to our rooms, which were all in a row. Another long passage, a little beyond the hall door, went the other way at right angles with the first, and along that were offices and servants' bedrooms. Next to the drawing-room came the dining-room, then Sir Thomas Biddulph's room, then the Duke's, then Brown's and Ross's (in one), then Louise's, then mine, then Emilie's and Annie's (in one), then, a little further back, Jane Churchill's and her maid's—all very comfortably and conveniently together. But though our maids had arrived, not a bit of luggage. We waited and waited till dinner-time, but nothing came. So we ladies (for Sir Thomas had wisely brought some things with him) had to go to dinner in our riding-skirts, and just as we were. I, having no cap, had to put on a black lace veil of Emilie's, which she arranged as a coiffure. I had been writing

A drear January day in Glen Feshie; watercolour by R. P. Leitch, 1862.
The royal party fording the Tarff in Glen Tilt; watercolour by W. Leitch.

and resting before dinner. The Duke (who remained at Glenfiddich) and Sir Thomas dined with us ladies.

None of the maids or servants had any change of clothing. Dinner over, I went with Louise and Jane to the drawing-room, which was given me as my sitting-room, and Jane read. While at dinner at half-past nine, Ross told us that Blake, the footman, had arrived with some of the smaller things, but none of the most necessary—no clothes, etc. The break with the luggage had finally broken down at Tomintoul; from thence Blake had gone with a cart to Dufftown, where he had got a small break, and brought the light things on, but the heavier luggage was coming in a cart, and they hoped would be here by twelve o'clock. At first it seemed as if no horses were to be had, and it was only with the greatest difficulty that some were at last obtained. Louise and Jane Churchill left me at near eleven o'clock.

I sat up writing and waiting for this luggage. A man was sent out on a pony with a lantern in search of it, and I remained writing till a quarter-past twelve, when, feeling very tired, I lay down on the sofa, and Brown (who was indefatigable) went out himself to look for it. At one, he came back, saying nothing was to be seen or heard of this luckless luggage, and urged my going to bed. My maids had unfortunately not thought of bringing anything with them, and I disliked the idea of going to bed without any of the necessary toilette. However, some arrangements were made which were very uncomfortable; and after two I got into bed, but had very little sleep at first; finally fatigue got the better of discomfort, and after three I fell asleep.

Tuesday, October 15, 1867

OUR BLESSED ENGAGEMENT DAY![25] A dear and sacred day—already twenty-eight years ago. How I ever bless it! A wet morning—most annoying and provoking!

At a quarter-past eleven in this distressing rain, which twice had given hopes of ceasing, I, with all the family and Janie Ely, drove to the spot, just above Middleton's Lodge, where were assembled all the servants and tenants, and the detachment of the 93rd Highlanders drawn up opposite, just behind the Statue. I and the children stood just in front of the Statue, which was covered. A verse of the 100th Psalm was sung, and Mr. Taylor then stepped forward and offered up a beautiful prayer (in pelting rain at that moment), after which the order was given to uncover the Statue; but (as happened at Aberdeen) the covering caught, and it was a little while before it could be loosened from the shoulder.

The soldiers presented arms, and the pipes played, as we gazed on the dear noble figure of my beloved one, who used to be with us here in the prime of beauty, goodness, and strength.

opposite above: The exterior of Blair Castle; watercolour by C. Landseer.
opposite below: Floors Castle; coloured engraving by an unknown artist, 1868.

Unveiling of the statue of Albert at Balmoral, October 15th, 1867.

Then Dr. Robertson stepped forward, and made a very pretty little speech in the name of the servants and tenants, thanking me for the gift of the statue. He spoke remarkably well. This was followed by the soldiers firing a *feu de joie*; then all cheered, and the whole concluded by "God save the Queen" being sung extremely well.

Thursday, October 1, 1868

AT NEARLY FOUR O'CLOCK left with Louise and Jane Churchill for the Glassalt Shiel. It was a beautiful evening, clear and frosty. We drove by Birkhall and the Linn of Muich, where we stopped to take tea; we had just finished when Arthur[26] arrived from Ballater with Grant, who had gone to meet him there. He had travelled straight from Geneva, and looked rather tired, having besides had a bad passage. After walking a little we drove on, Arthur getting into the carriage with us, and Grant going with Brown on the box. We arrived at half-past six at the Glassalt Shiel, which looked so cheerful and comfortable, all lit up, and the rooms so cozy and nice. There is a wonderful deal of room in the compact little house. A good staircase (the only one) leads to the upper floor, where are the rooms for Louise, Jane Churchill, her maid, and Arthur, in one passage; out of this there is another, where are three rooms for Brown, the cook, and another servant; in one of these Grant and Ross slept, and C. Thomson in the other. Below are my sitting-room, bedroom, and my maids' room; and on the other side of our little hall the dining-room; then a nice kitchen, small steward's room, store-closet, and another small room where two menservants slept. The small passage near my bedroom shuts off the rest, and makes it quite private and quiet. Good stables, and the keeper's cottage, where our gillies sleep, just outside at the back.

We dined at about half-past eight in the small dining-room. This over, after waiting for a little while in my sitting-room, Brown came to say all the servants were ready for the house-warming, and at twenty minutes to ten we went into the little dining-room, which had been cleared, and where all the servants were assembled, viz., my second dresser, C. Wilmore, Brown, Grant, Ross (who played), Hollis (the cook), Lady Churchill's maid, Maxted, C. and A. Thomson, Blake (the footman), the two housemaids, Kennedy, J. Stewart (the stableman), and the policeman (who only comes to do duty outside at night). We made nineteen altogether. Five animated reels were danced, in which all (but myself) joined. After the first reel "whisky-toddy" was brought round for every one, and Brown begged I would drink to the "fire-kindling". Then Grant made a little speech, with an allusion to the wild place we were in, and concluding with a wish "that our Royal Mistress, our good Queen", should "live long". This was followed by cheers given out by Ross in regular Highland style, and all drank my health. The merry pretty little ball ended at a quarter-past eleven. The men, however, went on singing in the steward's room for some time, and all were very happy, but I heard nothing, as the little passage near my bedroom shuts everything off.

Sad thoughts filled my heart both before dinner and when I was alone and retired to rest. I thought of the happy past and my darling husband whom I fancied I must see, and who always wished to build here, in this favourite wild spot, quite in amidst the hills. At Altnaguithasach I could not have lived again now—alone. It is far better to have built a totally new house; but then the sad thought struck me that it was the first Widow's house, not built by him or hallowed by his memory. But I am sure his blessing does rest on it, and on those who live in it.

Thursday, October 21, 1868

AT A QUARTER TO TWELVE I drove off with Louise and Leopold in the waggonette up to near the "Bush" (the residence of William Brown,[27] the farmer) to see them "juice the sheep". This is a practice pursued all over the Highlands before the sheep are sent down to the low country for the winter. It is done to preserve the wool. Not far from the burnside, where there are a few hillocks, was a pen in which the sheep were placed, and then, just outside it, a large sort of trough filled with liquid tobacco and soap, and into this the sheep were dipped one after the other; one man (James Brown,[28] my shepherd, the elder brother, who came up on purpose to help) took the sheep one by one out of the pen and turned them on their backs; and then William and he, holding them by their legs, dipped them well in, after which

Victoria's sketch of juicing the sheep at the Bush.

they were let into another pen into which this trough opened, and here they had to remain to dry. To the left, a little lower down, was a cauldron boiling over a fire and containing the tobacco with water and soap; this was then emptied into a tub, from which it was transferred into the trough. A very rosy-faced lassie, with a plaid over her head, was superintending this part of the work, and helped to fetch the water from the burn, while children and many collie dogs were grouped about, and several men and shepherds were helping. It was a very curious and picturesque sight.

Sunday, October 24, 1868

AT A QUARTER TO FOUR I drove, with Louise, Beatrice, and Lady Ely, to John Thomson the wood forester's house for the christening of their child, three weeks old. Here, in their little sitting-room, in front of the window stood a table covered with a white cloth, on which was placed a basin with water, a bible, and a paper with the certificate of the child's birth.

We stood on one side, and John Thomson in his Highland dress next the minister, who was opposite me at the head of the table. Barbara, his wife, stood next to him, with the baby in her arms, and then the old Thomsons and their unmarried daughter, the Donald Stewarts, Grants, and Victoria, Morgan and sister, and Brown.

Dr. Taylor (who wore his gown) then began with an address and prayer, giving thanks "for a living mother and a living child", after which followed another prayer; he then read a few passages from Scripture, after which came the usual questions which he addressed to the father, and to which he bowed assent. Then the minister told him—"Present your child for baptism." After this the father took the child and held it while the minister baptised it, sprinkling it with water, but not making the sign of the cross, saying first to those present: "The child's name is Victoria"; and then to the child:

Victoria, I baptise thee in the name of the Father, and of the Son, and of the Holy Ghost, One God blessed for ever.—Amen.

The Lord bless thee and keep thee! The Lord make His face to shine upon thee and be gracious unto thee! The Lord lift up His countenance upon thee and give thee peace!

The service was concluded with another short prayer and the usual blessing. I thought it most appropriate, touching, and impressive. I gave my present (a silver mug) to the father, kissed the little baby, and then we all drank to its health and that of its mother in whisky, which was handed round with cakes. It was all so nicely done, so simply, and yet with such dignity.

Wednesday, September 1, 1869

WE GOT UP AT HALF-PAST SEVEN, breakfasted at eight, and at half-past eight left Balmoral with Louise, Beatrice, and Jane Churchill (Brown as always, unless I mention to the contrary, on the box), for Ballater. A high and rather cold wind, but very bright sun, dreadfully dusty. Colonel Ponsonby[29] met us at the railway station. Emilie Dittweiler and Annie Macdonald, Ocklee (for the two girls), Jane Churchill's maid, Charlie Thomson, and the footman Cannon, went with us: Blake, Spong with the luggage, A. Thomson, with Sharp (my faithful collie dog), and Annie Gordon (house-maid), Kennedy, Arthur Grant, and Hiley (the groom) with the ponies, all went yesterday, and three cooks came from London. We had a saloon carriage, but not my own. It grew hot in the railway train. We stopped at Aberdeen and the Bridge of Dun, where Jane Churchill got into our carriage, and had luncheon with us; but we could have no one to help to pack and unpack it, which is now so comfortably arranged in my own railway carriage where there is a communication with the attendants.

Stopping a moment at Cupar-Angus, we passed through Perth, and had another short halt at Dunblane, where the people crowded very much. Here we got a view of the old Cathedral, and turned off to Callander, which we reached at a quarter-past three. There was a very well-behaved crowd at the quiet station. Mr. and Lady Emily Macnaghten, to whose house (which they had most kindly lent us) we were going, and Sir Malcolm and Lady Helen MacGregor (he is Miss MacGregor's nephew, she Lady Emily Macnaghten's niece), received us there. Their little girl gave me a nosegay. We at once got into our celebrated sociable, which has been to the top of the Furca in Switzerland,[30] etc., and had been sent on before, Colonel

Victoria with the dog "Sharp".

Invertrossachs House around the time of Victoria's visit.

Ponsonby and Brown going on the box. We drove off at once with post-horses through the small town of Callander, which consists of one long street with very few shops, and few good houses, but many poor ones. We drove on, and, after about three-quarters of a mile's drive, came to Loch Vennachar, a fine lake about four miles long, with Ben Venue and other high and beautiful mountains rising behind and around it. The road is thickly wooded with oak, birch, beech, mountain-ash, etc. The house stands extremely well on a high eminence, overlooking the loch and surrounded by trees, and you drive up through evergreens and trees of all kinds. Half an hour brought us to the door of the house, Invertrossachs,[31] which is small and comfortable. At the entrance is a nice little hall in which there is a small billiard table; to the left, beyond that, a very nice well-sized dining-room with one large window. To the right of the hall is the drawing-room, very much like the one at Invermark (Lord Dalhousie's); altogether the house is in that style, but larger. The staircase is almost opposite the hall-door, and there is a narrow passage which goes on to the left and right, along which are Louise's, Baby's (Beatrice's), my sitting-room (a snug little room), and my bedroom (very good size); and out of that, two little rooms which I use as dressing- and bath-rooms, and Emilie Dittweiler's. Further on, round a corner as it were, beyond Louise's, are Lady Churchill's, her maid's, and Colonel Ponsonby's rooms, all very fair-sized and comfortable. Close to my dressing-rooms is a staircase which goes upstairs to where Brown and our other people live. The rooms are very comfortably and simply furnished, and they have put down new carpets everywhere.

Thursday, September 2

A very fine, bright, warm morning. We decided to go on an expedition, but not to Loch Lomond, as we should have to start so early. Breakfasted in the drawing-room with Louise and Beatrice. Then writing, etc. At twenty minutes to twelve I started in the sociable with Louise, Beatrice, Jane Churchill, and Colonel Ponsonby and Brown on the box, and drove (excellent post-horses, always only a pair) to Callander, but turned to the right short of it, and went on some little way. On coming to the top of a hill we saw Ben Ledi, a splendid hill; to the north Ben Voirlich, and to the east the heights of Uam Var, a pink heathery ridge of no great elevation; and in the distance, rising up from the horizon, Dun Myat, and the Wallace Monument on the Abbey Craig, near Stirling. We went across a moor, and then soon passed Loch Ruskie, quite a small lake. The country about here is rather lowland, but as we proceeded it was extremely pretty, with very fine trees and cornfields, and harvesting going on; and soon after, descending a hill, we came upon the Loch of "Menteith" (the only loch in Scotland which is ever called lake). It reminds one very much of Loch Kinnord near Ballater, and very low blue and pink hills rise in the distance. There are two or three islands in it; in the large one, Inchmahome, you perceive amongst the thick woods the ruins of the ancient priory. Queen Marh[32] lived there once, and there are monuments of the Menteiths to be seen on it. To the right we passed the ruin of Rednock Castle, and to the left the gates of the Park of Rednock, with very fine large trees, where Mr. Graham, the proprietor, was standing. We went on and passed the Clachan of Aberfoyle (renowned in Sir Walter Scott's *Rob Roy*), and here the splendid scenery begins — high, rugged, and green hills (reminding me again of Pilatus), very fine large trees and beautiful pink heather, interspersed with bracken, rocks, and underwood, in the most lovely profusion, and Ben Lomond towering up before us with its noble range. We went on perhaps a quarter of a mile, and, it being then two o'clock, we got out and lunched on the grass under an oak at the foot of Craig More. It was very hot, the sun stinging, but there were many light white clouds in the blue sky, which gave the most beautiful effects of light and shade on this marvellous colouring. After luncheon and walking about a little, not finding any good view to sketch, we got into the carriage (our horses had been changed), but had not gone above a few yards when we came upon Loch Ard, and a lovelier picture could not be seen. Ben Lomond, blue and yellow, rose above the lower hills, which were pink and purple with heather, and an isthmus of green trees in front dividing it from the rest of the loch. We got out and sketched. Only here and there, far between, were some poor little cottages with picturesque barefooted lasses and children to be seen. All speak Gaelic here. Louise and I sat sketching for half an hour, Beatrice running about merrily with Jane Churchill while we drew. We then drove on, and certainly one of the most lovely drives I can remember, along Loch Ard, a fine long loch, with trees of all kinds overhanging the road, heather making all pink; bracken, rocks, high hills of such a fine shape, and trees growing up them as in Switzerland; the road rough and bad, with very steep bits of hill (but the post-horses went remarkably well) overhanging the loch, which reminded me very much of the drive along the Lake Zug in Switzerland. Altogether, the whole drive along Loch Ard, then by the

Ben Lomond and the island of Inveruglas in the late nineteenth century.

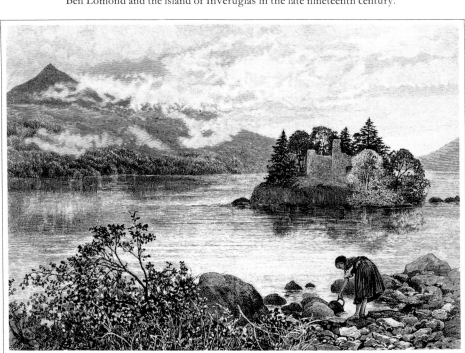

The walk by the shore of Loch Katrine.

very small Loch Dow and the fine Loch Chon, which is very long, was lovely. The heather in full bloom, and of the richest kind, some almost of a crimson colour, and growing in rich tufts along the road. One can see, by the mounds or heaps of stone, all along Loch Chon, where the Glasgow waterworks are carried, but they have not disfigured the landscape.

Emerging from this road we came upon the Loch Lomond Road, having a fine view of Loch Arklet, on the banks of which Helen MacGregor is said to have been born. The scene of our drive to-day is all described in *Rob Roy*. Loch Arklet lies like Loch Callater, only that the hills are higher and more pointed. Leaving this little loch to our left, in a few minutes we came upon Loch Katrine, which was seen in its greatest beauty in the fine evening light. Most lovely! We stopped at Stronachlachar, a small inn where people stay for a night sometimes, and where they embark coming from Loch Lomond and vice versa. As the small steamer had not yet arrived, we had to wait for about a quarter of an hour. But there was no crowd, no trouble or annoyance, and during the whole of our drive nothing could be quieter or more agreeable. Hardly a creature did we meet, and we passed merely a very few pretty gentlemen's places, or very poor cottages with simple women and barefooted long-haired lassies and children, quiet and unassuming old men and labourers. This solitude, the romance and wild loveliness of everything here, the absence of hotels and beggars, the independent simple people, who all speak Gaelic here, all make beloved Scotland the proudest, finest country in the world. Then there is that beautiful heather, which you do not see elsewhere. I prefer it greatly to Switzerland, magnificent and glorious as the scenery of that country is.

It was about ten minutes past five when we went on board the very clean little steamer *Rob Roy*—the very same we had been on under such different circumstances in 1859 on the 14th of October, in dreadful weather, thick mist and heavy rain, when my beloved Husband and I opened the Glasgow Waterworks. We saw the spot and the cottage where we lunched.

We took a turn and steamed a little way up the bay called Glen Gyle, where there is a splendid glen beautifully wooded, which is the country of the MacGregors, and where there is a house which belonged to MacGregor of Glen Gyle, which, with the property, has been bought by a rich Glasgow innkeeper of the same clan. We turned and went on, and nothing could be more beautiful than the loch, wooded all along the banks. The rugged Ben Venue, so famed in the *Lady of the Lake* (which we had with us as well as several guide-books, of which we find Black's far the best), rises majestically on the southern side of the lake, and looking back you see the Alps of Arrochar, which well deserve the name, for they are quite pointed and most beautiful; their names are Ben Vean, Ben Voirlich, Ben Eim, and Ben Crosh. Next came the well-known "Silver Strand", "Helen's Isle", which is most lovely, and the narrow creek so beautifully wooded below the splendid high hills, and the little wooden landing-place which I remembered so well; and very melancholy and yet sweet were my feelings when I landed and found on the path some of the same white pebbles which my dearest Albert picked up and had made into a bracelet for me. I picked up and carried off a handful myself.

We had taken our tea on board on deck. We now entered two hired carriages, the girls and I in the first, with Brown on the box, and Jane Churchill and Colonel Ponsonby in the second. The evening was lovely, and the lights and pink and golden sky as we drove through the beautiful Trossachs were glorious indeed

> So wondrous wild, the whole might seem
> The scenery of a fairy dream—

and along Loch Achray—the setting sun behind Ben Venue, which rose above most gloriously, so beautifully described by Sir W. Scott:

> The western waves of ebbing day
> Rolled o'er the glen the level way.
> Each purple peak, each flinty spire
> Was bathed in floods of living fire.

We passed the fine Trossachs Inn where Louise had stopped with Alice and Louis in 1865, and a lovely little church in a most picturesque position, and lastly the Brig of Turk. It is a long way round Loch Vennachar to Invertrossachs: you see the house for three-quarters of an hour before you can get to it. Home at eight. The drive back was lovely, for long after the sun had set the sky remained beautifully pink behind the dark blue hills. A most successful day. Dinner as yesterday. I felt very tired.

Saturday, September 4

Up by half-past seven, and breakfasting at a quarter to eight. Got on my pony Sultan[33] at nine, the others walking, and went through the wood to the loch's edge, where we three got into a small boat and were rowed across to the other side by the keeper and underkeeper, Brown sitting in the bow, Colonel Ponsonby and Jane Churchill going across in another very small boat rowed by one man. Here we got into our carriage as before. Dear Beatrice enjoys it all very much, and is so good and cheerful.

We drove on through the beautiful Trossachs to Loch Katrine. It was a very dark thick morning; no distance to be seen at all, and Ben Venue very imperfectly. We embarked by ten o'clock on board the steamer *Rob Roy*, and steamed off for Stronachlachar. No distant view was visible, and the colour of the sky was really that of a thick November fog. However, by the time we reached Stronachlachar, it was much lighter to the left, towards where we were going.

Here we got into two hired carriages again, Jane and Colonel Ponsonby preceding us this time. We drove along Loch Arklet, a lovely drive with pink heathered hills to the right, and gradually the mist cleared off, and allowed us to see rugged peaks above and in front of us. We met (as we had done from the first) several large coaches, but with only outside seats, full of tourists. This reminded me, as did the whole tour this day and on Thursday, of Switzerland and our expeditions there, especially now when we suddenly came upon Loch Lomond, and drove down a very steep hill to Inversnaid, where there is only one house (a small inn), and saw high mountains, looking shadowy in the mist (dry mist), rising abruptly from the loch. We went at once on board the fine steamer *Prince Consort* (a pleasant idea that that dear name should have carried his poor little wife, alas! a widow, and children, on their first sail on this beautiful lake which he went to see in 1847). She is a fine large vessel, a good deal larger than the *Winkelried* (in which we used to go on the Lake of Lucerne), with a fine large dining-cabin below, a very high upper deck, and a gallery underneath on which people can stand and smoke without incommoding the others above.

We steamed southward, and for the first half nothing could be finer or more truly Alpine, reminding me much of the Lake of Lucerne; only it is longer—Loch Lomond being twenty-two miles long. We kept close to the east shore, passing under Ben Lomond with its variously called shoulders—Cruachan, Craig a Bochan, and Ptarmigan—to Rowardennan pier, where there is a pretty little house rented from the Duke of Montrose (to whom half Loch Lomond belongs) by a Mr. Mair, a lovely spot from whence you can ascend Ben Lomond, which is 3,192 feet high, and well wooded part of the way, with cornfields below. After you pass this, where there are fine mountains on either side, though on the west shore not so high, the lake widens out, but the shores become much flatter and tamer (indeed to the east and south completely so); but here are all the beautifully wooded islands, to the number of twenty-four. Some of them are large; on Inchlonaig Island the yews are said to have been planted by Robert Bruce to encourage the people in the use of archery. Another, Inch Cailliach, is the ancient burial-place of the MacGregors.

On the mainland we passed Cornick Hill, and could just see Buchanan House, the Duke of Montrose's, and to the right the island of Inch Murrin, on which the Duke has his deer preserve. The sun had come out soon after we went on board, and it was blowing quite fresh as we went against the wind. At two o'clock we stopped off Portnellan for luncheon, which we had brought with us and took below in the handsome large cabin, where fifty or sixty people, if not more, could easily dine. Colonel Ponsonby also lunched with us. . . . This over, we went to the end of the lake to Balloch, and here turned. It became very warm. To the left we passed some very pretty villas (castles they resembled) and places, amongst others Cameron (Mr. Smollett)s), Arden (Sir J. Lumsden's, Lord Provost of Glasgow), Ross-Dhu (Sir J. Colquhoun's), the road to Glen Fruin, the islands of Inch Connachan, Inch Tavanach, the point of Stob Gobhlach, Luss, a very prettily situated village, the mountain of Ben Dubh, and the ferry of Inveruglas, opposite Rowardennan. Then Tarbet, a small town, where dearest Albert landed in 1847, and here began the highest and finest mountains, with splendid passes, richly wooded, and the highest mountains rising behind. A glen leads across from Tarbet to Arrochar on Loch Long, and here you see that most singularly shaped hill called the Cobbler, and a little further on the splendid Alps of Arrochar. All this and the way in which the hills run into the lake reminded me so much of the Nasen on the Lake of Lucerne.

The head of the lake with the very fine glen (Glen Falloch), along which you can drive to Oban, is magnificent. We (Louise and I) sketched as best we could, but it is most difficult to do so when the steamer keeps moving on; and we were afterwards much vexed we had not asked them to go more slowly, as we had to wait again for the *Rob Roy* steamer at Stronachlachar. From the head of Loch Lomond (where is the Hotel of Inverarnan) we turned; we were shown a hole in the rock, on the east side, which they called Rob Roy's Cave, and landed at Inversnaid. The people (quite a small crowd) threw bunches of heather as we passed. Heather is everywhere the decoration, and there is indeed no lovelier, prettier ornament. It was in such full bloom. The mountains here are peculiarly fine from the sharp serrated outline and wonderful clothing of grass and trees. It was a very bright warm evening, and the drive back, which we had to take slowly, not to arrive too soon, was extremely pretty. At Stronachlachar, both on embarking and disembarking, there were a few people collected. On board we had again our tea, and Mr. Blair, the very obliging gentleman-like host of the Trossachs Inn (and possessor of the Loch Katrine steamer), who was in attendance each time, gave us some clotted cream.

It was a splendid sail over this most lovely loch, and delightful drive back by the Trossachs. We got into the boat again where we left it this morning, and rowed across; but this time it was most unpleasant, for it blew and was very rough, and the little boat rolled and danced. The second smaller one with the two others shipped water. Rode back and got up to the house by half-past seven. This was the only *contretemps* to our most successful, enjoyable day. How dearest Albert would have enjoyed it!

Sunday, September 5

A dull muggy morning. Decided not to go to kirk, as it would have been very public. So at eleven rode (on Sultan) with dear Beatrice (on her little Beatrice) for an hour, first up at the back of the farm, and then a little way on the beautiful pink heathery and bracken hills just behind the house, and saw Loch Drunkie almost dry from the drought, and looked over to the Brig of Turk, then back by the stables to the house. Read the collect, epistle, and gospel, and the second lesson for the day, with the two girls, Beatrice reading the last-named.

While we were at luncheon it rained, but it soon ceased, and the afternoon became quite fine and was very warm. At half-past five walked out with Louise, Beatrice, and Jane Churchill, stopping at the lodge where McIsaacs, the keeper, and his wife live. Walked some way on, and then drove with Beatrice round a short way on the Trossachs Road, coming home at half-past seven.

Monday, September 6

Misty early, then beautiful and clear and very hot. Got up with a bad headache. At five minutes to eleven rode off with Beatrice, good Sharp going with us and having occasional "collie-shangies"[34] with collies when we came near cottages (A. Thomson and Kennedy following). We rode out the same way we came back yesterday, and then up the same hill overlooking Loch Drunkie—which really is nearly dry—and on down the other side of the hill, as fast as we could go along a rough but very pretty road, which brought us, over perfumed pink heather interspersed with bracken, to a spot where you get a lovely glimpse of Loch Achray and Ben Venue. We then continued along a wood past a few miserable cottages, but as private as if I were riding at Balmoral, out into the high road just at the Brig of Turk, and stopped at what is called "Fergusson's Inn", but is in fact the very poorest sort of Highland cottage. Here lives Mrs. Fergusson, an immensely fat woman and a well-known character, who is quite rich and well dressed, but will not leave the place where she has lived all her life selling whisky. She was brought out and seemed delighted to see me, shaking hands with me and patting me. She walks with a crutch, and had to sit down. We only stopped a very few minutes, and then went home as fast as we came, and got back by one.

Balmoral,
October 3, 1870

THIS WAS AN EVENTFUL DAY! Our dear Louise was engaged to Lord Lorne.[35] The event took place during a walk from the Glassalt Shiel to the Dhu Loch. She had gone there with Janie Ely, the Lord Chancellor (Lord Hatherley[36]), and Lorne. I had driven with Beatrice and the Hon. Mrs. Ponsonby to Pannanich Wells, two miles from Ballater, on the south side of the Dee, where I had been many years ago. Unfortunately almost all the trees which covered the hills have been cut down.

We got out and tasted the water, which is strongly impregnated with iron, and looked at the bath and at the humble but very clean accommodation in the curious little old inn, which used to be very much frequented. Brown formerly stayed there for a year as servant, and then quantities of horses and goats were there.

The same perfectly cloudless sky as on the two preceding days. We got home by seven. Louise, who returned some time after we did, told me that Lorne had spoken of his devotion to her, and proposed to her, and that she had accepted him, knowing

Princess Louise and the Marquess of Lorne, afterwards the Duke of Argyll.

that I would approve. Though I was not unprepared for this result, I felt painfully the thought of losing her. But I naturally gave my consent, and could only pray that she might be happy.

Tuesday, June 11, 1872

BROWN CAME IN SOON AFTER FOUR O'CLOCK, saying he had been down at the waterside, for a child had fallen into the water, and the whole district was out to try and recover it—but it must be drowned long before this time. I was dreadfully shocked. It was the child of a man named Rattray, who lives at Cairn-na-Craig, just above where the new wood-merchant has built a house, and quite close to the keeper Abercrombie's house, not far from Monaltrie Farmhouse in the street. At a little before five, set off in the waggonette with Beatrice and Janie Ely, and drove along the north side of the river. We stopped a little way beyond Tynebaich, and saw the people wandering along the riverside. Two women told us that two children had fallen in (how terrible!), and that one "had been gotten—the little een" (as the people pronounce "one"), but not the eldest. They were searching everywhere. While we were there, the old grandmother, Catenach by name, who lives at Scutter Hole, came running along in a great state of distress. She is Rattray's mother. We drove on a little way, and then turned round.

We heard from the people that the two boys, one of ten or eleven and the other only three, were at Monaltrie Burn which comes down close to the farmhouse and below Mrs. Patterson's shop, passing under a little bridge and running into the Dee. This burn is generally very low and small, but had risen to a great height—the Dee itself being tremendously high—not a stone to be seen. The little child fell in while the eldest was fishing; the other jumped in after him, trying to save his little brother; and before any one could come out to save them (though the screams of Abercrombie's children, who were with them, were heard) they were carried away and swept by the violence of the current into the Dee, and carried along. Too dreadful! It seems, from what I heard coming back, that the poor mother was away from home, having gone to see her own mother who was dying, and that she purposely kept this eldest boy back from school to watch the little one.

We drove back and up to Mrs. Grant's, where we took tea, and then walked up along the riverside, and heard that nothing had been found and that the boat had gone back; but as we approached nearer to the castle we saw people on the banks and rocks with sticks searching: amongst them was the poor father—a sad and piteous sight—crying and looking so anxiously for his poor child's body.

Wednesday, June 12

Drove up to the Bush to warn Mrs. William Brown never to let dear little Albert run about alone, or near to the burn, of the danger of which she was quite aware. She said her husband, William, had started off early at three this morning. Some people went down to Abergeldie and as far as the Girnoch to search, and others were up and below the castle.

No word of the poor child being found. All were to start early to search.

Thursday, June 13

At half-past ten drove out in the waggonette with Beatrice and Janie Ely, and drove beyond Mrs. Patterson's "shoppie" a little way, and turned up to the right off the road behind the wood-merchant's new cottage, and got out just below Abercrombie the keeper's house, and walked a few paces on to the small cottage called Cairn-na-Craig, at the foot of Craig Noerdie, in a lovely position, sheltered under the hill, yet high, with a beautiful view of Lochnagar. Brown went in first, and was received by the old grandmother; and then we went in, and on a table in the kitchen covered with a sheet which they lifted up, lay the poor sweet innocent "bairnie", only three years old, a fine plump child, and looking just as though it slept, with quite a pink colour, and very little scratched, in its last clothes—with its little hands joined—a most touching sight. I let Beatrice see it, and was glad she should see death for the first time in so touching and pleasing a form.

Then the poor mother came in, calm and quiet, though she cried a little at first when I took her hand and said how much I felt for her, and how dreadful it was. She checked herself, and said, with that great resignation and trust which it is so edifying to witness, and which you see so strongly here, "We must try to bear it; we must trust to the Almighty."

The poor little thing was called Sandy. She herself is a thin, pale, dark, very good, and respectable-looking woman. She had no wish to go away that day, as the old grandmother told us, but her husband wished her to see her mother. She has one boy and two girls left, and the eldest and youngest are taken.

They were playing at the burnside, but some way above the road, where there is a small bridge. As we were leaving I gave her something and she was quite overcome, and blessed me for it.

We walked down again, and then drove back, and walked at once past the stables to the riverside, where, on both sides, every one was assembled, four in the boat (Donald Stewart and Jemmie Brown amongst them), and all with sticks, and up and down they went, searching under every stone. They had been up to the boat pool and back, but nothing appeared. I remained watching till one o'clock, feeling unable to tear myself away from this terrible sight. The poor father was on our side, William Brown amongst the others on the other side. I sat on the bank with Janie Ely for some time (Beatrice having gone in earlier than I), Grant as well as Brown standing near me. When they came to that very deep pool, where twenty-two years ago a man was nearly drowned when they were leistering for salmon, they held a piece of red cloth on a pole over the water, which enabled them to see down to the bottom. But all in vain. The river, though lower, was still very high.

At four took a short drive in the single pony carriage with Janie Ely, and back before five. Saw and talked to the schoolmaster, Mr. Lubban, a very nice little man, and he said that this poor child, Jemmie, the eldest, was such a good, clever boy. Every one shows so much feeling and kindness. It is quite beautiful to see the way in which every one turned out to help to find this poor child, from the first thing in the morning till the last at night—which, during these long days, was very hard work— and all seemed to feel the calamity deeply. We heard by telegraph during dinner that the poor boy's body had been found on an island opposite Pannanich, below Ballater, and that steps would be taken at once to recover it.

Saturday, June 15

After luncheon, at a quarter to three, drove with the two children up as far as the West Lodge, and then just descried the sad funeral procession slowly and sadly wending its way along the road; so we drove back again, catching glimpses of it as we went along, and drove on a little way beyond the bridge, when, seeing the first people not far off, we turned and drove back, stopping close to the bridge, and here we waited to see them pass. There were about thirty people, I should say, including the poor father, Jemmie and Willie Brown, Francie's brother, Alick Leys, Farmer Patterson, etc. The poor father walked in front of one of the coffins; both covered with white, and so small. It was a very sad sight.

Tuesday, August 13, 1872

AT SIX I LEFT SWEET OSBORNE WITH LEOPOLD and Beatrice, and the Duchess of Roxburghe, Flora Macdonald,[37] Colonels Ponsonby and De Ros, Mr. Collins,[38] and Fräulein Bauer.[39]

The Royal Company of Archers marching out of the forecourt of the Palace of Holyrood, Edinburgh; oil painting by W. S. Cumming, 1886.

We had our own usual large travelling railway carriages, which are indeed charming. It was a splendid night. Sir W. Jenner joined us at Basingstoke, and at Banbury at half-past ten we stopped for refreshments, and lay down before twelve.

Wednesday, August 14

I had a good deal of rest, and was up and dressed by eight, or a little past. But we had already passed Melrose, and there was so much fog, and the air so thick, that we could see very little. The last station (not in a village or town) was Fountainhall, where old Mr. Lawson, the former Lord Provost of Edinburgh and famous seedsman, came up to the carriage, and some little girls presented Baby (as Beatrice is always called by us still) with a nosegay. We passed Portobello, and a few minutes more brought us to the very station—the private one, outside Edinburgh—which for eleven years my beloved Albert and I had always arrived at, and where we left it together eleven years ago. There it was, all unaltered, and yet all so altered!

The General, Sir J. Douglas,[40] the Lord Provost, and other official people received us there, and we got into our carriage. The two children and the Duchess of Roxburghe went in the carriage with me.

It was a dull, gloomy, heavy morning, but a great many people were out, and all most enthusiastic, reminding me forcibly and sadly of former days. We had an escort of the Scots Greys. We drove up to the door of the old, gloomy, but historical Palace of Holyrood, where a guard of honour with a band of the 93rd Highlanders were stationed in the quadrangle of the court. We got out, walked up the usual stairs, and passed through two of the large gloomy rooms we used to occupy, and then went past some passages up another and very steep staircase to the so-called "Argyll rooms", which have been arranged for me, with very pretty light paper, chintz, and carpets (chosen by Louise). There is a suite, beginning with a dining-room (the least cheerful) at the farthest end, and then my sitting-room, a large and most cheerful room, the nicest of all, with very light paper; next to this the bedroom, almost too large a room, and out of this the dressing-room. All open one out of the other, and have, except the dining-room, the same pretty carpets and chintzes (red geraniums on a white ground). The page's room and a wardrobe and dresser's room are just opposite, across a small passage.

We three took breakfast directly in the dining-room. Our rooms are above the old rooms, and have the same look-out.

It cleared up, and though still thick and hazy, the sun shone out brightly, and at a quarter to twelve I went out into the garden, going through our old rooms, which looked sadly deserted: all open and some few things removed from them; the gloomy bedroom with its faded tapestry and green silk bed, and the wretched little dark boxroom in which I undressed at night, all full of many recollections. I went through the long picture gallery, down the small steps into the garden, where I met Beatrice, who walked with me. We walked about the garden, which is improved, but terribly overlooked, and quite exposed to public view on the side looking towards the street. We walked about the fine old chapel with its beautiful window

Inveraray Castle, on the shore of Loch Fyne.

Arthur's Seat, in Edinburgh.

and its tombstones, and then went in—Beatrice and I with Brown (who was much interested by all)—conducted by the keeper, an intelligent sensible man called Anderson[41] and visited the rooms of Queen Mary, beginning with the Hamilton apartments (which were Lord Darnley's rooms) and going up the old staircase to Queen Mary's chamber. In Lord Darnley's rooms there are some fine old tapestry and interesting portraits of the Royal family, and of the Dukes and Duchesses of Hamilton. There are some other curious old pictures in this room.

We saw the small secret staircase which led up in the turret to Queen Mary's bedroom, and we went up another dark old winding staircase at the top of which poor Rizzio was so horribly murdered—whose blood is still supposed to stain the floor. We entered the Presence Chamber, the ceiling of which, in panels, is from the time of Queen Mary, and contains her mother's and her own initials and arms as Dauphine of France and Queen of Scotland, with Darnley's initials. Here is the bed provided for Charles I when he came to Holyrood to be crowned King of Scotland. Thence we were shown into poor Queen Mary's bedroom, where are the faded old bed she used, the baby-basket sent her by Queen Elizabeth when King James I was born, and her work-box. All hung with old tapestry, and the two little turret rooms; the one where she was supping when poor Rizzio was murdered, the other her dressing-room. Bits of the old tapestry which covered the walls at the time are hung up in frames in the rooms. Beatrice is immensely interested by all she sees, and delighted with everything.

At half-past five drove off in the open landau and four with Beatrice, Leopold, and the Duchess of Roxburghe, the two equerries riding. We drove up through the Canongate, that curious old street with its very high-storied houses, past Knox's House and quaint old buildings, with the lowest, poorest people about, down Bank Street, and eastward along Princes Street, that splendid street with its beautiful shops, hotels, etc., on one side, and its fine monuments on the other, the gardens and institutions and other parts of the town rising above it and crowned by the picturesque Castle; then by Saint Andrew Street, across Saint Andrew Square (where Lord Melville's statue is), along George Street, a fine wide street, at the end of which is Charlotte Square, where my dear one's Monument is to be placed, and where I was to have stopped to look at the site. But the crowd, which was very great everywhere and would run with us (facilitated by the great steepness and slipperiness of the streets), as well as the great number of cabs and vehicles of all kinds which would drive along after us everywhere, made this impossible. We turned to the left with some difficulty — one or two carriages coming in contact with ours — and went on by Hope Street, Queen's Ferry Street, where we took a wrong turn, and went by Clarendon Crescent and Forres Street till we got to the Water of Leith, where we found we could not go on.

We had to turn, with considerable difficulty, owing to the narrowness of the road, and go back again by Moray Place, Heriot Row, and thence down by Pitt Street on to Inverleith Row (outside the town), past the Botanic Garden, then along the Queen's Ferry Road, Pilrig Street and Leith Walk (which I remembered from our having taken the same drive in 1861), then along a broad street, under the Calton Hill, and Regent Terrace, past Holyrood, into the beautiful Queen's Drive, right round Arthur's Seat with its fine grass, its rocks and small lochs. Unfortunately, however, no clear distant view could be obtained on account of the fog. Home to Holyrood at half-past seven. It was a fatiguing drive.

The crowds were very great, but the people behaved remarkably well; only they kept cheering and shouting and running with us, for the postilions drove very slowly whenever there was the slightest descent, and there were many in the town, and one long one coming down home from the Queen's Drive. A good many flags were out, but there were hardly any decorations. The equerries kept extremely well close up to the carriage which was no easy task.

Thursday, August 15

Again a very foggy morning. Breakfasted at half-past nine Beatrice and Leopold started to go and see Roslin Chapel. Walked a little in the garden at half-past ten, and then sat for half an hour under the only tree which afforded shade and was not overlooked by the street, a thorn, with very overhanging long branches, on a small grassy mound or "hillock". Here I read out of a volume of Poems by the "Ettrick Shepherd", full of beautiful things (which Brown had given me some years ago), and wrote till half-past twelve.

At half-past five I started as yesterday with Beatrice, Leopold, and the Duchess of Roxburghe, the two equerries riding, and took a very long — rather too long — drive. It would have been quite beautiful and most enjoyable from the very fine scenery with rich vegetation, fine trees, and hills, and dales, with the Pentlands in

The Earl of Dalhousie.

the distance, had it not been for a dark, heavy, leaden fog and sky like November, but warmer, which obscured all the distance in the most provoking way, and at one time even came down in a rather heavy shower. We went out by the Queen's Drive, going to the right as we left Holyrood. Numbers of people surrounded the entrance, and, as there is a long ascent part of the way, some of them, especially boys, ran along with us. We proceeded by the Liberton Road, on past the villages Straiton, Lasswade (very picturesque, and which I well remember from 1842), and Bonnyrigg, to Dalhousie Castle, where we had visited the late Marquis and Marchioness from Dalkeith in 1842 (the Duchess of Buccleuch drove me over), an old Scotch castle in red stone, where, however, we did not get out. It had been raining, but we did not shut the carriage, and just as we had thought of doing so the rain ceased. From here we drove under a very fine viaduct along the South Esk, past Newbattle (not into the grounds)—which there is an arch which was built for George IV to drive through, but he never went there—on through the small town of Dalkeith, where many people, as indeed in almost every other place, had collected, into the Park of Dalkeith. Here, as well as everywhere in the neighbourhood, there are beautiful trees, especially some very fine sycamores. We drove up to the house, and got out, as I wished the children to see the rooms where we had lived. The staircase and the gallery where I held the Drawing-room I

Dalhousie Castle.

remembered well, as also the dining-room. Our former rooms were shown us; but though the bed and even the washing-basin still exist, the rooms which had been arranged for us are altered.

We visited it last in September 1859. The population of Dalkeith and of all the villages about here are colliers and miners, and are very poor. We came home straight, coming into the same road as we started by, and going down the hill of the Queen's Drive. We collected again a goodly and most good-humoured crowd, and saw the little boys and girls rolling down the steep hill, and people pouring in from the town to get a sight of us.

Friday, August 16

A thoroughly wet day. At half-past eleven I walked out with Flora Macdonald (whose name attracted great attention in Edinburgh), right across the court to the stables, which are very good, and saw all belonging to them—harness-room, coach-house, etc. Then I looked into the guard-room next door, where the guard, who were called out and drawn up thinking I was coming by, did not know us. I went in behind them, and I found a sergeant (I think) of the 93rd in full dress, with four medals, and I asked him his years' service, which were twenty, and where he came from—"Perthshire". Two other men, who were cooking and had their coats off, were in the room where they also slept. The newspapers have reported an absurd conversation of mine with them, but none took place. We then walked back

The arrival of Queen Victoria and the Prince Consort on board the *Royal George* at Granton in 1842 for their first visit to Scotland.

through the house into the garden, and finally came home through the chapel at half-past twelve.

It was raining hard, but nevertheless we started at half-past four in the open landau, Beatrice and the two ladies with me, the two equerries riding. We drove by way of Princes Street, which overlooks the Mound with its gardens and fine buildings, and is always so animated and full of people on foot and in carriages; crossed the Dean Bridge, which commands a most beautiful view, though then it was obscured by the pelting rain; passed Stewart's Asylum, a fine new building, getting from the road a good view of another fine institution, Fettes College, built only within the last few years; and so on to the edge of Barnton Park, where we turned back to Granton. By this time it had begun to blow most violently, in addition to the rain, and the umbrellas dripped and the carriage became soaked. Our road lay close to the sea, past Granton Pier where we had landed in 1842; Trinity came next, a place with some good houses, and then Newhaven—where we saw many fishwives who were very enthusiastic, but not in their smartest dress—and then Leith, where there were numbers of people looking out for us in spite of the dreadful rain; but indeed everywhere the poor people came out and were most loyal. We took a wrong turn here, and had to come back again to go to the Albert Docks—new and very splendid large docks, with the ships all decked out. We stopped a moment to speak to the Provost of Leith, who said the people were very grateful for my coming; and I have since had repeated expressions of thanks, saying the good people felt my coming out in the rain more than anything. We drove on

Edinburgh in the late nineteenth century: in the foreground is Waverley Station crossed by
Waverley Bridge.

along the shore, with a distant view of the Island of Inchkeith, by Leith Links, the
London Road, the Cavalry Barracks, St. Margaret's Station and Queen's Park,
home. We got home by ten minutes past seven. We were all more or less wet, and
had to change our things. The waterproofs seemed not to have done their work.
After dinner, at twenty minutes past eleven, we left Holyrood; a gardener presented
me with a bouquet, and said it was "the proudest day in his life". It did not rain, so
we had the carriage open. The two children and the Duchess of Roxburghe were in
our carriage, and we had an escort. Numbers of people were out. The whole way
was splendidly lit up by red, blue, and yellow lights from Salisbury Crags and
Arthur's Seat, and the effect was most dazzling and beautiful. There were besides
some torches near the station, which was the same we arrived at. The Provost
hoped I "was leaving well", and I thanked him for the very kind reception which I
had met with, and for the beautiful illuminations.

Saturday, August 17

Did not sleep much or well—it was so very hot, and I was too much excited, and
then we had to be roused up and to dress hurriedly before seven, by which time we
were at Ballater. There were many people out, and so there were at Balmoral, where
we arrived at a quarter to eight. The heather beautiful, but not completely out yet.
The air sweet and soft.

Beloved Mama's birthday! That dear, dear mother! so loving and tender, so full of kindness! How often I long for that love! She frequently spent this day at Abergeldie, but we were not here then.

Friday, September 6, 1872

ADULL BUT FAIR MORNING. Breakfasted with the children before nine o'clock, and at half-past nine I left dear Balmoral in the open landau and four with Beatrice and Leopold, Jane Churchill, Fräulein Bauer, and Lord Granville, and drove to Ballater, where Colonel Ponsonby, Sir W. Jenner, and Mr. Collins met us. Besides Brown, who superintends everything for me, Emilie Dittweiler, Annie Macdonald, Jemmie Morgan, my second piper Willie Leys, Beatrice's, Leopold's, and Lady Churchill's attendants, three footmen and Goddard went with us. We passed into the station at Aberdeen, which was immensely crowded. An address and the keys were presented by Provost Leslie; then Lord Kintore[42] (who gave me a nosegay and some fruit) and young Lord Aberdeen[43] were presented. The day was becoming fine, and it was excessively hot. From Aberdeen we went by a line totally new to me—past Inverurie, close past the hill of Benachie, and got a good sight of the Buck of Cabrach and the surrounding hills, past Huntly and the ruined Castle of Huntly to Keith, where the Banff Volunteers were drawn up and there were many people close to the station, but no one on the platform. Here we were delayed by one of the doors, from the bedroom into the little dressing-room, refusing to open. Annie had gone through shortly before we got to Keith, and when she wanted to go back, the door would not open, and nothing could make it open. Brown tried with all his might, and with knives, but in vain, and we had to take in the two railway men with us, hammering and knocking away as we went on, till at last they forced it open. We were at Keith at 1.20, and at Elgin at 1.58. The station here was beautifully decorated; there were several arches adorned with flowers and heather, and a platform with raised seats for many ladies. The Provost and the Duke of Richmond and Lord March were there. The Provost presented an address, and then I spoke to the Duke of Richmond, who told me that dear Uncle Leopold[44] had received the freedom of the city when he was staying in the neighbourhood in 1819. The ruins of the Cathedral are said to be the finest in Scotland, and the town is full of ancient recollections. No British sovereign has ever been so far north. The Provost's daughter presented me with a nosegay.

We stopped here about ten minutes. It was broiling hot. The corn and oats looked ripe, and were cut in many places. After this we took our luncheon (cold), and as we were sitting at the small table we suddenly found ourselves passing slowly, without stopping, the station of Forres, near which is the wild "muir" which Shakespeare chose as the scene of Macbeth's meeting with the witches. Nairn lies very prettily on the shore of the Moray Firth. We passed Culloden, and the moor where that bloody battle, the recollection of which I cannot bear, was fought. The heather beautiful everywhere, and now the scenery became very fine. At half-past three we were at Inverness, the capital of the Highlands, the position of which is lovely. We stopped here for ten minutes, but outside the station. There was an immense crowd, but all very well managed, and no squeeze or crush. There were numbers of seats in galleries filled with ladies, among whom I recognised Mrs. Cluny Macpherson. Cluny Macpherson himself was in command of the Volunteers. On the platform to the left (the Volunteers and the galleries with seats were to the right) was the Provost, Dr. Mackenzie, a fine-looking old man in a kilt, with very white hair and a long white beard, who presented an address. Lord Seafield, the Master of Lovat, Mr. Baillie of Dochfour, and his son Mr. Evan Baillie, were all there, and I said a word to each. The Provost's grand-daughter presented a bouquet. There was an immense crowd at the back of the platform.

As our train proceeded, the scenery was lovely. Near the ruins of the old Priory of Beauly the river of the same name flows into the Beauly Frith,[45] and the frith looks like an enormous lake with hills rising above it which were reflected on the perfectly still water. The light and colouring were rather grey, but had a charming effect. At twenty minutes to four we reached Dingwall, where there were Volunteers, as indeed there were everywhere, and where another address was presented and also flowers. Sir J. Matheson, Lord Lieutenant of the county, was named to me, also the Vice-Lieutenant; and some young ladies gave Beatrice nosegays. The position of Dingwall, in a glen with hills rising above it, is extremely pretty, and reminds me of a village in Switzerland. The head of the Cromartie Frith appears here. After this and passing slowly Tain and St. Duthus (called after the

Late nineteenth-century photograph of Dunrobin Castle.

Cathedral there), we thought, as we did not stop, and were not to do so, that we would take our tea and coffee—which kept quite hot in the Norwegian kitchen— when suddenly, before we had finished, we stopped at Bonar Bridge, and the Duke of Sutherland[46] came up to the door. He had been driving the engine(!) all the way from Inverness, but only appeared now on account of this being the boundary of his territory, and the commencement of the Sutherland railroad. He expressed the honour it was to him that I was coming to Dunrobin. Lord Ronald L. Gower[47] also came up to the carriage door. There was a most excited station-master who would not leave the crowd of poor country-people in quiet, but told them to cheer and "cheer again", another "cheer", etc., without ceasing.

Here the Dornoch Frith, which first appears at Tain, was left behind, and we entered the glen of the Shin. The railway is at a very high level here, and you see the Shin winding below with heathery hills on either side and many fine rocks, wild, solitary, and picturesque. The Duchess of Sutherland's[48] own property begins at the end of this glen. At six we were at Golspie station where the Duchess of Sutherland received us, and where a detachment of the Sutherland Volunteers, who look very handsome in red jackets and Sutherland tartan kilts, was drawn up. I got into the Duchess's carriage, a barouche with four horses, the Duke riding, as also Lady Florence and their second son Lord Tarbat, and drove through the small town—one long street like Dufftown—which is inhabited chiefly by a fishing population, and was extremely prettily decorated with heather and flowers, and where there were many triumphal arches with Gaelic inscriptions (which I annex) and some very pretty English ones.

> Ar Buidheachas do 'n Bhuadhaich.
> Our gratitude to Victoria.
> Na h-uile lath chi's nach fhaic, slainte duibh 'is solas
> Health and happiness, far or near.
> (Literally—Every day see we you, or see we not,
> health to you and happiness.)
> Ceud mile failte do Chattaobh.
> A hundred thousand welcomes to Sutherland.
> Failte do 'n laith Buidhe.
> Hail to the lucky day.
> Better lo'ed you canna' be;
> Will you no come back again?

Everywhere the loyalty and enthusiasm were very great. In about ten minutes we were at Dunrobin Castle. Coming suddenly upon it as one does, or rather driving down to it, it has a very fine imposing appearance with its very high roof and turrets, a mixture of an old Scotch castle and French château. Constance Westminster (the Marchioness of Westminster, the Duke's youngest sister) was at the door, and Annie Sutherland's little girl in the hall, which is, as also the staircase, all of stone, with a sort of gallery going round opening into a corridor. But I will describe this and the rooms to-morrow.

The Duchess took me to my rooms, which had been purposely arranged and handsomely furnished by the dear late Duke and Duchess[49] for us both, and consist of a sitting-room next to the drawing-room, with a little turret communicating by a small passage with the dressing-room, which opens into the bedroom and another room which is my maid's room, and was intended for dearest Albert's dressing-room. I went to see Beatrice's room, which is close by, down three steps in the same passage. Fräulein Bauer, and Morgan, her dresser, are near her. Brown lives just opposite in the room intended for Albert's valet. It was formerly the prison.

Rested a little while, for I felt very tired. Dined at half-past eight alone in my sitting-room with Beatrice and Leopold, Brown waiting. Shortly afterwards Annie Sutherland came to see us for a little while, and later Jane Churchill. The children went early to bed.

Sunday, September 8

A fine bright morning. Breakfast as yesterday. Directly after it, at a quarter-past ten, walked with Beatrice along the Lady's Walk, as it is called, which commences near the Castle and goes for a mile and a half entirely amongst trees, very shady, and overlooking the sea, and with paths leading down to the sea, and seats commanding lovely views of the sea and distant coast. It was very warm, and the thickness of the adjoining woods made the air feel close. We walked back the same way, and got home at a quarter-past eleven. At twelve there was quite a short service performed by Dr. Cumming in the gallery which runs round the staircase, Dr. Cumming being opposite to us. It was over by a quarter to one. Annie then took me up to her room, which is a very pretty one; long, but not high, and very light, with a very fine view above all the trees; very simply furnished. Her dressing-room and bedroom equally nice and airy, like those they have at Stafford House. The Duke's dressing-room is very simply and plainly furnished; he is wonderfully plain and simple in his tastes. The Duchess took me along the passage to where Florence lives, and to the nursery where we saw little Alix in her bed, and then by a staircase, which belongs to the very old part of the Castle, to the rooms which were the dear late Duke's and Duchess's, though the last time she came here she lived in my rooms. Everywhere prints of ourselves and of people I know. After this came down again. Luncheon as yesterday.

At twenty minutes past four walked to the nearest seat in the Lady's Walk, and sketched the view, and about half-past five drove out in the waggonette with Beatrice and Lady Granville. We drove through the Uppat Woods, along the big burn drive, past the Pictish Tower up to Mr. Loch's[50] Memorial, which has the following inscription on it by the late Duchess:

TO THE HONOURED MEMORY OF
JAMES LOCH,
WHO LOVED IN THE SERENE EVENING OF HIS LIFE
TO LOOK AROUND HIM HERE.

May his children's children gather here, and think of him whose life was spent in virtuous labour for the land he loved and for the friends he served, who have raised these stones, A.D. 1858.

OBIIT JUNII 28° 1855.

The heather is very rich all round here. We got out and went into it, and there is a very fine view looking up Dunrobin Glen and over the sea, and Birk Head, which is the extreme point of the land which runs into the sea. You also get a very pretty glimpse of the Castle at the end of a path cut through the wood. We drove down again, and before we were out of the lower wood, which is close down upon the sea-shore, we stopped to take our tea and coffee, but were half devoured by midges.

Monday, September 9

At twenty-five minutes past twelve I started with the two children and Annie for the laying of the first stone of the Memorial to be raised by the clansmen and servants to the memory of my dear Duchess of Sutherland, who was adored in Sutherland. We drove in the barouche and four. The rain had quite ceased. Everyone else had gone on before; the Duke waited to help us in, and then ran on followed by MacAlister, his piper, valet, and confidential servant—a short stout man of sixty, I should say—an excellent man, and first-rate piper. We got out, and I went up on a platform, which was covered over and close to the stone, with the children, Annie, the Duke, Constance, and Jane Churchill. All the others, and many spectators, stood around. Mr. Joass, the minister there, offered up a short prayer, and after it presented (but did not read) the Address. I then answered what I had thought over, but spoke without reading:

"It gives me great pleasure to testify on this occasion my love and esteem for the dear Duchess, my valued friend, with whose children I am happy to be now staying, and I wish also to express my warm thanks for the loyal and hearty welcome I have met with in Sutherland."

This made me very nervous, but it was said without hesitating. Then the usual ceremony of spreading the mortar and of striking the stone with a mallet was gone through. The Duke gave me a drawing of the intended Memorial, which is to be an Eleanor cross, with a bust of the dear Duchess, and a medal of her which Ronald L. Gower had struck. After this we got into the carriage again, amid the cheers of the people, and drove back. Only Leopold walked, and Constance took his place in the carriage. We were in before one. Almost directly afterwards Beatrice and I went into the ante-room (where all the company who afterwards had luncheon were assembled) with Annie and the Duke, who presented some people to me; amongst others a very old lady, Mrs. Houston by name, who is between eighty and ninety, and was a great friend of the dear Duchess and of the Duchess of Norfolk. She was quite overcome, and said, "Is that my dear Queen", and, taking the Duke's hand, "and my darling Duke?"

Luncheon as usual. After it saw Lord Granville. At a quarter-past four drove out in the waggonette, drawn by four of the Duke's horses, with Beatrice, Annie, and Constance. It was fine though not very bright weather, and windy. We drove to the top of Benabhraghie, or the Monument Hill, on which is the very colossal statue of the Duke's grandfather, the first Duke, who married the Countess of Sutherland, from whom this enormous property came. She died in 1839, and I remember her quite well as a very agreeable, clever old lady. We drove through part of the wood by the way we went the previous days, up the big burn drive and through Bacchies,

The memorial erected to the Duchess of
Sutherland at Dunrobin Castle.

looking up Dunrobin Glen, which is very wild; and the pink heathery hills, though
not very high, and the moor, with distant hills, were very pretty. It is a long pull
upwards on a grass drive, which makes it very hard work for the horses. Halfway up
we stopped to take tea and coffee; and before that, Brown (who has an
extraordinary eye for it, when driving quite fast, which I have not) espied a piece of
white heather, and jumped off to pick it. No Highlander would pass by it without
picking it, for it is considered to bring good luck. We got a very extensive view,
though not quite clear, of endless hills between this and the west coast—all the
Duke's property—where the Westminsters have two if not three forests of the
Duke's.

In fine weather seven counties are to be seen in the other direction, looking
towards Ross-shire and the Moray Frith, but it was not clear enough for this. We
saw distinctly Ben Rinnes, a highish hill that rises in the distance above a long
stretch of low land extending into the sea which belongs to the Duke of Richmond.
We drove down the hill the same way, but afterwards took a different turn into the
high-road, and home by Golspie and the Lodge by seven. The dear pretty little girl
came to see me. Beatrice brought in Lilah Grosvenor, who had just arrived. Dined

at a quarter-past eight in the dining-room, as on Saturday. The same people exactly, with the addition of Colonel Ponsonby. We had some sheep's head, which I tasted for the first time on Sunday, and think really very good. Remained a little while in the drawing-room, and the Duke presented Mr. Stanley,[51] the discoverer of Livingstone. He talked of his meeting with Livingstone, who he thinks will require eighteen months to finish the work on which he is bent.

Tuesday, September 9, 1873

Got up at ten minutes to seven, and breakfasted with Beatrice at twenty minutes past seven. The morning was splendid. At five minutes past eight I left Balmoral with Beatrice and Jane Churchill in the landau and four (Brown on the rumble) for Ballater, whither General Ponsonby and Dr. Fox had preceded us. We had our own comfortable train; Jane Churchill came with us. Emilie Dittweiler, Annie Macdonald, Morgan, and Maxted (Jane's maid) went in the dresser's compartment, and Francie with dear Noble,[52] with Brown next to me. After crossing the Bridge of Dun, where we were at half-past eleven, we had some cold luncheon, and by a quarter to one we were at Stanley Junction, where we left the main line from Aberdeen to the south, and turned into the Highland Railway. Here, alas! the distance became indistinct, the sky grey, and we began fearing for the afternoon. At one we passed the really beautiful valley of Dunkeld, catching a glimpse of the cathedral and the lovely scenery around, which interested Beatrice very much, and made me think of my pleasant visits and excursions thence; then passed opposite St. Colme's, the Duchess's farm, by Dalguise, and saw the large Celtic cross at Logierait, put up to the late Duke of Athole; then Pitlochry; after which we passed through the magnificent Pass of Killiekrankie, which we just skirted in our long drive by Loch Tay and Loch Tummel, in 1866. The dull leaden sky which overhung Dunkeld continued, and soon a white veil began to cover the hills, and slight rain came down.

We passed close by Blair, which reminded me much of my sad visit there in 1863, when I came by this same line to visit the late Duke; and I could now see the great improvements made at the Castle. From here the railway (running almost parallel with the road by which *we* went so happily from Dalwhinnie the reverse way in 1861) passes Dalnaspidal Station—a very lonely spot—then up Drumouchter, with Loch Garry and Loch Ericht, fine and wild, but terribly desolate and devoid of woods and habitations, and so veiled by mist and now beating rain as to be seen to but very little advantage. Next comes Dalwhinnie Station, near the inn where we slept in 1861, having ridden over from Balmoral to Glen Fishie, and thence down by Newton More; consequently, the distance across the hill is comparatively nothing, though, to avoid posting in uncertain weather, we had to come all this way round. At thirty-five minutes past two we reached Kingussie. The station was decorated with flowers, heather, and flags, and the Master of Lovat (now Lord Lieutenant of Inverness-shire) and Cluny Macpherson (both of course in kilts) were there. We waited till all our things were put into our carriage, and then got out, in heavy rain at that moment. We three went in the sociable, General Ponsonby and Brown on the box, Dr. Fox and my maids in the waggonette, the other maids and

Francie with the dog and the remainder following in two other carriages. We passed through the village of Kingussie, where there were two triumphal arches and decorations, and some of Cluny's men drawn up, and then turned sharp to the left up amongst the hills, through the very poor long village of Newton More (which Annie Macdonald, whose late husband came from there, had never seen, but which *we* had driven through in 1861), and on amongst desolate, wild, heathery moors. The road skirts the Spey, which meanders through a rich green valley, hills rising grandly in the distance and on either side. We passed the rock of Craig Dhu, and a castle amongst trees, where there was an arch, and the owner and his family standing near it, and where a nosegay was presented to me. Next we came to Cluny Castle, at the gate of which stood Mrs. Macpherson with her family. We stopped after we had gone past, and she came and presented me with a nosegay.

From here the road was known to me, if I can call going once to see it in 1847 knowing it. Very few inhabitants, and not one village after Newton More, only miserable little cottages and farmhouses, with a few people, all very friendly, scattered about here and there. We changed horses first at Laggan Bridge, having crossed the Spey over a large stone bridge, which I well remember; it is near Strathmashie. Here we stopped a few minutes; and a little girl presented me with a nosegay, and the innkeeper gave Brown a bottle with some wine and a glass. We were preceded the whole way by the postmaster of Banavie, who supplied the horses; he was called McGregor, and wore a kilt. We had only a pair of horses all along and after the first stage—excellent ones. The roads admirable—hardly any hills, though we drove through such a hilly, wild country. The rain had ceased, and only occasional showers came on, which did not prevent our seeing the very grand scenery, with the high finely pointed and serrated mountains, as we drove along. Shortly after changing horses we left the river and came to the beautiful Loch Laggan, seven miles in length, along which the drive goes under birch, mountain-ash laden with bright berries, oak, alders, in profusion, and is really beautiful. I was quite pleased to see the loch again after twenty-five years—recognised it and admired its beauty, with the wooded promontories, its little bays, and its two little islands, its ferry (the only communication to the other side) and the noble hills, the two Ben Alders.

We stopped, soon after passing the ferry, in a very secluded spot at five, and had our (made) tea in the carriage, which was very refreshing. We at length came opposite Ardverikie, which I so well remember, recalling and relating, as we now drove along, many of the incidents of our month's stay there, which was as wet as this day. Sir John Ramsden,[53] who has bought the property, was standing with some other people by the roadside. At the head of the loch is Moy Lodge, a pretty little place in the style of Ardverikie, at which Mr. Ansdell,[54] the artist, is staying. A little beyond this we changed horses at Moy (only a single house), and drove along through Glen Spean, which is very fine and grand in some parts, the road looking down upon the rapid, rushing, gushing river, as it whirls along imbedded in rocks and overhung with wood, while high ranges of hills, fine and pointed in shape, are seen in the distance rising peak upon peak. Along this road I had driven, but I had forgotten it. Before coming to the Bridge of Roy Inn, we saw some of the celebrated Parallel Roads quite distinctly, which are more clearly seen farther on, and which are very interesting to all geologists as being supposed to mark the beaches of an inland lake, which was pent back by a great glacier in Glen Spean, and subsided to different levels, as the glacier sank or broke away at three successive periods.

The rain ceased, and we walked a little before coming to the Bridge of Roy, where we changed horses for the last time, and directly afterwards passed a triumphal arch with heather and inscriptions, pipers playing, etc., and Highlanders as well as many other people drawn up, but we unfortunately drove past them too quickly. There was an inscription in Gaelic on one side, and on the other "Loyal Highlanders welcome their Queen". The papers say that it was put up by Mrs. McDonell of Keppoch.

About three miles farther on we reached Spean Bridge, and it was already getting dark. Here there is only an inn, and Lord and Lady Abinger and their tenantry met us. Lord Abinger[55] said he had been requested to express the people's thanks for my honouring their country with a visit, and his little girl presented me with a large nosegay in the name of the tenantry. We then drove on through rather desolate moors, and the rain began to fall again very heavily. It became quite dark, and we could just descry mountains under which we drove. At ten minutes past eight we arrived at Inverlochy, entering by a lodge, which was lit up and looked cheery enough. The house is entered through a small, neat-looking hall, and I have three nice rooms upstairs, with the maids close by, and Beatrice and Morgan also, just at the other side of the passage. My sitting-room is very nice. It was nine before we got to dinner, which I took with Beatrice and Jane, Brown waiting on us as well as Cannon (the footman). The drawing-room is a large, rather handsome and well-furnished room. We soon went up to our rooms, and all were glad to go to bed.

Inverlochy Castle,
Wednesday, September 10

Mist on all the hills, and continuous rain! Most disheartening, but the views from the house beautiful, especially from my sitting-room, which has a bow-window, with two small ones on either side, looking towards Ben Nevis (which is close in front of it), and commands a lovely view of Fort William (farther to the right), and of Loch Linnhe, etc., a portion of Loch Eil (pronounced Loch Eel) which runs up a long way, nearly twelve miles, with the fine Moidart range, close to Glen Finnan, as a background; and this, with Banavie and the hotel, close to the Caledonian Canal, is distinctly seen from the other window. This very pretty little room does not open into any other; next to it is Emilie Dittweiler's, next to that my dressing-room, and Annie's room, all narrow and long, and next again is a really large and also long room, my bedroom, in which I had my own bed, which has been to Switzerland, Invertrossachs, Sandringham,[56] and Baden. Downstairs is the dining room, a good-sized room (in which the gentlemen dine), also the drawing-room, and a small library, in which *we* take our meals. No room in the house opens into another. Though some of the bedrooms are larger than those at Invertrossachs, the servants are not so well off. After breakfast (which, as well as luncheon, Beatrice and I always took alone) at half-past nine, went upstairs again and looked at Brown's room, which is a few steps lower than mine, in fact, only a very small bathroom. Beatrice is just opposite where I am, or rather round the corner. Jane Churchill and the two gentlemen, upstairs, have also good rooms.

A late nineteenth-century view of Ben Nevis across the loch.

Friday, September 12

A most beautiful bright sunshiny day. After breakfast Mr. Newton, the artist, brought some lovely sketches. Sketched and painted, for the views are quite lovely, from my room. At eleven drove in the waggonette with Beatrice and Jane Churchill, General Ponsonby being on the box with Brown, to and through Fort William, which is three miles and a half from Inverlochy, passing the celebrated Ben Nevis Distillery, which is two miles from here, and through a triumphal arch, just beyond the bridge over the Nevis Burn, by an old, very neglected graveyard, to the right, in which is an obelisk to McLachlan, a poet, and past the Belford Hospital, a neat building, built by a Mr. and Mrs. Belford; then a little farther on, entered the town, where there was a triumphal arch, the fort, now private property, belonging to Campbell of Monzie. Here Glencoe came to take the oath to King William III.

The town of Fort William is small, and, excepting where the good shops are, very dirty, with a very poor population, but all very friendly and enthusiastic. There are four churches (Established, Free Church, Episcopalian, and Roman Catholic). We drove on along Loch Eil (called Loch Linnhe below Corran ferry) a mile, and turned at Achintee, and down to old Inverlochy Castle, which is nearer to Fort William than the new castle. We got out to look at the ruin, but it is uninteresting, as there is so little of it and literally nothing to see. About a quarter of a mile from the house we got out and walked; home by half-past twelve.

Friday, September 12

At a quarter-past three, the day being most splendid, started with Beatrice and Jane Churchill, the two gentlemen following in the waggonette (with Charles Thomson on the box), and drove by Banavie, the same road we came home yesterday, as far as where we crossed the canal at Gairlochy—only, instead of going down to it, we kept above, and went to the left: it is a beautiful road, coming in sight of Loch Lochy, which, with its wooded banks and blue hills, looked lovely. Leaving the main road, we turned into a beautiful drive along the river Arkaig, in Lochiel's property, reminding one very much of the Trossachs.

As you approach Achnacarry, which lies rather low, but is surrounded by very fine trees, the luxuriance of the tangled woods, surmounted by rugged hills, becomes finer and finer till you come to Loch Arkaig, a little over half a mile from the house. This is a very lovely loch, reminding one of Loch Katrine, especially where there is a little pier, from which we embarked on board a very small but nice screw steamer which belongs to Cameron of Lochiel.

He received us (wearing his kilt and plaid) just above the pier, and we all went on board the little steamer. The afternoon was beautiful, and lit up the fine scenery to the greatest advantage. We went about halfway up the Loch (which is fourteen miles long), as we had not time to go farther, to the disappointment of Lochiel, who said it grew wilder and wilder higher up. To the left (as we went up) is the deer forest; to the right he has sheep.

Both sides are beautifully wooded all along the lower part of the fine hills which rise on either side, and the trees are all oaks, which Cameron of Lochiel said were the "weed of the country", and all natural—none were planted. A good many grow up all the hollows and fissures of the hills and rocks. Right ahead, where we turned, was seen a fine conical-shaped hill called Scour-na-nat, and to the left Glenmally, to the north Muir Logan, and Giusach and Gerarnan on either side. Before we came to the turning we three had our tea, which was very refreshing. I tried to sketch a little, but the sun shone so strongly that I could not do much.

Mr. Cameron, who was with Lord Elgin[57] in China, came and explained everything, and talked very pleasantly. His father had to let this beautiful place, and Lord Malmesbury had it for fifteen years. The Cannings[58] used to go there, and I often heard Lady Canning speak of its beauties, and saw many pretty sketches which she made there. Thirteen years ago his father died, and he has lived there ever since. Alfred was there in 1863.

It was, as General Ponsonby observed afterwards, a striking scene. "There was Lochiel," as he said, "whose great-grand-uncle had been the real moving cause of the rising of 1745—for without him Prince Charles would not have made the attempt—showing your Majesty (whose great-great-grandfather he had striven to dethrone) the scenes made historical by Prince Charlie's wanderings.[59] It was a scene one could not look on unmoved."

Yes; and *I* feel a sort of reverence in going over these scenes in this most beautiful country, which I am proud to call my own, where there was such devoted loyalty to the family of my ancestors[60]—for Stewart blood is in my veins, and I am *now* their representative, and the people are as devoted and loyal to me as they were to that unhappy race.

We landed at the little pier, but walked over the small bridges (the carriages following)—on which a piper was playing—a few hundred yards to a gate (on the side opposite to that by which we came), where we got into the carriages again. We drove through a beautiful road called the Dark Mile—dark from the number of very fine trees which overhang it, while on the left it is overshadowed by beetling rocks with a rich tangled undergrowth of bracken and heather, etc. The heather grows very richly and fully in these parts, and in thick tufts. We saw here the cave in which Prince Charles Edward was hid for a week. We came out of this road at the end of Loch Lochy, which looked lovely in the setting sun, and drove along the water's edge till nearly where we joined the road by which we had come. It is all Lochiel's for a long way—a splendid possession.

And now came the finest scene of all—Ben Nevis and its surrounding high hills, and the others in the direction of Loch Laggan, all pink and glowing in that lovely after-glow (Alpenglühen), which you see in the Alps. It was glorious. It grew fainter and fainter till the hills became blue and then grey, and at last it became almost quite dark before we reached Banavie, and we only got home at a quarter-past eight. As we drove out I sketched Ben Nevis from the carriage.

Quantities of letters. The post comes in after eight and goes out at ten, which is very inconvenient.

Our usual little dinner only, about nine.

Saturday, September 13

Another splendid morning, of which we were very glad, as we meant to go to Glencoe, which was the principal object of our coming here. Our nice little breakfast as usual. Sketching.

At eleven we started, just as yesterday, Francie Clark[61] and Cannon going on the box of the second carriage. We drove through Fort William, on as we did yesterday morning by Achintee, and down the eastern side of Loch Eil, which was beautifully lit, the distant hills intensely blue. The cottages along the roadside here and there hardly deserve the name, and are indeed mere hovels—so low, so small, so dark with thatch, and overgrown with moss and heather, that if you did not see smoke issuing from them, and some very ragged dirty old people, and very scantily clothed, dishevelled children, you could not believe they were meant for human habitations. They are very picturesque and embedded in trees, with the heathery and grassy hills rising above them. There were poor little fields, fuller of weeds than of corn, much laid by the wet, and frequently a "calvie" or "coo" of the true shaggy Highland character was actually feeding in them.

The road, which runs close above the loch, commands an excellent view of the fine noble hills on the opposite side of the loch. At Corran Ferry (eleven miles) are seen across the loch Conaglen, and Ardgour, Lord Morton's,[62] at the entrance of a very fine glen. He has bought a large property in these parts, which formerly belonged to the Macleans. South of Corran Ferry the loch is called Loch Linnhe, and the road turns inland westwards, soon after passing up along the shore of Loch Leven, which is, in fact, also an arm of the sea. After three miles we passed a few cottages called Onich, the high hills of Glencoe beginning already to show. All was so bright and green, with so much wood, and the loch so calm, that one was in perpetual admiration of the scenery as one went along. Four miles more from

Highland cottages—"indeed mere hovels", according to Victoria—from a painting by Landseer.

Corran Ferry brought us to Ballachulish at a little before one o'clock. The situation of the hotel—the large one—on the opposite side, at the foot of the hills close to the ferry, is extremely pretty. There was a smaller and less handsome inn on the north side, by which we had come. Here we got out after all our things—cloaks, bags, luncheon baskets, etc.—had been removed from the carriage, which we had to leave, and walked down to the boat. The small number of people collected there were very quiet and well behaved. Beatrice and Jane Churchill and I, with General Ponsonby and Brown, got into the boat, and two Highlanders in kilts rowed us across to the sound of pipes. On the opposite side there were more people, but all kept at a very respectful distance and were very loyal. A lady (a widow), Lady Beresford, who owns the slate quarries, and her daughter, in deep mourning, were at the landing-place, and one of them presented me with a bouquet. We got at once into two carriages (hired, but very fair ones), Beatrice, Jane, and I in a sort of low barouche, Brown on the box. We had a pair of horses, which went very well. The two gentlemen occupied the second carriage. The drive from Ballachulish, looking both ways, is beautiful, and very Alpine. I remember Louise, and also Alice, making some sketches from here when they went on a tour in 1865.

We went on, winding under the high green hills, and entered the village of Ballachulish, where the slate quarries are, and which is inhabited by miners. It was very clean and tidy—a long, continuous, straggling, winding street, where the poor people, who all looked very clean, had decorated every house with flowers and bunches or wreaths of heather and red cloth. Emerging from the village we entered the Pass of Glencoe, which at the opening is beautifully green, with trees and cottages dotted about along the verdant valley. There is a farm belonging to a Mrs. MacDonald, a descendant of one of the unfortunate massacred MacDonalds. The Cona flows along the bottom of the valley, with green "haughs", where a few cattle are to be seen, and sheep, which graze up some of the wildest parts of this glorious glen. A sharp turn in the rough, very winding, and in some parts precipitous road, brings you to the finest, wildest, and grandest part of the pass. Stern, rugged, precipitous mountains with beautiful peaks and rocks piled high one above the other, two and three thousand feet high, tower and rise up to the heavens on either side, without any signs of habitation, except where, halfway up the pass, there are some trees, and near them heaps of stones on either side of the road, remains of what once were homes, which tell the bloody, fearful tale of woe. The place itself is one which adds to the horror of the thought that such a thing could have been conceived and committed on innocent sleeping people. How and whither could they fly? Let me hope that William III knew nothing of it.

To the right, not far on, is seen what is called Ossian's Cave; but it must be more than a thousand feet above the glen, and one cannot imagine how any one could live there, as they pretend that Ossian[63] did. The violence of the torrents of snow and rain, which come pouring down, has brought quantities of stone with them, which in many parts cover the road and make it very rough. It reminds me very much of the Devil's Bridge, St. Gothard, and the Göschenen Pass, only that is higher but not so wild. When we came to the top, which is about ten miles from Ballachulish, we stopped and got out, and we three sat down under a low wall, just below the road, where we had a splendid view of those peculiarly fine wild-looking peaks, which I sketched.

Their Gaelic names are Na tri Peathraichean (the Three Sisters), but in English they are often called "Faith, Hope, and Charity."

We sat down on the grass (we three) on our plaids, and had our luncheon, served by Brown and Francie, and then I sketched. The day was most beautiful and calm. Here, however—here, in this complete solitude, we were spied upon by impudently inquisitive reporters, who followed us everywhere; but one in particular (who writes for some of the Scotch papers) lay down and watched with a telescope and dodged me and Beatrice and Jane Churchill, who were walking about, and was most impertinent when Brown went to tell him to move, which Jane herself had thought of doing. However, he did go away at last, and Brown came back saying he thought there would have been a fight; for when Brown said quite civilly that the Queen wished him to move away, he said he had quite as good a right to remain there as the Queen. To this Brown answered very strongly, upon which the impertinent individual asked, "Did he know who he was?" and Brown answered he did, and that "the highest gentlemen in England would not dare do what he did, much less a reporter"—and he must move on, or he would give him something more. And the man said, "Would he dare say that before those other men (all reporters) who were coming up?" And Brown answered "Yes," he would before "anybody who did not behave as he ought." More strong words were used; but the others came up and advised the man to come away quietly, which he finally did. Such conduct ought to be known. We were there nearly an hour, and then began walking down a portion of the steep part.

The parish clergyman, Mr. Stewart, who had followed us up, and who had met us when we arrived at Ballachulish, explained the names of the hills, and showed the exact place of the dreadful massacre. He also said that there were many Episcopalians there from the old Jacobite feeling, and also Roman Catholics.

There was seldom frost in the glen, he said, but there was a good deal of snow.

A short distance from where Ossian's cave is shown there is a very small lake called Loch Treachtan, through which the Cona flows; and at the end of this was a cottage with some cattle and small pieces of cultivated land. We drove down on our return at a great pace. As we came through Ballachulish the post-boy suddenly stopped, and a very respectable, stout-looking old Highlander stepped up to the carriage with a small silver quaich,[64] out of which he said Prince Charles had drunk, and also my dearest Albert in 1847, and begged that I would do the same. A table, covered with a cloth and with a bottle on it, was on the other side of the road. I felt I could hardly refuse, and therefore tasted some whisky out of it, which delighted the people who were standing around. His name, we have since heard, is W. A. Cameron.

We drove to the same small pier where we had disembarked, and were rowed over again by two Highlanders in kilts. The evening was so beautiful and calm that the whole landscape was reflected in the lake. There is a high, conical-shaped hill, the commencement of the Pass of Glencoe, which is seen best from here; and the range of hills above Ardgour and Corran Ferry opposite was of the most lovely blue. The whole scene was most beautiful. Three pipers played while we rowed across, and the good people, who were most loyal and friendly, cheered loudly. We re-entered our carriages, and drove off at a quick pace. When we were on the shores of Loch Eil again, we stopped (but did not get out) to take tea, having boiled the kettle. The setting sun cast a most glorious light, as yesterday, on Ben Nevis and the surrounding hills, which were quite pink, and gave a perfectly crimson hue to the heather on the moor below. The sky was pink and lilac and pale green, and became richer and richer, while the hills in the other direction, over Fort William, were of a deep blue. It was wonderfully beautiful, and I was still able to make, or at least begin, a sketch of the effect of it, after we came home at a quarter to seven, from Beatrice's window.

Sunday, September 14

At five drove out with Beatrice and Jane Churchill in the waggonette. We drove past the distillery; and then just beyond the bridge, which must be very little over two miles from Inverlochy, we turned off the main road. We drove up for four miles along the Nevis, a fine rapid burn rolling over large stones and almost forming cascades in one or two places, under fine trees with very steep green hills rising on either side, and close under and along the base of Ben Nevis, which rose like a giant above us. It was splendid! Straight before us the glen seemed to close; halfway up we came to a large farm, the drive to which is under an avenue of ash trees. But there is no other habitation beyond this of any kind; and soon after the trees become fewer and fewer, though still a good many grow at the burnside and up the gullies of the hills. Sheep were grazing at a great height. The road became so rough and bad that we got out and walked almost a mile, but could go no farther. We were delighted with the solemn solitude and grandeur of Glen Nevis; it is almost finer than Glencoe.

Dinner as usual. My favourite collie Noble is always downstairs when we take our meals, and was so good, Brown making him lie on a chair or couch, and he never attempted to come down without permission, and even held a piece of cake in his mouth without eating it, till told he might. He is the most "biddable" dog I ever saw, and so affectionate and kind; if he thinks you are not pleased with him, he puts out his paws, and begs in such an affectionate way.

Monday, September 15

The mist hung about the hills, but the sun struggled through. It was very mild and became beautiful. We decided to go up Glenfinnan and to lunch out. Painted and finished two other sketches looking up Loch Eil and towards Banavie, and then wrote, after which at a quarter to twelve took a short turn in the grounds with Beatrice.

At twenty minutes to one started with Beatrice and Jane Churchill in the sociable (Brown going each day of course with us on the box), the two gentlemen following (with Francie Clark and Charlie Thomson), and drove past Banavie through Corpach and up Loch Eil. When we had come to the head of the loch, the road turned towards the right, winding along through verdant valleys, with that noble range of Moidart before you, rather to the left. In one valley, which became very narrow after passing a large meadow in which they were making hay, we turned into a narrow sort of defile, with the stream of the Finnan flowing on as slowly as an English river, with trees and fir trees on the rocks, and unlike anything I had seen in Scotland, and then you come at once on Loch Shiel (a freshwater loch), with fine very high rugged hills on either side. It runs down twenty miles.

At the head of the loch stands a very ugly monument to Prince Charles Edward, looking like a sort of lighthouse surmounted by his statue, and surrounded by a wall. Here it was that he landed when he was brought by Macdonald of Borradale— whose descendant, now Macdonald of Glenaladale, has a house here (the only habitation to be seen)—to wait for the gathering of the clans. When Prince Charlie arrived at the spot where the monument stands, which is close to the loch and opposite to Glenfinnan (the road we came going past it and on up a hill to Arisaig, twenty-five miles farther on), he found only a dozen peasants, and thought he had been betrayed, and he sat down with his head in his hands. Suddenly the sound of the pipes aroused him, and he saw the clans coming down Glenfinnan. Soon after the Macdonalds appeared, and in the midst of a cheering host the Marquis of Tullibardine (Duke of Athole but for his attainder) unfurled the banner of King James. This was in August 1745. In 1746 poor Prince Charles was a fugitive hiding in the mountains on the side of Loch Arkaig and Loch Shiel. As we suddenly came upon Loch Shiel from the narrow glen, lit up by bright sunshine, with the fine long loch and the rugged mountains, which are about 3,000 feet high, rising all around, no habitation or building to be seen except the house of Glenaladale, which used to be an inn, and a large picturesque Catholic church, reminding one, from its elevated position to the right and above the house, of churches and convents abroad, I thought I never saw a lovelier or more romantic spot, or one which told its history so well. What a scene it must have been in 1745! And here was *I*, the descendant of the Stewarts and of the very king whom Prince Charles sought to overthrow, sitting and walking about quite privately and peaceably.

We got out and scrambled up a high hillock off the road, where I lunched with Beatrice and Jane Churchill and then sketched, but did not attempt to colour. We walked about a little, and then came down to the road to speak to Mr. Macdonald of Glenaladale, whom General Ponsonby had been to speak to, and who had never seen me. He is a stout, robust-looking Highlander of about thirty and a widower. He is a Catholic, as are all the people in this district. The priest is his uncle, and lives with him. He showed me some curious relics of Charles Edward. An old-fashioned, strange silver snuff "mull" which had been given by him to Macdonald's ancestor, with the dates 1745 and 1746 engraved on it, for at Borradale Prince Charlie slept for the last time in Scotland; a watch which had belonged to him, and a ring into which some of his fair hair had been put, were also shown.

This is the district called Moidart, and from the highest hills the Isle of Skye is seen distinctly. Lord Morton's property comes up close to Loch Shiel, and to the right are Lochiel, etc., and Macdonald of Glenaladale's in front, at the head of the loch. The family used to live at Borradale near Arisaig, but acquired Glenaladale from the former Macdonalds of Glenaladale who emigrated to Prince Edward's Island after the Forty-five.

Beatrice, Jane Churchill, and Brown went up with Mr. Macdonald to the top of the monument, but said the ascent was very awkward and difficult. General Ponsonby had been into the church, and said it was very expensively and handsomely decorated, but we have since heard there are only about fifty people in the neighbourhood. We left this beautiful spot about half-past four, having spent two hours there. The evening was not so bright as on Friday and Saturday, and there was no after-glow on the hills, Ben Nevis having its top covered with mist, as it often has. The horses were tired, and went rather slowly. I observed a flower here, which I have not seen with us at Balmoral, viz., instead of the large white daisies[65]— "Marguerites", as the French call them, and of which such numbers are seen in the fields in England—there is a large yellow one,[66] just the same in form, only the petals are bright yellow.

The heather, as I before observed, is of a very full and rich kind, and, as we drove along, we saw it on the old walls, growing in the loveliest tufts. We met those dreadful reporters, including the man who behaved so ill on Saturday, as we were coming back. We got home at twenty minutes past six. Had some tea. Wrote and put everything in order. All had been settled about money to be given, etc. Our last nice little dinner, which I regretted. Came up directly after and wrote.

Tuesday, September 16

Had to get up by seven, and Beatrice and I breakfasted at a quarter to eight. The morning was fine.

We drove to Banavie, where a good many people were assembled, and stepped on board the steamer which was on the Caledonian Canal. Here were Lord and Lady Abinger, whom I thanked very much for their kindness. I left an illustrated copy of my book and prints of Albert's and my portraits at Inverlochy for Lord Abinger.

Part of the Caledonian Canal in the 1870s.

She is an American lady from the Southern States, a Miss Macgruder, and they have five children, of whom one only is a boy. They left the steamer, and we began moving. The steamer is called the *Gondolier*. It is built on the same principle as the one we had on Loch Lomond, with a fine large cabin with many windows, almost a deck cabin (though it is down one flight of steps), which extends through the ship with seats below, open at the sides far forward. In this large cabin sixty-two people can dine. We remained chiefly on deck. We steamed gently along under the road by which we had driven from Gairlochy and Achnacarry, Lochiel's to the left or west, and Lord Abinger's to the right. Ben Nevis, unfortunately, was hid in the mist, and the top invisible, which we hear is very generally the case.

We came to one lock, and then shortly afterwards to Gairlochy, after which you enter Loch Lochy. The Caledonian Canal is a very wonderful piece of engineering, but travelling by it is very tedious. At each lock people crowded up close to the side of the steamer. As the river rises from Banavie to Loch Oich (which succeeds Loch Lochy), the canal has to raise the vessels up to that point, and again to lower them from Loch Oich to Inverness. The vessel, on entering the lock from the higher level, is enclosed by the shutting of the gates. The sluices of the lower gates are raised by small windlasses (it was amusing to see the people, including the crew of the steamer, who went on shore to expedite the operation, which is not generally done, run round and round to move these windlasses), and holes are thus opened at the bottom of the lower gates, through which the water flows till the water in the lock sinks to the lowest level. The lower gates are then opened, as the water is on the lowest level, while the upper gates keep back the water above. The same process raises the ships in the lock which ascend. About five or six feet can be raised or depressed in this manner at each lock. (I have copied this from an account General Ponsonby wrote for me.)

As we entered Loch Lochy, which looked beautiful, we saw where Loch Arkaig lay, though it was hid from us by high ground. The hills which rise from Loch Lochy are excellent pasture for sheep, but the lower parts are much wooded. After eight miles' sail on Loch Lochy we came to Loch Oich, which is entered by another lock at Laggan. Here Mr. and Mrs. Ellice (who is a first cousin of the Greys) were waiting, and came on board. They had wished me to get out and drive round their fine place, Invergarry, to rejoin the steamer at the next lock, but I declined, preferring to remain quietly on board, though the process of going through the locks is slow and necessarily tedious. It is nervous work to steer, for there is hardly a foot to spare on either side. Mrs. Ellice went on shore again, having given us some fine grapes, but Mr. Ellice remained on board till the next lock, Cullochy. A road much shaded runs along the side of the loch, and here we passed the small monument by its side, put over the well into which a number of heads of some of the MacDonalds, who had murdered two of their kinsmen of Keppoch, were thrown after they had been killed in revenge for this act, by order of MacDonald of the Isles. It was erected in 1812. We next came to the old ruined castle of Invergarry, embosomed in trees, close to which, but not in sight, is Mr. Ellice's new house. He has an immense deal of property here on both sides. The hills rise high, and one conically shaped one called Ben Tigh towers above the rest. At Cullochy Mr. Ellice left the steamer. Mr. Brewster, formerly Lord Chancellor of Ireland and nearly eighty years old, was standing on the shore here. Francie and one of the policemen got out with good Noble, and walked to meet us again at Fort Augustus. While we were stopping to go through one of the locks, a poor woman came and brought us a jug of milk and oat-cake, which with their usual hospitality the country people constantly offer.

After this, and at about ten minutes past twelve, Beatrice, Jane Churchill, and I went below and had some hot luncheon. The people from the locks looked down upon us, but it was unavoidable. We had now reached Fort Augustus, where there was again some delay and a great many people, and where there was a triumphal arch. Here on this very day thirty-six years ago my beloved Albert passed, and he saw poor Macdonald the Jäger here, and took a liking to him from his appearance, and, being in want of a Jäger, inquired after him and engaged him. He was keeper to Lord Digby and Colonel Porter then, and brought some game for dearest Albert from them, and Albert was greatly struck by his good looks. He was very handsome, especially in the kilt, which he habitually wore.

There had been a heavy shower, but it was over when we came up on deck again. We entered Loch Ness here. It is twenty-four miles long, and broad, the banks wooded, with many pretty places on them. We passed Invermorriston in Glen Morriston, the seat of Sir G. Brooke Middleton, formerly Grant property. (So many of the finest, largest estates in the Highlands have passed into English hands, chiefly by purchase, but also often by inheritance.) Foyers, the celebrated falls, which are much visited, could just be seen, but not the falls themselves. Everywhere, where there were a few houses or any place of note, people were assembled and cheered.

Next, to the left comes the very fine old ruin of Castle Urquhart, close upon the Lochan Rocks, where there were again a great many people. The Castle has stood

Urquhart Castle.

several sieges, and one in particular in the fourteenth century in the reign of Edward I. It belongs to Lord Seafield (head of the Grants), who has a very large property here, and whose own shooting-place, Balmacaan, is up in the glen just beyond. The fine mountain of Mealfourvonie rises above it. It is 2,700 feet high, but the peak alone is seen from here. I tried to sketch a little, but in vain, the wind in my face was so troublesome.

At about twenty minutes to four (or half-past three) we passed Dochfour House, Mr. Baillie's, which I think stands rather low, and in which Albert passed this night twenty-six years ago. A few minutes more brought us to Dochgarroch, quite a quiet place, but where a good many people had assembled. We waited to see every one and all our luggage landed and packed in and off before we stepped on shore. It was an amusing sight. There must have been two or three carriages besides ours. The last to drive off was the one in which Morgan, Maxted, and Lizzie Stewart[67] got, with Francie Clark and Noble on the box. Mr. Baillie and Lady Georgiana, whom I had not seen for long, were at the end of the landing platform, as well as Mr. Evan Baillie and Mrs. Colville, their son and daughter. Two little girls put down bunches of flax for me to walk upon, which it seems is an old Highland custom. There is a small village where we landed. Lady Georgiana Baillie is quite an old lady, aunt of the Duke of Manchester, and grand-daughter of the celebrated Duchess of Gordon.

Beatrice, Jane, and I got into a hired (not very beautiful) open landau (on the rumble of which Brown sat, as in crowds it is much safer to have a person close behind you) with a pair of post-horses and a postilion. In the second carriage went General Ponsonby, Emilie Dittweiler (sitting next to him), Dr. Fox, and Annie, every available place being necessary. We were escorted by the 7th Dragoon Guards, which was thought better on account of the great crowds in Inverness,

Inverness in the mid nineteenth century.

where no Sovereign had been seen since my poor ancestress Queen Mary.

The mixture of half state and humble travelling (we being in our common travelling dresses) was rather amusing.

The evening was beautiful, and Inverness looked extremely well on the blue Moray Frith. We passed a magnificent building, which is the county Lunatic Asylum. We had to drive six miles to the town, through a small portion of which only we passed, and had to drive quickly, as it was late. The streets were full of decorations and arches, and lined with volunteers. Great order prevailed, and the people were most enthusiastic. The fine-looking old Provost was there, and the Master of Lovat, who walked up along the station with us. A great squeeze, which Brown, having a great heap of cloaks etc. to carry, had some difficulty in getting through. But everyone, including the dog, got safe in, and we travelled by train as before. We went the same way as last year, but never stopped till we got to Keith, where last time our door got wrong. After this, about six, we had some warm tea and cold meat, which was very refreshing. A fine evening.

We reached Ballater at five minutes to nine, and started at once in the open landau and four, preceded by the outrider with the lamp. There were a few drops of rain, but very slight. At twenty minutes to ten we reached Balmoral safely, very thankful that all had gone off so well.

⁂

Tuesday, September 21, 1875

W E HAD A FAMILY DINNER at twenty minutes to nine. At a quarter past ten left Balmoral with Beatrice and Jane Churchill, Brown on the rumble. We reached Ballater by eleven, when we took the railroad. The horses (six) with Bourner, Hutchinson, and Goddard with the luggage, had gone on in advance. We started immediately, and very soon after lay down. We went steadily and slowly, but I did not sleep very well.

Inverary,
Wednesday, September 22

At eight we reached Tyndrum, a wild, picturesque, and desolate place in a sort of wild glen with green hills rising around. Here we breakfasted in the train, Brown having had the coffee heated which we had brought made with us, and some things coming from the nice-looking hotel. The morning was beautiful, just a little mist on the highest hills, which cleared off. There are a few straggling houses and a nice hotel at this station, where we got out and where Lord[68] and Lady Breadalbane met us, as this is his property. The day was beautiful.

We got into the sociable (that is Beatrice, Jane Churchill, and I) with a pair of posthorses, Brown and Francie Clark on the box, the two gentlemen and four maids in a waggonette following, and further behind the unavoidable luggage with the footmen, etc. The road lay up a broad glen, with green hills on either side, on one of which are lead mines belonging to Lord Breadalbane. It was very winding, very rough, and continually up and down, and we went very slowly. Looking back, behind Tyndrum was a fine range of hills which are in the forest of the Black Mount. Passed the entrance of a broad glen with many trees called Glenorchy (the second title of Breadalbane), and saw all along where the railway is being made. A small stream flows at the bottom. To the left we saw Ben Luie; then as we descended, the country became more and more beautiful, with trees and copsewood sprinkled about, till we came to Dalmally, lying embosomed in trees, with Ben Cruachan and its adjacent range rising close before us, with the bluest shadows and tints on all the heights, and the sky pure and bright with a hot sun, though a good deal of air. Looking back we still saw the other green hills from which we had come.

As it approaches Dalmally the road goes under trees till you reach the inn, which stands quite alone. The church is beautifully situated at the bottom of the glen, and is surrounded by trees. There was no large crowd here, and the people behaved very well. Dalmally is thirteen miles from Tyndrum. Four horses were put on here to drag us up the first hill, which was long and high, and brought us in view of Loch Awe, which looked beautiful. Here the leaders were taken off. Loch Awe extends back a good way, and we could just see Kilchurn Castle, of historic celebrity, and the beautiful head of the loch with high hills on the right, and the islands of Innishail and Ardchone, besides many smaller ones. On the first-named of

Ardrishaig Harbour, on Loch Fyne, in the late nineteenth century.

these is said to be buried an ancestor of the Argylls. The loch is thirty miles in length, and as it stretches out and widens the hills become much flatter. We drove quite round the head of Loch Awe, then passed Cladich, and here the ground became very broken, and high hills were seen in the background, towering above the nearer ones. Bracken with birch and oak, etc., grow profusely among the green hills and rocks, much as they do near Inverlochy, Loch Eil, etc. Here and there were small knots of people, but not many. About five or six miles before Inveraray, at a place called Crais-na-Schleacaich, at the foot of Glen Aray, where the Duke's property begins, four of our own horses were waiting, and here dear Louise and Lorne[69] met us, looking pleased and well. Lorne rode, and dear Louise got into her pony-carriage and drove after us. We soon after came to an arch with a Gaelic inscription—"Ceud mille Failte do'n Bhan Rhighinn do Inerara" (A hundred thousand welcomes to the Queen to Inveraray). A very stout tenant's wife, Mrs. McArthur, presented me with a nosegay, which a child she held in her arms gave me.

On we went along Glen Aray, the road as we approached Inveraray Castle being bordered on either side by trees. When we reached the gate there were two halberdiers, whilst others were posted at intervals along the approach, dressed in Campbell tartan kilts with brown coats turned back with red, and bonnets with a black cock's tail and bog-myrtle (the Campbell badge). With them were also the pipers of the volunteers. In front of the house the volunteers in kilts and red jackets, and the artillery volunteers in blue and silver, of whom Lorne is the colonel, were drawn up, and a good many spectators were assembled. The Duke and Duchess of Argyll[70] and their six girls were at the door: the outside steps are now under glass and made into a sort of conservatory.

The Duke and Duchess took us upstairs at once to our rooms, part of which are Louise's; very comfortable, not large but cheerful, and having a beautiful view of Loch Fyne. It was one when we arrived, and we lunched at two, only Louise, Beatrice, and Lorne, in a nice room (in fact the Duchess's drawing-room) with tapestry, at the foot of the stairs. Brown (who has attended me at all the meals since we came here) waited, helped by two or three of the Duke's people. After lunch we went into the large drawing-room, next door to where we had lunched in 1847, when Lorne was only two years old. And now I return, alas! without my beloved Husband, to find Lorne my son-in-law!

Thursday, September 23

A fine morning. Breakfasted in my sitting-room at a quarter to ten with Louise and Beatrice. My sitting-room is generally Louise's bedroom, which had been specially arranged by her for me, and in the recess the Duchess had placed a picture of Balmoral, copied from A. Becker's picture. This opens into a small apartment, generally used as Lorne's dressing-room, in which my maid Annie sleeps and the two maids sit, next to which comes the bedroom, at the end of which is the nice cozy little turret-room with two windows, one of which looks on the loch with the very fine Ardkinglass Range in front, and the other on the front door, the bridge, and splendid trees. My dresser, Emilie Dittweiler, is next door to my bedroom, and Beatrice next to her in Louise's sitting-room.

At a little after eleven I walked out with Louise and Beatrice along the approach, and then turned up through the wood and up the lower walk of Dunaquoich, the hill opposite the house, which is wooded nearly to the top, on which is a tower, and walked along under magnificent trees, chiefly beeches and some very fine spruces, that reminded me of Windsor Park and Reinhardtsbrunn. We walked on some way, passed a well and a small cottage, where the poultry is kept, where there is a funny good-natured woman called Mrs. McNicholl, who kissed Louise's hand and knelt down when I came up, and said to Louise, when she heard I was coming, "How shall I speak to her?" We went into the little cottage, where another old woman of eighty lives. She looked so nice and tidy with a clean white mutch. We then walked down and came back along the river, which flows quite close to the house into the sea, and is full of fish. We were in at twenty minutes to one. Luncheon at two, just like yesterday. The day was dull, but quite fair and clear. Drawing and painting.

At a quarter-past four drove out with Louise, Beatrice, and the Duchess, in my waggonette, driven by Bourner. After going for some distance the same way as yesterday afternoon, we turned into a wooded drive, leading to the Glen of Essachosan, where there are the most beautiful spruces, and some silver firs which reminded me in height and size of those on the road to Eberstein, near Baden, and on by what they call the Queen's drive, made for me in 1871, past Lechkenvohr, whence there is a fine view of the loch and surrounding hills, Ben Een, Ben Buie, etc. The road is very steep going down to the Curling Pond and Black Bull Cottage; then over Carlonnan Bridge down to some falls, and back along the approach to the Dhu Loch, under the avenue of fine old beeches, which, joining as they do, almost form an aisle. Eleven, alas! were blown down two years ago: they were planted by the Marquis of Argyll two hundred years ago. You come rapidly upon the Dhu Loch, a small but very pretty loch—a complete contrast to our Dhu Loch, for this is surrounded by green and very wooded hills, with the extremely pretty and picturesque Glen Shira in the background, which is richly wooded. We drove along the right bank of the Shira River, up as far as the small farm of Drum Lee, most prettily situated on the hillside some way up, passing one or two other farms—one especially, a very strange old building. We took our (made) tea, and Elizabeth (the Duchess) greatly admired the convenient arrangement (viz. the bag into which cups etc. are fitted), and then drove back the same way and along the shore road.

Friday, September 24

At a quarter-past five, after tea, started with Louise, Beatrice, and Jane Churchill in the rain, which turned to a heavy downpour. We drove up the way we had previously walked, by the private road, under trees the whole way, to Lynn a Gluthen, the highest fall of the Aray, which is very pretty. There we had to get out to walk over a wooden bridge, which Louise said they did not like to drive over, and came back by the high road. By this time the weather had quite cleared, and so we drove on past the inn of Inveraray, through a gate which is always left open, and up what is called the "Town Avenue", consisting entirely of very old beeches joining overhead and nearly a mile long, at the back of the town. We came back by the lime avenue in the deer park, and in by a gate close to the pleasure-ground at half-past six. The halberdiers, all tenants of the Duke, kept guard the whole day.

We dined at a quarter-past eight on account of the ball—only Louise, Beatrice, Jane Churchill, and I. Went into the drawing-room for a moment, where the Duke presented Sir Donald Campbell of Dunstaffnage and his wife, and J. A. Campbell of New Inverawe (Loch Awe). Sir Donald Campbell is deputy-keeper of Dunstaffnage Castle, and wears a key in consequence.[71] He is between forty and fifty, and wore a kilt, as did also Malcolm of Poltalloch and the other gentlemen. At a quarter-past ten we drove across to the temporary pavilion, where the ball to the tenants was to take place. Louise, Beatrice, and Jane Churchill went with me in the Duke's coach. The Duke, Lorne, and Colin received us, and the Duchess and all the girls and the other ladies were inside at the upper end on a raised platform, where we all sat. It is a very long and handsome room, I believe a hundred and thirty feet long, and was built at the time of Louise's marriage. It was handsomely decorated with flags, and there were present between seven and eight hundred people—tenants with their wives and families, and many people from the town; but it was not like the Highland balls I have been accustomed to, as there were many other dances besides reels. The band could not play reels (which were played by the piper), and yet came from Glasgow! The ball began, however, with a reel; then came a country dance, then another reel. Louise danced a reel with Brown, and Beatrice with one of the Duke's foresters; but the band could only play a country dance tune for it. Another reel with pipes, in which Jane Churchill danced with Brown, and Francie Clark with

opposite above: Strathtummel; in the distance is Schiehallion.
opposite below: The Three Sisters of Glencoe: Buchaille Etive Bheag, Beinn Fhada and Aonach Dubh.

The valley of the River Dee above Braemar.

Annie (Mrs. Macdonald, my wardrobe maid), Louise and Beatrice dancing in another reel with one of the other people and Mr. John Campbell. Then came a "*schottische*", which seemed to be much liked there, and more reels, and lastly a "*tempête*", in which Louise and Beatrice danced. In the early part a Gaelic song was sung by some of the people, including Mr. John Campbell. I remember some which were sung by the boatmen on Loch Tay in 1842. After the "*tempête*" we came away at nearly half-past twelve.

Saturday, September 25

A pouring morning. Breakfast as usual with my two dear children—dear Louise so kind and attentive, so anxious I and all my people should be comfortable, thinking of everything. It cleared, and at half-past eleven I walked out with Louise (Beatrice walked with Jane Churchill and the girls) to the kennel, along the River Aray, which had risen a great deal since Thursday, when it was as low as possible. We went to the kennel and saw the dogs and the eagle; from here we went to the kitchen-garden, which is large. There are very fine peaches and a wonderful old laurel and thuja, which have spread to an immense size. Home at twenty minutes to one. Luncheon as before.

Louise introduced me to a good old lady, a Miss McGibbon, who was too ill to come out and see me; she patted Louise on the shoulder and said, "We are all so fond of the Princess; she is a great pet." Louise said, "Lorne was her great pet"; and she answered, "Yes; he is, and so you are a double pet."

At ten minutes past four drove out with Louise, Beatrice, and the Duke in the waggonette, and took a charming drive, the afternoon being very fine and bright. We went out the same way we had been on Wednesday, and once or twice besides, along the avenue called Ballachanooran, by the deer park (a great many gates having to be opened, as they must be kept locked to prevent the deer getting out), and struck into the Lochgilphead Road beyond Cromalt. We then passed, as on the first day, Dalchenna and Killean, Achnagoul and Achindrain. The last two places are old Highland villages, where a common old practice, now fallen into disuse, continues, of which the Duke gave me the following account:

In the *Highlands* of *Scotland* up to a comparatively recent date the old system of *village communities* prevailed as the common system of land tenure. Under this system the cultivators were collected into groups or villages, the cottages being all built close together on some one spot of the farm. The farm itself was divided into *pasture land* and *arable land*. The pasture land was held in *common* by all the families, and the arable land was divided *by lot* every year, so that each family might get its turn or its chance of the better and the worse qualities of soil. This very rude system is quite incompatible with any improved culture, but is an extremely ancient one. Sir Henry Maine has lately published a very interesting little book on the subject, showing that it once prevailed all over Europe, and does still actually prevail over the greater part of India. It has now almost entirely disappeared in the Highlands where such *crofters* or very small cultivators as remain are generally separate from each other—each living on his own *croft*— although there are still remaining many cases of pasture or hill land held in common among several crofters.

Achnagoul, near Inveraray, is one of the old *primitive villages*, where all the houses are built close together, and where, as late as the year 1847, the old rude practice still held—that of an *annual casting of lots* for the patches of arable land into which the farm was divided. At that time there were sixteen families, and each of them cultivated perhaps twenty different patches of arable land separated from each other. About that year the families were persuaded with much difficulty to give up this old semi-barbarous system and to divide the arable land into fixed divisions, one being assigned to each tenant, so that he could cultivate on an improved system. But the village remains as it was, and is one of the comparatively few of that class which now remain in the Highlands.

They are said to be the only two villages of the kind in existence in the Highlands. The inhabitants are very exclusive, and hardly ever marry out of their own villages.

The morning was very wet, so decided after our usual nice breakfast not to go out, but wrote, etc. At a quarter to twelve we attended divine service in the house in the large dining-room, which is a long room. Dr. MacGregor performed the service. Went afterwards into the drawing-room and the two libraries, the newer of which had been arranged by Louise and Lorne. There are some fine pictures in the drawing-room—one of the Marquis of Argyll who was beheaded,[72] of Field-Marshal Conway[73] by Gainsborough, of Duke Archibald, who built the house, etc.,[74] also of the present Duke's handsome grandmother,[75] who married first a Duke of Hamilton, secondly a Duke of Argyll.

Monday, September 27

It was a dreadfully rough night, pouring and blowing fearfully, and we heard it had thundered and lightened. After our nice little breakfast and writing, I went out at eleven with Louise, and met the Duke and the rest in the pleasure-grounds, where I planted a small cedar of Lebanon, the seed of which Lady Emma McNeill had brought back from the East. Then went on a little farther to where the road turns near the river, and planted a small silver fir, opposite to a magnificent one which my beloved Albert had admired in 1847. Beatrice walked up meanwhile with Jane Churchill, Evelyn, and Frances Campbell, to the top of the fine hill of Dunaquoich, opposite the Castle, after seeing the trees planted, and was to plant one herself when she came down. I drove off with Louise past the Creitabhille Lodge, the granite quarry (not, of course, the large ones which we saw on Saturday in the deer forest), and then got out and walked up a long steep path in the wood to obtain a view, of which, however, we did not see much. I am sure we walked a mile and a half up to the top, and it was a long pull, but I walked well. However, in going down, the wet grass and moss made me slip very much, having no nails to my boots, and twice I came down completely.

Tuesday, September 28

Bright and then showery. At a little past eleven drove with Louise and Beatrice along the sea-shore as far as Douglas Water Point, where we stopped to sketch between the frequent showers the view being lovely and the lights so effective.

Home through the town by a quarter to one.

Painting. Luncheon as each day, after which again painting. At a quarter to four started off in a shower in the waggonette, with Louise, Beatrice, and Jane Churchill, for Glen Shira. We drove by the approach through the fine old avenue of beeches which suffered so much two years ago. This time along the right side of the Dhu Loch, which is three-quarters of a mile long, up to the head of Glen Shira, which is seven miles distant from the upper end of the loch, and is lovely. We had driven up a good way last Thursday, as far as Drumlee. It is a lovely glen, wilder and much shut in as you advance, with fine rocks appearing through the grassy hills, and thickly wooded at the bottom. We passed two farms, and then went up to where the glen closes, and on the brae there is a keeper's cottage, just above which are the remains of a house where Rob Roy[76] lived for some time concealed, but on sufferance. His army or followers were hidden in Glen Shira.

We got out here to look at some fine falls of the river Shira, a linn falling from a height to which footpaths had been made. Then drove on a little farther, and stopped to take our tea. We stopped twice afterwards to make a slight sketch of this lovely green glen, so picturesque and peaceful-looking, and then to take another view from the lower end of the Dhu Loch, in which Louise helped me. She also sketched the glen, and had done a sketch this morning. She has such talent, dear good child, and I felt so sad to leave her.

Wednesday, September 29

Vicky's and Fritz's engagement day—already twenty years ago! God bless them!

Got up before eight, and at half-past eight breakfasted for the last time with dear Louise and Beatrice. Then dressed before half-past nine and went downstairs. The early morning was fair, though misty, but unfortunately by half-past eight the mist had come down and it rained. It was decided that the horses should go back overland (having had such a terrible journey from the difficult embarkation and landing) by Dalmally, stopping all night at Tyndrum and coming on next day. The van was to go by sea. Some of the things belonging to our toilettes (which were in far too cumbrous boxes) we kept with us. I took leave of the whole family,[77] including the MacNeills, and, with a heavy heart, of my darling Louise. It rained very much as we drove off, and for some time afterwards, to make it more melancholy.

We left Inveraray at half past nine, and drove out by the same gateway as on our arrival, but afterwards went along the sea-shore to the head of the loch. We then turned to the right, still along the lochside, and changed horses at twenty minutes to eleven at a small inn called Cairndow, where the dear little Campbell children are staying, and who were at the window—such lovely children! There were a few people collected, and the harness as well as the horses had to be changed, and a pair of leaders put on to pull us up the long steep ascent in Glenkinglass. This caused a delay of ten minutes or a quarter of an hour. It rained rather heavily, the mist hanging over the hills most provokingly. We passed Ardkinglass (Mr. Callander's), and then turned up to the left through the very wild and desolate Glenkinglass. The high green hills with hardly any habitations reminded me of the Spital of Glenshee. The mist lifted just enough to let one see the tops of the hills below which we were passing. The road was steep, and, just as we were getting near the top, the leaders, which had repeatedly stopped, refused to pull any farther, reared and kicked and jibbed, so that we really thought we should never get on, and should perhaps have to sleep at some wayside inn. But we stopped, and Brown had the leaders taken off near a small tarn, called Loch Restel, and he and Francie walked. We then got on much better. A little farther on we passed a few scattered huts, and at last we reached the top of this long ascent. The rain, which had been very heavy just when our plight was at its worst, stopped, and the day cleared.

At the summit of the pass is the spot called Rest and be thankful, from an inscription cut upon a stone by the regiment that made the road, which was one of the military roads to open up the Highlands constructed by Government under the superintendence of Marshal Wade. The stone still remains, but the words are much defaced. Here we came upon the splendid steep wild pass of Glen Croe, something like Glencoe, but not so fine and the road much steeper. It reminds me of the Devil's Elbow, and even of the Devil's Bridge in the Göschenen Pass on the St. Gothard. We got out and walked down the road, which goes in a zigzag. A few people who had walked up from the coach were standing there. As at Glencoe the stream flows in the hollow of the pass, and there were some cattle and a house or two. The sun even came out all at once and lit up the wild grand scene. We got into the carriage near the bottom, and drank Fritz and Vicky's healths.

There was no more heavy rain, though there were frequent showers succeeded by most brilliant sunshine. We drove on under and by trees, and saw high hill-tops, including the peak of Ben Lomond, and then came upon Loch Long, a sea loch, which we sailed up in 1847, and drove part of the way along the shore, on the opposite side of which lie Arrochar and several pretty villas. We went round the head of the loch, where stood Lady Welby (formerly Victoria Wortley) and her children, and drove along under an arch near the bridge, passing through the village of Arrochar, which is in Dumbartonshire, and here had a very good view of the celebrated Cobbler, or Ben Arthur. We next changed horses at Tarbet, quite a small village, where there was a sort of arch, composed of laurels and flowers stretched across the road. There were a good many people here, who pressed in upon us a good deal. Here General Ponsonby presented Mr. H. E. Crum Ewing, Lord Lieutenant of Dumbartonshire. He preceded us a little way in his carriage, and then followed us.

The drive along Loch Lomond, which we came upon almost immediately after Tarbet, was perfectly beautiful. We wound along under trees on both sides, with the most lovely glimpses of the head of the loch, and ever and anon of Loch Lomond itself below the road; the hills which rose upon our right reminding me of Aberfoyle, near Loch Ard, and of the lower part of the Pilatus.[78] Such fine trees, numbers of hollies growing down almost into the water, and such beautiful capes and little bays and promontories! The loch was extremely rough, and so fierce was the wind, that the foam was blown like smoke along the deep blue of the water. The gale had broken some trees. The sun lit up the whole scene beautifully, but we had a few slight showers. As we proceeded, the hills became lower, the loch widened, and the many wooded islands appeared. We next changed horses at Luss, quite a small village—indeed the little inn stands almost alone, and they drove us close up to it, but there was a great crowding and squeezing, and some children screamed with fright; two presented nosegays to Beatrice and me, and a poor woman offered me a bag of "*sweeties*".

From here we drove along past the openings of Glen Luss and Glen Finlas, which run up amongst the fine hills to the right, the loch being on our left, and the road much wooded. There are slate quarries close to Luss. About two miles from Luss we drove through Sir J. Colquhoun's place, Rossdhu, which commands a beautiful view of Ben Lomond and the loch, and drove up to the house, where Highland volunteers were drawn up, and where we stopped without getting out of the carriage, and I received a nosegay from Sir J. Colquhoun's little girl and a basket of fruit. His uncle was drowned two years ago in the loch, crossing over from an island where he had been shooting, and the body was not found for a fortnight; the keepers with him were also drowned. We drove on, passing several other places, and everywhere were arches of flowers, flags, etc., and the poorest people had hung out handkerchiefs for flags. We were followed by endless "machines" full of people, and many on foot running, and our horses were bad and went very slowly. However, as we approached Balloch, through which we did not pass, but only went up to the station, though the crowds were very great, perfect order was kept. The militia was out, and we got quite easily into the train at a quarter-past three.

Our next stoppage was at Stirling, where there was an immense concourse of people, and the station prettily decorated. The evening was very fine, the pretty scenery appearing to great advantage, and the sky lovely. After this it got rapidly dark. We stopped at Perth and at the Bridge of Dun, where Jane Churchill got into our carriage and we had some tea; and then at Aberdeen, where it poured. At twenty minutes to ten we arrived at Ballater, and at once got into our carriage, and reached Balmoral at twenty-five minutes to eleven.

Holyrood,
August 17, 1876

BELOVED MAMMA'S BIRTHDAY.
How often she came to Edinburgh for a few days on her way to and from Abergeldie, and how much she always liked it!

We arrived yesterday morning at Edinburgh at eight o'clock. Had had a good night. Unfortunately the weather was misty, and even a little rain fell. No distance could well be seen. Dear Arthur[79] came to breakfast (always in uniform). At eleven o'clock went and sat out till half-past twelve, under an umbrella and with screens, on the side of the Abbey facing Arthur's Seat. Wrote and signed, Brown always helping to dry the signatures.

Read also in the papers a very nice account given in the *Courant* of what passed yesterday. Many interruptions. The day improving. Crowds flocking into the town, troops marching, bands playing—just as when any great event takes place in London.

The last time that my dearest Albert ever appeared in public was in Edinburgh on October 23 [1861], only six weeks before the end of all, when he laid the first stone of the new Post Office, and I looked out of the window to see him drive off in state, or rather in dress, London carriages, and the children went to see the

The memorial to Albert in Edinburgh,
as photographed in the late nineteenth century.

ceremony. It was in Edinburgh, too, that dearest Mama[80] appeared for the last time in public—being with me at the Volunteer Review in 1860, which was the first time she had driven with me in public for twenty years!

Dear Arthur could not come to luncheon, as he was on duty. At half-past three we started in three carriages: Beatrice, Leopold, and I in the third; Brown (in full dress) and Collins[81] behind; Leopold in the Highland dress; dear Arthur, commanding the full Sovereign's escort of the 7th Hussars, riding next to me.

We drove out to the right—by Abbey Hill, the Regent Road, Princes Street, then turning into St. Andrew Square, along George Street to Charlotte Square. Enormous crowds everywhere clustering upon the Calton Hill and round and upon all the high monuments. The decorations were beautiful along the streets and on the houses, Venetian masts with festoons of flags on either side of Princes Street and St. Andrew Street. St. Andrew Square also was beautifully decorated, and the few inscriptions were very touching and appropriate. The day was quite fair, though dull (which, however, under the circumstances, was better than a very scorching sun like yesterday) and heavy, and not clear as to distance. The crowd, which was all along most hearty and enthusiastic, was densest at Charlotte Square. The Duke of Buccleuch received us, and the Royal Archers kept the ground.

We walked up to a dais handsomely arranged, where I stood between Beatrice and Leopold (who were a little behind me). Dear Arthur's sense of duty was so great, that he would not dismount and stand near me, but remained with the escort which he commanded, and which waited near our carriage. The ladies and gentlemen, Mr. Cross[82] (Home Secretary), etc., standing behind them; the Committee, with the Duke of Buccleuch at their head, below. A large enclosure railed off was full of spectators, including all the highest and principal people, the Duchesses of Athole and Roxburghe, the Dowager Lady Ruthven, Sir Thomas Biddulph,[83] etc.; and our maids also were there, but I saw none of them.

The ceremony began by a short prayer (which was somewhat disturbed by a great noise made by the crowd) offered up by Dr. Milligan, one of the Deans of the Chapel Royal. Then my dearest Albert's Chorale, with words like a National Anthem, was beautifully sung by a choir, accompanied by the band of the 79th, led by Professor H. Oakeley, Mus. Doc. and Professor of Music in the University of Edinburgh. The Duke of Buccleuch then presented the Executive Committee, of which he himself is Chairman, and which consisted of Sir J. McNeill, G.C.B., Sir William Gibson Craig, Sir Daniel McNee, Dr. Lyon Playfair, and Mr. William Walker. After this, the Duke of Buccleuch read a very pretty address, in which, besides my beloved Husband, dear Mama was alluded to, and I read a reply.

Mr. Cross then declared that I wished the Statue (an equestrian one) to be unveiled, which was done most successfully, without a hitch. The effect of the monument as a whole, with the groups at the angles of the pedestal, is very good. The Coburg March was played, and its well-known strains[84] ever bring back dear and sweet memories.

Mr. Steell, the sculptor, was presented, and this was followed by the singing of another beautiful chorale, with touching words and music, the latter composed by Professor Oakeley, who is a wonderful musician, and plays beautifully on the organ. We then, followed by our own suite, the Committee, and Mr. Steell, walked round the Statue and examined the groups of bas-reliefs. The three sculptors who had executed the groups were also presented. Brown followed us round, having stood behind us the whole time. He was delighted with the reception.

We drove back by South Charlotte Street and Princes Street. The horses of the Yeomanry and even some of the Hussars were very restive, and kept plunging and whirling round upon our horses. One of the Hussars, in particular, got in between our horses, and nearly caused an accident.

Wednesday, September 12, 1877

A DULL MORNING, VERY MILD. Had not a good night. Up at a quarter-past eight, breakfasting at a quarter to nine (I had packed my large boxes with papers etc., with Brown, before breakfast on Monday, as all the heavier luggage had to be sent on in advance), and at a quarter-past nine left Balmoral with Beatrice and the Duchess of Roxburghe, leaving Leopold, who was himself to start at ten A.M. for Dunkeld. Brown on the rumble of the landau, his leg now really fairly well, but he looks pulled.[85] It began to rain very soon, and went on till we almost reached Ballater, when we got into the railway. Here General Ponsonby and Sir William Jenner met us. Wilmore, Morgan, Cannon, Francie Clark (with darling Noble), and Heir went with us. Annie Macdonald, Hollis the cook, Lockwood, Seymour (who replaced poor Goddard), and Lizzie Stewart (the housemaid) went on before us on Monday.

The day cleared and gradually became very fine. Passed through Aberdeen, which looked very handsome, and where we much admired a new tower added to a college. Stopped at Dyce Junction at nineteen minutes to twelve. Near Aberdeen we saw the corn already cut, which is unusually early. Passed close under Benachie, the heather beautiful everywhere. At one o'clock we had our luncheon, and dear Noble came in and was so good and quiet. At twenty-five minutes past one stopped at Keith, where we had stopped in 1872, and where we had then been obliged to take two people into the carriage to open a door through which the maids passed, and which had got fixed. The volunteers and a number of people were waiting for us here. About Keith the corn was sadly destroyed, but around Elgin it was better. Soon after this appeared the lovely hills of the Moray Frith—really beautiful: the land-locked sea so blue, with heavy fields of yellow corn (harvesting going on) in the undulating ground, with trees and woods here and there, formed a lovely picture. An old ruined church (Kinloss Abbey) we passed to the right, and Forres at eighteen minutes past two. Then Nairn, lying low on the Frith, but very picturesque with the hills rising around. The heather was so brilliant, and the sea, though very rough, was blue, which had a lovely effect; but the bracken, and even the trees, have begun to turn here, as well as with us. Good crops about here. We passed near Fort George, which lies very prettily on the shore of the Frith, but where we did not stop, and Culloden. At three minutes past three passed through Inverness, where many people were out, and went quickly past Beauly. As far as Dingwall we had travelled precisely the same way in going to Dunrobin in 1872. At twenty minutes to four reached Dingwall, charmingly situated in a glen, where we stopped, and where there were a good many people waiting for us.

Here Sir Kenneth and Lady Mackenzie of Gairloch met us with their three children, two boys and a girl. He is a pleasing courteous person, and wore the kilt. He has an immense property about here, and all round is the Mackenzie country. Lady Mackenzie is the elder sister of Lady Granville, and excessively like her. Soon after this we took tea, which was pleasant and refreshing. From Dingwall we turned to the left, and, instead of going on by the main line to Tain, went through the celebrated Strathpeffer, which is extremely pretty—a wooded glen with houses and cottages dotted about; then on through a wild glen, with hills, partly rocky, but with grass, heather, and bracken, and some trees running up amidst them. The railway goes along above and at some distance from the village, proceeding by way of Strath Bran and Loch Luichart. There were occasional showers, with gleams of sunshine always between.

We left the railway at Achnasheen, where we arrived at a quarter to five, and where there are only a small station and two or three little cottages. We three ladies got into the sociable (Brown and Cannon on the box), the two gentlemen and three maids following in the waggonette, and the other servants in "traps". Sir Kenneth Mackenzie came as far as this small station, where there were a Gaelic inscription and some plaids arranged in festoons. The twenty miles drive from here, through a desolate, wild, and perfectly uninhabited country, was beautiful, though unfortunately we had heavy showers. The first part winds along Loch Rusque (Gaelic *Chroisg*), a long narrow loch, with hills very like those at the Spital and at Glen Muich rising on either side. Looking back you see the three high peaks of

Harvest time in the Highlands, from a painting by Landseer.

Scour-na-Vuillin. The road continues along another small loch; and then from the top of the hill you go down a very grand pass called Glen Dochart. Here Loch Maree came in view most beautifully. Very shortly after this you come upon the loch, which is grand and romantic. We changed horses at Kinlochewe, a small inn, near to which is a shooting-lodge, which was for some time rented by Lady Waterpark's son-in-law, Mr. Clowes, and he and his wife used to live there a good deal. They are now living near Gairloch, at Flowerdale, another shooting-lodge of Sir Kenneth Mackenzie.

The drive along the lochside, for ten miles to the hotel of Loch Maree, is beautiful in the extreme. The hills to the right, as you go from Kinlochewe, are splendid— very high and serrated, with wood at the base of some of them. The windings of the road are beautiful, and afford charming glimpses of the lake, which is quite locked in by the overlapping mountains. There are trees, above and below it, of all kinds, but chiefly birch, pine, larch, and alder, with quantities of high and most beautiful heather and bracken growing luxuriantly, high rocks surmounting the whole. Here and there a fine Scotch fir, twisted, and with a stem and head like a stone-pine, stands out on a rocky projection into the loch, relieved against the blue hills as in some Italian view. Part of the way the road emerges altogether from the trees, and passes by a mass of huge piled-up and tumbled-about stones, which everywhere here are curiously marked, almost as though they were portions of a building, and have the appearance of having been thrown about by some upheaving of the earth. We had several heavy showers, which produced a most brilliant rainbow, with the reflection of a second, quite perfect. Then it quite cleared up, and the sky was radiant with the setting sun, which gave a crimson hue to all the hills, and lit up Ben

Sleach just as I remember having seen it light up Ben Nevis and the surrounding hills at Inverlochy.

It was a little after seven when Loch Maree Hotel, which stands close to the loch and to the road and is surrounded by trees, was reached. At the entrance there is no gate, merely a low wall open at either side to admit carriages etc. It is a very nice little house, neatly furnished. To the left, as you enter, are two good rooms—a large one called the coffee-room, in which we take our meals, and the other smaller, next to it, in which the gentlemen dine. Up the small but easy short winding staircase to the right come small, though comfortable, rooms. To the left Beatrice's, and Brown's just opposite to the right. Then up three steps is a small passage; at the end, to the left, is my dear little sitting-room, looking on to the loch, and to Ben Sleach and the road; it is very full with my things. At the other end is my bedroom, with two small rooms between for Wilmore and Annie.

Thursday, September 13

It had rained a great deal through the night, and the morning was dull. Had slept well. Beatrice and I breakfasted together downstairs, where we also lunched. Began to sketch, though there was no light and shade; but the splendid mountain was clear. At eleven walked out with Beatrice on the road to Kinlochewe, about a mile, and back, greatly admiring the magnificent hills. There is a bridge over a stream called Talladale, and near it was a cottage, a miserable hovel, in which an old man lived; he wore a coat and a high hat, and was much pleased to see me, but said he "had very little English", which is the case with most people here. We gave him something, and when Brown took it to him he asked the old man the names of some of the hills.

Saturday, September 15

A fair morning. Up early after a very good night. There is a perfect plague of wasps, and we are obliged to have gauze nailed down to keep these insects out when the windows are open, which, as the climate is so hot, they have to be constantly. I had to put on quite thin things again. Decided, after some little doubt, to make an expedition for the day to Torridon, described as fine and wild. There was a heavy shower before we started. Had been sketching and painting.

At half-past twelve we started in the waggonette, with Beatrice, the Duchess (who is delighted with everything), and General Ponsonby and Brown on the box. The day was very fine; we had only two or three showers, which lasted a few minutes. We drove on to Kinlochewe, where we took fresh horses, and a capital pair of bay ones we had. The sun was brilliant, and lit up the magnificent scenery beautifully. Halfway we crossed the bridge of Grudie (from which Ben Sleach is seen to advantage), a very pretty rapid burn, with fine fir trees, and a glen running up to the right—i.e. to the south. At Kinlochewe we turned up to the right by the stream of Garry, mountains towering up, as we advanced, like mighty giants, and coming one by one and unexpectedly into view. To the left we passed a pretty, small loch, called Loch Clare, which runs back into a wooden glen at the foot of high hills.

Highland cattle on a misty morning.

Sir Ivor Guest has a shooting-lodge near, and you can just see a small house amongst the trees.

Soon after this the grand, wild, savage-looking, but most beautiful and picturesque Glen of Torridon opened upon us, with the dark mural precipices of that most extraordinary mountain Ben Liughach, which the people pronounce Liarach. We were quite amazed as we drove below it. The mountains here rise so abruptly from their base that they seem much higher than our Aberdeenshire mountains, although, excepting Ben Sleach (3,216 feet) and a few others, the hills are not of any remarkable height, and the level of the country or land itself is barely a hundred feet above the sea, whereas Balmoral is eight hundred feet to begin with. All the hills about Loch Maree and this glen, and elsewhere in this neighbourhood, are very serrated and rocky. Ben Liarach is most peculiar from its being so dark, and the rocks like terraces one above the other, or like fortifications and pillars—most curious; the glen itself is very flat, and the mountains rise very abruptly on either side. There were two cottages (in one of which lived a keeper), a few cattle, and a great many cut peats.

We came to the Upper Loch Torridon, which is almost landlocked and very pretty. In the distance the hills of Skye were seen. Village there really is none, and the inn is merely a small, one-storied, "harled" house, with small windows. We drove beyond the habitations to a turn where we could not be overlooked, and scrambled up a bank, where we seated ourselves, and at twenty minutes to three took our luncheon with good appetite. The air off the mountains and the sea was delicious, and not muggy. We two remained sketching, for the view was beautiful. To the right were the hills of Skye, rising above the lower purple ones which closed in the loch. To the south, nearly opposite to where I sat, was Applecross (formerly Mackenzie property), which now belongs to Lord Middleton, and the high mountains of Ben Hecklish and Ben Damph, with, in the distance northwards, the white peaks of Ben Liarach. We were nearly an hour sitting there, and we got down unwillingly, as it was so fine and such a wild uncivilised spot, like the end of the world. There was a school, standing detached by itself, which had been lately built. The property here belongs to a Mr. Darroch, whose two little boys rode past us twice with a groom. An old man, very tottery, passed where I was sketching, and I asked the Duchess of Roxburghe to speak to him; he seemed strange, said he had come from America, and was going to England, and thought Torridon very ugly!

We walked along, the people came out to see us, and we went into a little merchant's shop, where we all bought some trifles—just such a "shoppie" as old Edmonston's, and the poor man was so nervous he threw almost everything down. I got some very good comforters, two little woven woollen shawls, and a very nice cloak. We had spoken to a woman before, but she could not understand us, only knowing Gaelic, and had to ask another younger woman to help.

A little farther off the road, and more on the slope of the hill, was a row of five or six wretched hovels, before which stood barelegged and very ill-clad children, and poor women literally squatting on the ground. The people cheered us and seemed very much pleased. Hardly any one ever comes here. We had now to get into the carriage, and one of the horses was a little restive; but we soon started off all right much interested by our adventures. We admired the splendid mountain again on our way back, and enjoyed our expedition very much. One very short shower we had, before coming to Kinlochewe, where we again changed horses, and were home at our nice little house by nearly seven, when Beatrice and I had some welcome tea. Later our usual dinner; then Beatrice played, and we afterwards played together.

Sunday, September 16

A most beautiful bright morning, with a slight cloud overhanging Ben Sleach, which is very often not clear at the top. There was a heavy shower, which came on quite unexpectedly. We walked out at half-past eleven, and after some three hundred yards turned up a path to the right, off the road to Kinlochewe, under oak and rowan trees, through very wet grass and fern, to where stood two very poor-looking low cottages. We looked into one, out of which came a tidy-looking woman, but who could hardly understand or speak a word of English. We then looked into the second, where Baldry lodged; it was wet and muddy almost to the door, and the inside very low and close, but tidy. The "gudewife" came up and spoke to us, also like a foreigner, with difficulty. She was a nice, tidy-looking woman, and gave her name as Mrs. McRae, and the place is called "Sliorach". She knew us—at least Brown told her it was the "Bhan Righ" with her daughter, and gave her some money.

We returned as we had come, and went on some way in the other direction, coming in at twenty minutes to one. Read prayers, etc. There is no kirk nearer than Kinlochewe and Gairloch, and people had been seen passing on foot as early as half-past seven to Gairloch. At half-past four Beatrice, the Duchess of Roxburghe, and I started in a four-oared gig, steered by Hormsby the landlord, a very nice, quiet, youngish man, and rowed to the Isle of Maree ("Eilan Maree"), which is not visible from the house, being concealed by some of the larger islands. Contrary to what is stated in the *Guide*, it is the smallest of them. It was delightful rowing through these wooded and rocky islands, with the blue, calm loch—not another sound but the oars—the lovely blue and purple distant hills on the one side, and the splendid peaks of Ben Sleach and its surrounding mountains on the other.

The boat was pushed on shore, and we scrambled out and walked through the tangled underwood and thicket of oak, holly, birch, ash, beech, etc., which covers the islet, to the well, now nearly dry which is said to be celebrated for the cure of insanity. An old tree stands close to it, and into the bark of this it is the custom, from time immemorial, for every one who goes there to insert with a hammer a copper coin, as a sort of offering to the saint who lived there in the eighth century, called Saint Maolruabh or Mulroy. The saint died near Applecross in 722, and is said to have rested under a rock, which is still shown, close to Torridon. Some say that the name of Maree was derived from "Mulroy", others from "Mary". We hammered some pennies into the tree, to the branches of which there are also rags and ribbons tied. We then went on to where there are some old grave-stones: two belonged to the tomb of a Norwegian or Danish princess, about whose untimely death there is a romantic story. There are also modern graves, and only eight years ago one of the family of the McLeans was buried there, the island being their burying-place. The remains of the old wall of the monastery are still to be seen. The island is barely a quarter of a mile across at the widest part, and not above half a mile in circumference. Some of the larger islands have red deer on them. We walked along the beach and picked up stones, then rowed back as we had come. It took about twenty minutes. Four very respectable-looking men (one a very good-looking young farmer) rowed the boat. After landing, we got into the waggonette and drove to a bridge just beyond where the trees cease on the Gairloch Road, about two miles from the hotel. Here we first took our tea, and then got out and scrambled up a steep bank to look at a waterfall, a pretty one, but very inferior to those in our neighbourhood at Balmoral; walked down again and drove home by a quarter-past seven.

Reading; writing. Beatrice's room is a very pretty one, but very hot, being over the kitchen. Brown's, just opposite, also very nice and not hot, but smaller. After dinner the Duchess of Roxburghe read a little out of the newspapers. Saw Sir William Jenner.

Monday, September 17

A splendid bright morning, like July! Have had such good nights since we came, and my own comfortable bed. Sketched and painted after breakfast. At ten minutes past eleven walked out with Beatrice the same way as yesterday, and turned up to the right and looked at the farm, where the horses for the coach are kept. This coach is like a great break, and is generally full of people; we met it each morning when out walking. We then went on past Talladale, where lives the old man to whom we spoke on Thursday, and whom we saw get off the coach this morning, having been to Gairloch for church, of which he is an elder. Here three or four very poorly dressed bairns were standing and sitting about, and we gave them biscuits and sandwiches out of the luncheon-box. The midges are dreadful, and you cannot stand for a moment without being stung. In at twenty minutes to one. I remained sketching the lovely views from the windows in the dining-room, and then sketched the beautiful mountain also.

After luncheon some doubt as to what should be done, but decided not to go to Pool Ewe, beyond Gairloch, but on to Kerrie's Bridge to meet the good people who had asked permission to come over from Stornoway, in the Isle of Lewis, to see "their beloved Queen". Drew again. At ten minutes past four we two and the Duchess of Roxburghe started in the waggonette, General Ponsonby and Brown on the box. We went by the same pretty winding road; but the Kerrie Falls were not nearly so full as on Friday after the heavy rain.

As we approached Kerrie's Bridge, we saw a number of people standing on the road, and we drew up to where they were and stopped the carriage. General Ponsonby presented the minister, Mr. Greenfield, who had come over with them. They sang "God save the Queen", with most loyal warmth; and their friendly faces and ringing cheers, when we arrived and when we left, were very gratifying. It took them three hours to come over, and they were going straight back. There were two hundred and fifty of them of all classes, from the very well dressed down to the poorest, and many fishermen amongst them. We met many of these on Saturday coming back from having sold their fish, and also on the coaches. As we returned we met the coach where there was only just room to pass.

Tuesday, September 18

A wet, misty morning, no hills whatever to be seen. Got up early and breakfasted at half-past eight, and at a quarter to nine we left with regret our nice cozy little hotel at Loch Maree, which I hope I may some day see again. Changed horses at Kinlochewe. The beautiful scenery was much obscured, but it got better as we went on, though it was not a really fine day. At a little before half-past eleven we reached Achnasheen, where Mr. (now Sir Alexander) Matheson, M.P. (who is chairman of the railway company, and has property farther north), met us. Here we got into the train, and went on without stopping to Dingwall; Strathpeffer, and Castle Leod, which belongs to the Duchess of Sutherland, partly hidden among trees, looked very pretty. The lochs of Luichart and Garve are most picturesque. We stopped at Dingwall, and Keith, and Dyce Junction as before. We had our luncheon at one o'clock, before coming to Keith, and tea after the Dyce Junction. Dear Noble was so good on the railway, and also at Loch Maree, where he came to our meals; but he was lost without his companions.

We reached Ballater at six. A very threatening evening. Such dark, heavy clouds, and the air much lighter than at Loch Maree. We reached Balmoral at a quarter to seven. Dear Arthur received us downstairs, and came up with us and stayed a little while with me. He had been out deer-stalking these two days, but got nothing.

The Prince Imperial: son of Napoleon III.

Balmoral Castle, Thursday, June 19, 1879

At twenty minutes to eleven Brown knocked and came in, and said there was bad news; and when I, in alarm, asked what, he replied, "The young French Prince is killed"; and when I could not take it in, and asked several times what it meant, Beatrice, who then came in with the telegram in her hand, said, "Oh! the Prince Imperial[86] is killed!" I feel a sort of thrill of horror now while I write the words.

I put my hands to my head and cried out, "No, no! it cannot, cannot be true! It can't be!" And then dear Beatrice, who was crying very much, as I did too, gave me the annexed telegram from Lady Frere:[87]

Government House, Cape Town, June 19, 1879.
To General Sir Henry Ponsonby, Balmoral Castle.—For the Information of
Her Majesty the Queen.

The melancholy tidings have been telegraphed from Natal, that the Prince Imperial, when out on a reconnaissance from Colonel Wood's[88] camp on the 1st of June, was killed by a number of Zulus concealed in a field in which the Prince Imperial and his party had dismounted to rest and feed their horses. No official particulars yet received by me. The Prince Imperial's body found and buried with full military honours at Camp Itelezi, and after being embalmed will be conveyed to England. This precedes the press telegrams by one hour. I have sent to Lord Sydney[89] to beg him, if possible, to break the sad intelligence to the Empress before the press telegrams arrive.

To die in such an awful, horrible way! Poor, poor dear Empress! her only, only child—her all gone! And such a real misfortune! I was quite beside myself; and both of us have hardly had another thought since.

We sent for Janie Ely, who was in the house when he was born, and was so devoted to him; and he was so good! Oh! it is too, too awful! The more one thinks of it, the worse it is! I was in the greatest distress. Brown so distressed; every one quite stunned. Got to bed very late; it was dawning! and little sleep did I get.

Friday, June 20

Had a bad, restless night, haunted by this awful event, seeing those horrid Zulus constantly before me, and thinking of the poor Empress, who did not yet know it. Was up in good time.

My accession day, forty-two years ago; but no thought of it in presence of this frightful event.

Had written many telegrams last night. One came from Lord Sydney, saying he was going down early this morning to break this dreadful news to the poor afflicted

Ben Arthur ("The Cobbler"),
with Loch Long in the middle ground, Dumbartonshire.

mother. How dreadful! Received distressed and horrified telegrams from some of my children. Heard by telegram also from Sir Stafford Northcote[90] that the news arrived in the House of Commons; that much sympathy had been shown. It came to Colonel Stanley. Telegraphed to many.

Packed my boxes with Brown. Was so horrified. Always, at Balmoral in May or June, dreadful news, or news of deaths of Royal persons, come, obliging the State parties to be put off.

At twenty-minutes past eleven drove to Donald Stewart's and got out to say "Good-bye", as well as to the Profeits, and stopped at the door of the shop to wish Mrs. Symon good-bye, and also at Brown's house, to take leave of the Hugh Browns. Home at twenty minutes past twelve. Writing.

Received a telegram from Lord Sydney, saying that he had informed the poor dear Empress of this dreadful news. She could not believe it for some time, and was afterwards quite overwhelmed.

How dreadful! Took luncheon with Beatrice in my darling Albert's room. Beatrice was much upset, as indeed we all were. Even those who did not know them felt the deepest sympathy, and were in a state of consternation. He was so good and so much beloved. So strange that, as last time, our departure should be saddened, as, indeed, it has been every year, at least for three or four years, by the occurrence of deaths of great people or of relations.

We left Balmoral at half-past one, Janie Ely and Leila Erroll[91] (full of feeling) going with Beatrice and me. It was a pity to leave when everything was in its greatest beauty. The lilacs just preparing to burst. Near Ballater there was a bush of white lilac already out. The dust dreadful. Very little whin, and far less of that beautiful broom, out, which was always such a pretty sight from the railway at this time of the year. We reached Aberdeen at twenty-eight minutes to four, and soon after had our tea.

At the Bridge of Dun we got newspapers with some of the sad details. Thence we turned off and passed again close to the sea by Arbroath, East Haven, Carnoustie (where poor Symon went and got so ill he had to be taken back), all lying low, with golf links near each, and the line passing over long grass strips with mounds and small indentations of the sea, such as are seen near sands, where there are no rocks and the coast is flat; but the ground rises as you approach Dundee.

We reached the Tay Bridge station at six. Immense crowds everywhere, flags waving in every direction, and the whole population out; but one's heart was too sad for anything. The Provost, splendidly attired, presented an address. Ladies presented beautiful bouquets to Beatrice and me. The last time I was at Dundee was in September 1844, just after Affie's birth, when we landed there on our way to Blair, and Vicky, then not four years old, the only child with us was carried through the crowd by old Renwick. We embarked there also on our way back.

We stopped here about five minutes, and then began going over the marvellous Tay Bridge, which is rather more than a mile and a half long.[92] It was begun in 1871. There were great difficulties in laying the foundation, and some lives were lost. It was finished in 1878.

Mr. Bouch, who was presented at Dundee, was the engineer. It took us, I

opposite above: Invercauld Bridge, Royal Deeside.

opposite below: The Bass Rock from the coast near North Berwick.

The Tay Bridge, before and after the great disaster.

Divers working from Steam launch

Lochleven Castle, with the Lomonds in the background.

should say, about eight minutes going over. The view was very fine.

The boys of the training-ship, with their band, looked very well. The line through the beautifully wooded county of Fife was extremely pretty, especially after Ladybank Junction, where we stopped for a few minutes, and where Mr. Balfour of Balbirnie brought a basket of flowers. We met him and his wife, Lady Georgiana, in Scotland in 1842. We passed near Loch Leven, with the ruined castle in which poor Queen Mary was confined (which we passed in 1842), stopping there a moment and in view of the "Lomonds", past Dollar and Tillicoultry, the situation of which, in a wooded green valley at the foot of the hills, is quite beautiful, and reminded me of Italy and Switzerland, through Sauchie, Alloa, all manufacturing towns, and then close under Wallace's Monument. We reached the Stirling Station, which was dreadfully crowded, at eighteen minutes past eight (the people everywhere very enthusiastic), and after leaving it we had some good cold dinner.

We got Scotch papers as we went along, giving harrowing details (all by telegraph) from the front, or rather from Natal to Cape Town, then by ship to Madeira, and thence again by telegraph here. Of nothing else could we think. Janie Ely got in at Beattock Summit, and went with us as far as Carlisle. She showed us a Dundee paper, called the *Evening Telegraph*, which contained the fullest and most dreadful accounts. Monstrous! To think of that dear young man, the apple of his mother's eye, born and nurtured in the purple, dying thus, is too fearful, too awful; and inexplicable and dreadful that the others should not have turned round and fought for him. It is too horrible![93]

The Duke of Connaught.

Monday, September 8, 1879

A FINE MORNING. BREAKFASTED WITH BEATRICE, Arthur, and Louischen[94] in the garden cottage, and at eleven we started for Arthur's Cairn, I on my pony "Jessie", Beatrice walking to the top. We were met by Arthur and Louischen, and went on to near the cairn, to the right of Campbell's path. I got off when we were near it; and here were assembled all the ladies and gentlemen, also Dr. Profeit, the keepers and servants belonging to the place with their families, and almost all our servants from the house. When we had got to the top and had our glasses filled, and were standing close to the cairn, Dr. Profeit, with a few appropriate words complimentary to Arthur, and with many good wishes for both, proposed their health, which was drunk with three times three. Then Arthur, with great readiness, returned thanks in a little speech. My health followed, also with loud cheering; and then Brown said they ought to drink the health of Princess Beatrice, which Cowley took up and proposed; and it was received with many cheers. Fern (who with the other dogs was there) resented the cheering, and barked very much. We all placed a stone on the cairn, on which was inscribed:

ARTHUR DUKE OF CONNAUGHT AND STRATHEARNE,
Married to Princess Louise Margaret of Prussia,
March 13, 1879.

After a few minutes we left, I walking down the whole way. We stopped at Dr. Profeit's on our way down, and here I got on my pony again.

Empress Eugenie: a sketch by Queen Victoria.

Abergeldie Castle.

Victoria and "Bertie" process at the gillies' ball at Abergeldie Castle; behind are the Princess of Wales and the Duke of Hesse.

Balmoral, October 6, 1879

AT TEN MINUTES PAST FOUR drove with the Empress Eugenie[95] (who had driven up from Abergeldie) in the victoria to the Glen Gelder Shiel,[96] or Ruidh na Bhan Righ (the Queen's Shiel). The evening was perfectly beautiful, warm, and clear, and bright. The Empress was pleased with the little Shiel, which contains only two small rooms and a little kitchen. It stands in a very wild solitary spot looking up to Loch-na-Gar, which towers up immediately above the house, though to reach Loch-na-Gar itself would take a very long time. We walked on along the footpath above the Gelder for a mile and a half, the dogs, which had come up, following us, and the Empress talked a great deal, and most pleasantly, about former times.

When we came back to the little Shiel, after walking for an hour, we had tea. Brown had caught some excellent trout and cooked them with oatmeal, which the dear Empress liked extremely, and said would be her dinner. It was a glorious evening—the hills pink, and the sky so clear.

We got back at twenty minutes past six, and the Empress drove back to Abergeldie with her lady.

LONDON AND NORTH WESTERN RAILWAY.

ARRANGEMENT OF CARRIAGES

COMPOSING

HER MAJESTY'S TRAIN

From BALLATER to WINDSOR,

ON TUESDAY, THE 6TH, AND WEDNESDAY, THE 7TH NOVEMBER, 1900.

	GUARD.	FOR MEN SERVANTS.	DRESSERS AND LADIES MAIDS.	COUNTESS OF LYTTON. HON. MRS. MALLET. HON. EVELYN MOORE. MISS BULTEEL.	Her Majesty AND PRINCESS HENRY OF BATTENBERG.	QUEEN'S DRESSERS.	PERSONAL SERVANTS.	PRINCESS VICTORIA OF BATTENBERG. FRAULEIN MARGRAF. HON. HARRIET PHIPPS.	PRINCE LEOPOLD AND MAURICE OF BATTENBERG AND ATTENDANTS. MR. THEOBALD.	SIR ARTHUR BIGGE. SIR THOMAS DENNEHY. CAPT. PONSONBY. SCROBON BANKART.	MAJOR COLBORNE. HERR VON PFYFFER. INDIAN ATTENDANTS.	FOR PAGES AND UPPER SERVANTS.	DIRECTORS.	DIRECTORS.	FOURGON.	GUARD.
ENGINE.	VAN. No. 210.	CARRIAGE No. 870.	SALOON. No. 73.	SALOON. No. 153.	Royal Saloon.			SALOON. No. 56.	SALOON. No. 50.	SALOON. No. 131.	SALOON. No. 71.	SALOON. No. 72.	SALOON. No. 180.	CARRIAGE No. 306.	TRUCK No. 100.	VAN. No. 272.

‹·············· 192 feet 8 inches ··············› ‹·············· 403 feet 5 inches ··············›

CONCLUSION

The two years after the death of John Brown were the saddest in the whole Balmoral story, and it was not to be until 1885 that laughter was heard again at Balmoral. In July Princess Beatrice married gay Prince Henry of Battenberg, whose elder brother Louis, serving in the British Navy, was already married to the Queen's favourite granddaughter, Victoria of Hesse.[1] Prince Henry conceded to the Queen's wish that he and his wife should live with her. In September the couple received a welcome on Deeside that rivalled the days when the Dukes of Edinburgh, Connaught and Albany first brought their wives to Scotland, and a new chapter of happiness began for the Queen. To her, the presence of a man about the house was an essential. Prince Henry exactly fitted the bill. He swept away the cobwebs, and he made her laugh.

The four children of Prince and Princess Henry of Battenberg—Alexander,[2] Ena,[3] Leopold[4] and Maurice[5]—provided the most important factor in the domestic life of their grandmother during her closing years. She gave to them an intimacy and understanding beyond that which she had extended to her own offspring.

Two of the Battenberg children—Ena and Maurice—were born and christened at Balmoral. The Princess was the first royal child to be born in Scotland since 1600, and there had not been a royal christening there since that of Prince Henry, son of James VI, in 1594. Prince Maurice was given the additional name of Donald, in compliment to Scotland.

Once again children rode their ponies up the tracks of Lochnagar. Once again there were picnics at Altnagiuthasach and the Glassalt Shiel. There were visits to the circus on Ballater moor, and in the evening entertainers came to the Castle.

In 1887, the Jubilee year, when commemorative brooches were presented to the staff and the tenants, and the Prince of Wales unveiled the statue of his mother in the grounds, a new interest came into the life of the Queen. It was while she was at Balmoral that she decided to engage some Indian servants. Sir Henry Ponsonby commented that she was as excited about them as a child would be with a new toy. Two were quickly picked out for particular favour. Their names were Abdul Karim and Mahomet.

From *The Queen*

Balmoral, Sep. 12, 1887

Sir Henry will see what he (Lord Dufferin) says about Indian servants. It is just what the Queen feels and she cannot say what a comfort she finds *hers*. Abdul is most handy in helping when she *signs* by drying the signatures. He learns with extraordinary assiduity and Mahomet is wonderfully quick and intelligent and understands everything.

Abdul Karim advanced to become the Queen's Indian Secretary and was thereafter known as the Munshi Hafiz Abdul Karim. A cottage was built for him near to the stables. The Munshi and the Indian attendants stayed with the Queen until the

The Queen's goodbye. Visiting the cottages, October 1900. S. Begg.

end of her reign. Their attentiveness, silence and premeditation of her every wish suited the Queen well in her declining years.

In 1889 a romance strengthened the Queen's family relations with Scotland, and also with the former owners of Balmoral. Princess Louise, eldest daughter of the Prince of Wales, and afterwards Princess Royal, became engaged to "Macduff", sixth Earl of Fife. On his wedding to Princess Louise at Buckingham Palace in July, the sixth Earl was created Duke of Fife. The Queen was delighted with the match in every way. In a letter to the Empress Frederick she wrote: "It is a very brilliant Marriage in a worldly point of view as he is immensely rich." When "Macduff" succeeded his father in 1879 his estates extended over 257,657 acres in Banffshire, Aberdeenshire, Morayshire and Forfarshire, with an annual rental of £78,000.

Although the Queen's age and health would no longer permit her to make expeditions by pony through the hills, she enjoyed long carriage drives, and nothing better than visiting her many friends in the cottages. Each year she made a round and distributed presents.

22nd Oct. 1888.—In the afternoon drove with Beatrice in the victoria, stopping to see good old Mrs. Leys, an aunt of Brown's, who is such a fine old woman. She said she was quite well, but her old husband was "dottled, and some bad in the temper." I brought her a shawl, and some tea and tobacco, which she particularly likes.

Visitors to Balmoral were now welcomed more warmly than had been the case during the Queen's long years of mourning. They included the Crown Prince of Germany,[6] the Rao of Kutch and the Queen of Roumania.

26th Aug. 1887—Dear Fritz came over from Braemar to luncheon—where he has been staying at the Fife Arms. It has done him so much good and he is wonderfully better, still hoarse, but not without any voice, as when he arrived in England. He seemed in excellent spirits.

27th Aug.—Breakfast in the Cottage, and afterwards drove to the village to call on some of the people, and bring them my annual presents, then back to the Cottage to write ... Fritz came over to luncheon again, and kindly helped me in receiving the Rao of Kutch and his brother, who have been staying for a month in the Highlands, having taken a moor. They lunched with us, but touched nothing but vegetables and fruit. They are very strict Hindus. They wore beautiful clothes and jewels. The Rao is most amiable, gentle, and unaffected, speaking very good English. His brother, who is seventeen, is also handsome, but very shy. Fritz took tea with us under the trees near the Cottage. It was so fine and warm and quite delightful. Drove Fritz back to Braemar, Beatrice and Irene[7] going with us. It was a most lovely evening.

2nd Oct. 1890.—I was delighted to see the Queen [of Roumania] again, which I had not done since '63. She has the same charming smile and bright eyes she always had, but her hair is very grey, and she wears it cut short ... After talking a little while we took the Queen to her rooms. Lunched at half-past one, and Bertie, Alix, Eddy,[8] and Victoria[9] were there. Bertie was staying at Sinaia with the King and Queen two years ago. She came up afterwards to my room, and sat some time talking with me. She is so full of cleverness and charm. She writes a great deal, poems, prose, plays, and all under the name of Carmen Silva. Her writings are immensely thought of. She spoke a great deal of her stay in Wales, with which she is delighted, and which she says has done her health so much good. She is full of sympathy and kindness, and takes a keen interest in everything. Drove to the Garrawalt and had tea at *Dantzig*.[10] Before dinner there was a torchlight procession, and reels were danced in front of the castle.

From 1890 until the death of Prince Henry of Battenberg in 1896, from fever contracted while serving with the Ashanti Expedition, the Queen recaptured some of the gaiety and zest for living which had been so apparent in her during her husband's lifetime.

11th Oct. 1890.—After dinner, the other ladies and gentlemen joined us in the Drawing-Room, and we pushed the furniture back and had a nice little impromptu dance, Curtis's band being so *entraînant*. We had a quadrille, in which I danced with Eddy!! It did quite well, then followed some waltzes and polkas.

Sir Henry Ponsonby recalled that the following year, when she was seventy-two, she danced on such an evening with Prince Henry of Battenberg—"light airy steps in the old courtly fashion; no limp or stick but every figure carefully and prettily danced."

The nights of the Gillies' ball were most important to the Queen, and if necessary she would postpone her departure from Scotland in order to attend. Formerly organised by John Brown, they were somewhat rowdy affairs attended by shouting. Licence was granted to the staff, and no comment was made if gait was unsteady or soup spilt at table. To the Queen they were more of rite than revelry. Her Private Secretary found them somewhat tiring and on one occasion absented himself on the grounds of work. "I didn't get back [to the ball] till 11.30 when I found some asperity at my absence. Explanations ensued, culminating in my dancing a Hooligan with the Queen."

To Balmoral, now, were bidden the strolling players. The first professional performance in the Castle was staged in 1891, the D'Oyly Carte Company presenting *The Mikado*, an achievement which necessitated considerable orchestral compression in the ballroom.

Two years later a distinguished company arrived on Deeside.

26th Oct. 1893.—The Empress [Eugenie] came directly after dinner and we all went down to the ballroom, where the play *Diplomacy*, translated from Sardou's *Dora*, was performed. It is in four acts, and was most admirably given by Mr. Hare's Company. Mr. Hare,[11] as "Henry Beauclerc", the elder brother of "Julian" (Mr. Forbes Robertson),[12] Mr. Arthur Cecil as "Baron Stein", and Mr. Bancroft[13] as "Count Orloff", as well as Mrs. Bancroft[14] as "Lady Henry Fairfax", and Miss Rorke as "Dora", were all excellent. The play is a most thrilling one, and the interest never flags for a moment. Mrs. Bancroft is a most clever and amusing actress; and her part, which in fact has nothing to do with the plot, helped to relieve the tension and severity of the piece. It took three hours, but seemed much less from being so deeply interesting. We went up as before to the Drawing-room and all the Company came in. The performers were all presented and I spoke to most of them. Miss Rorke, a pretty person, I spoke to about her old aunt, the celebrated Miss Woolgar, whom I had seen act in former days. Mr. Hare is a very modest, nice little man.

It was on 18th June 1895 that the Queen was present at the opening and dedication of the new Crathie Kirk. The cost of the building, some £6,000, had been met by private donations, including one from the Queen, and also by the considerable proceeds from a bazaar which had been held at Balmoral the previous September.

It was a most extraordinary bazaar. Its attendance was swelled by the aid of special trains run to Ballater, it was visited by the Queen five times in the two days of its duration, and the takings were near to £2,400. Princesses and royal Duchesses were among the stallholders, the two youngest being the daughters of the Duke of Connaught, "Daisy"[15] and "Patsy".[16] Princess Ena of Battenberg, dressed as "the old woman", sold dolls from the giant shoe. Her father took photographic studies at five shillings a time. Prince Arthur of Connaught picked out the winning raffle ticket.

The range of goods offered for sale was wide, from a plough valued at fifty pounds at one end of the scale to a penny "heather scrubber" at the other. Old women from the bothies contributed pieces of exquisitely worked lace and the lairds weighed in with grouse and haunches of venison.

A royal group at Balmoral in 1898: from left to right Princess Victoria of Schleswig-Holstein, the Princess Leiningen, Princess Victoria of Wales, Queen Victoria, Princess Henry of Prussia, Prince Waldemar of Prussia, Prince Maurice of Battenberg.

The Queen's autumn holiday in Scotland in 1896 was to include three events outstanding in the Balmoral story. The Emperor Nicholas II and the Empress Alexandra Feodorovna of Russia paid a visit to the Castle, being accompanied by a staff so large that a special village had to be built to house them. The Queen celebrated the day on which she had reigned longer than any other British Sovereign. And Mr. Downey took a moving picture of the Queen and her family and guests, thus making history as the first royal news film.

The Queen had wished to make it a quiet and informal visit, but the Prince of Wales considered it necessary to impress Russia and to foster good relations on account of British military activity in the Sudan. The result was a processional march from Ballater station which, long after, the Marquess of Carisbrooke was to describe as one of the most impressive sights he had ever witnessed. There were bonfires on every hill and the church bells were ringing as an escort of Scots Greys led the cavalcade of carriages along the Deeside road. Blazing torches, held high by Highland troops, made a path through the night, and at the approach to the Castle the Queen's pipers took their place, their music filling the valley.

22nd Sept. 1896.—Heard of Nicky and Alicky's safe disembarkation, and of their departure from Leith . . . Went down soon after half-past seven into the visitors' rooms, and waited there till we heard the church bells ringing and the pipes playing.

Punctually at eight, the procession reached the door. The escort of Scots Greys came first, then the pipers and torchbearers, and finally the carriage containing Nicky, Alicky, Bertie and Arthur. I was standing at the door. Nicky got out first, whom I embraced, and then darling Alicky, all in white, looking so well, whom I likewise embraced most tenderly. She went round and shook hands with everybody who was standing in the hall. A very smart Cossack had previously arrived, and was at the door. We all went into the Drawing-room, and Nicky's suite came in, Count Woronzoff Dashkoff, Prince Galitzine, Count Benckendorff. The dear baby[17] was then brought in, a most beautiful child, and so big, after which Nicky and Alicky went to their rooms, and I quickly dressed for dinner, to which we sat down a little before nine. It was a family one; Nicky, Alicky, Bertie, Arthur and Louischen, Beatrice, Georgie and May,[18] George Cambridge,[19] Thora[20] and Franzjos,[21] all the Princes being in uniform. Georgie, May and George C. came over from Glen Muick, where they are staying. It seems quite like a dream having dear Alicky and Nicky here.

23rd Sept.—To-day[22] is the day on which I have reigned longer, by a day, than any English sovereign, and the people wished to make all sort of demonstrations, which I asked them not to do until I had completed the sixty years next June. But notwithstanding that this was made public in the papers, people of all kinds and ranks, from every part of the kingdom, sent congratulatory telegrams, and they kept coming in all day. They were all most loyally expressed and some very prettily.

3rd Oct.—At twelve went down to below the terrace, near the ballroom, and we were all photographed by Downey[23] by the new cinematograph process,—which makes moving pictures by winding off a reel of films. We were walking up and down, and the children jumping about. Then took a turn in the pony chair, and not far from the garden cottage Nicky and Alicky planted a tree. In the afternoon drove out with them alas! for the last time, and went to Invercauld and back by the Balloch Bhui. It was rather showery and dark.

More and more now did the Queen turn, for her amusement and her relaxation, towards the youngest of her grandchildren and the great-grandchildren who followed so soon upon them. A particular favourite was the eldest child of the Duke and Duchess of York, born in 1894.

BALMORAL, 28th Sept. 1896.—Dear little David[24] with the baby[25] came in at the end of luncheon to say good-bye. David is a most attractive little boy, and so forward and clever. He always tries at luncheon time to pull me up out of my chair, saying, "Get up, Gangan," and then to one of the Indian servants, "Man pull it," which makes us laugh very much.

So she came to her Diamond Jubilee year, visiting Deeside in the spring to gather strength for the ardours which lay ahead. She liked to be at Balmoral for her birthday, and to take flowers, as she always did, to the statue of the Prince Consort and the grave of John Brown.

24th May 1897.—A fine morning. Dear Beatrice came in to me early, as usual on this day. My poor old birthday again came round, and it seems sadder each year, though I have such cause for thankfulness, and to be as well as I am, but fresh sorrow and trials still come upon me. My great lameness, etc., makes me feel how age is creeping on. Seventy-eight is a good age, but I pray yet to be spared a little longer for the sake of my country and dear ones.

Before breakfast the little children, Lenchen and Beatrice, gave me flowers and took me to my birthday table, which was covered with presents. I received some lovely things. Beatrice gave me such a pretty water-colour sketch, done by herself, of the place in front of the Monastery at Cimiez, bringing in the old cross. Innumerable kind letters and telegrams. Got out very late with Lenchen, Beatrice, and the two eldest children. On coming home the telegrams began to pour in in a most extraordinary manner, and this continued till late at night, not only from all relations, connections, and friends, but from all sorts of individuals, Public Bodies, Societies, etc.

Scotland had particular plans for the celebration of Jubilee day, 22nd June. For two weeks beforehand ten ponies carried materials for a bonfire on Ben Nevis. Brushwood came from the deer forest in Glen Nevis, and loads of peat from the Distillery mosses. A shower of "May" rockets was the signal for those in charge of bonfires on neighbouring hills to be ready. A few seconds before half past ten, Mrs. Cameron Campbell of Monzie touched a wire at the foot of the hill, and seconds later the huge beacon was a sheet of flame. Within minutes fires were blazing from hill and mountain top throughout Scotland.

The visits of Queen Victoria to Balmoral during the last three years of her life were dominated by anxiety over the military operations in which British troops were engaged in many areas, in the Sudan, at Fashoda, in India, in China, and—the territory which most concerned her—in South Africa, where the Boer War broke out on 11th October 1899. Balmoral moved onto a war footing, the Gillies' ball was cancelled, and the Queen's engagements were limited to inspecting troops before their departure for South Africa. Among them were her own guard of Gordon Highlanders.

19th Oct. 1899.—Drove with Anna and Franzjos[26] round by the Pass of Ballater, Beatrice following, driving herself with Louisa [Antrim].[27] Went back through Ballater to the barracks, where my guard of Gordon Highlanders were drawn up, having to start off for Edinburgh to join the rest of the regiment and embark for South Africa. I drove down the line, they marched past me and reformed in line. I addressed them a few parting words as follows: "I desire to wish you Godspeed. May God protect you! I am confident that you will always do your duty, and will ever maintain the high reputation of the Gordon Highlanders." The men then gave three cheers, and I called up Captain Kerr, who seemed much moved, and could hardly speak. I

Queen Victoria presenting colours to the 2nd Battalion of the
Seaforth Highlanders at Balmoral in
September 1899.

shook hands with him, and wished him a safe return, and I felt quite a lump in
my throat as we drove away, and I thought how these remarkably fine men
might not all return.

The Queen travelled to Windsor through the night of 10th November, and in
the morning inspected the composite Household Cavalry regiment. The years
seemed to have fallen away from her and her energy was unbounded. Then the tide
turned for the British forces, news of victories came in, and Mafeking was relieved.
True to her routine, the Queen travelled north so that she might spend her birthday
on Deeside.

BALMORAL, 24th May 1900.—Again my old birthday returns, my
eighty-first! God has been very merciful and supported me, but my trials and
anxieties have been manifold, and I feel tired and upset by all I have gone
through this winter and spring. Beatrice came in early with a nosegay to
congratulate me. Had my present table in my sitting-room, and received so
many pretty things. Bertie and Alix gave me a lovely chain to wear in the day-
time, a beautiful screen, and the Duke of Wellington's hands in bronze, from
the Peel sale, which I am very glad to have. I have not the time to describe all
the other gifts. All in the house dined, including Sir Walter Parratt and Mr.

Forbes. After my health had been drunk, I proposed that of the Army in South Africa. We had some nice music after dinner.

The number of telegrams to be opened and read was quite enormous, and obliged six men to be sent for to help the two telegraphists in the house. The answering of them was an interminable task, but it was most gratifying to receive so many marks of loyalty and affection. Some of the telegrams were very touchingly worded, and they came from every part of the world. I had a nice one from Lord Roberts, and from the Household Cavalry.

The Queen was losing her appetite, but Lord James, who was in attendance, found her unchanged in mind, very cheerful, smart in conversation and still able to enjoy an anecdote. Her thoughts were entirely absorbed with the war. But when he returned to the same duty at Balmoral in the autumn he found a very different woman. "The Queen had lost much flesh, and had shrunk so as to appear about one-half of the person she had been. Her spirits, too, had apparently left her . . ."

17th Sept. 1900.—Drove with Irène and May to the Birkhall approach, where we took our tea, which for me consists of arrowroot and milk. I have not been feeling very well these last days, and can eat very little. This has been a great trouble for some time past.

She had been further depressed by the death, in July, of her second son, the Duke of Saxe-Coburg and Gotha, and by the sufferings of the Empress Frederick, who had developed cancer. A further blow came at the end of October when her grandson, Prince Christian Victor, who was serving in South Africa, died of enteric fever.

1st Nov. 1900.—This morning the beloved boy was to be laid to rest, with the soldiers he loved so well, and there were to be services at St. George's Chapel and at the Chapel Royal. We went at twelve to the church here, where there was a simple touching service, much the same as we had for dear Affie at Osborne. I was much moved. A great number of people were present, all the neighbours, and my own people, who show the greatest feeling. The sun was shining brightly, which was very pleasant, and made it less gloomy, but my tears flowed again and again.

A few more days to go before she went back to Windsor. She drove round the cottages, saying goodbye. A little girl told a magazine reporter: "One of the men came to the door and told my grandmother the Queen wished to see her. My grandmother was washing, and she wiped her hands and went round to where the Queen was waiting. The Queen said: 'I have come to say good-bye to you, and I hope you will have a comfortable winter, and keep well till I come back.'"

But Queen Victoria was very tired, and she did not come back—she died on 22nd January, 1901.

NOTES

Part one

1 Lady-in-waiting.
2 Maid of Honour.
3 Equerry to the Queen.
4 Equerry to Prince Albert.
5 Private Secretary to Prince Albert.
6 Lord Steward of the Household.
7 Lord-in-waiting.
8 Physician to the Queen.
9 Adolphus, son of George III.
10 Master of the Horse.
11 First Lord of the Admiralty.
12 Colonel Commandant of the Royal Regiment of Artillery.
13 Senior Naval Lord, afterwards Admiral of the Fleet.
14 Daughter of William Darling, keeper of the Longstone lighthouse. When the *Forfarshire* struck the Farne Islands in September 1838, with the loss of 43 lives, father and daughter rowed to the wreck in their coble and rescued four men and a woman. Both received the Gold Medal of the Humane Society. Grace Darling died of consumption on 20th October 1842.
15 5th Duke (1806–1884). Captain-General of the Royal Company of Archers. Lord Lieutenant of Mid-Lothian and Co. Roxburgh.
16 Afterwards 8th Earl of Wemyss. Lord Lieutenant of Peeblesshire.
17 Shortly before there had been a case of scarlet fever in the family of Lord Strathmore, who had apartments in Holyrood Palace, and the doctors considered that there was risk of infection to visitors.
18 Shortly after the royal procession had passed along Bank Street, a temporary stand collapsed. Fifty people were injured, two fatally.
19 4th Earl (1783–1868). Lord Lieutenant of Linlithgowshire.
20 Royal governess.
21 8th Marquess (1832–1870). His father had died the previous year.
22 10th Earl. Created Marquess of Dalhousie in 1849 (1812–1860).
23 In 1400.
24 5th Earl (1803–1843).
25 In 1568.
26 10th Earl (1785–1866). Lord Lieutenant of Perthshire.
27 4th Earl (1806–1898). Lord Lieutenant of Co. Clackmannan.
28 The long absence of sovereigns from Scotland created problems for the Lord Provost, C. G. Sidey, who demanded guidance from the Lord Chamberlain's Department as to which side of the carriage the Queen sat, which knee was to be bent, the position of his carriage in the procession, and when he was to put on his *Chapeau de bras*.
29 Afterwards 6th Duke of Atholl (1814–1864).
30 2nd Marquess and 5th Earl (1796–1862). Lord Lieutenant of Argyllshire. As the Queen reached the door she called to him: "Keeper, what a quantity of fine Highlandmen you have got."
31 Sir Neil Menzies (1780–1844). Lieutenant-Colonel, Royal Highland Perthshire local militia.
32 Afterwards Duchess of Argyll.
33 Afterwards 8th Duke of Argyll (1823–1900).
34 A new wing had been built and opened in honour of the visit. The initials and date, "V.R. 1842", are painted on the ceiling of the apartments used by the Queen.
35 To the delight of the woman in charge, the Queen accepted some milk and a piece of bread.
36 Lairig Eala.
37 19th Baron Willoughby de Eresby (1782–1865). Married the daughter and sole heiress of James Drummond, 1st Lord Perth.

38   The Queen's half-brother, Prince Leiningen (1804–1856).

39   8th Viscount (1767–1851). Restored his honours by Act of Parliament, 1824.

40   8th Earl. Murdered by the King's own hands, 22nd February 1452.

41   2nd Earl (1795–1873).

42   656 horses were engaged in conveying the Queen and her suite to and from Taymouth Castle.

43   On this day the Freedom of the City of Edinburgh was conferred on Prince Albert. Dr Lee, Principal of the University, also delivered to him the diploma of an honorary LLD.

44   Died 1342, being starved to death in Hermitage Castle by Sir William Douglas.

45   Duchess of Kent.

46   Princess Alice, born 25th April 1843.

47   Prince Alfred, born 6th August 1844.

48   The name by which the Prince of Wales was known in the family.

49   Victoria, Princess Royal.

50   Hon. Charlotte Stuart, eldest daughter of Lord Stuart de Rothsay.

51   Afterwards Lady Caroline Courtenay. Maid of Honour.

52   4th Earl of Aberdeen (1784–1860). Foreign Secretary.

53   Composed of honey, whisky and milk.

54   "The Humble Petition of Bruar Water to Noble Duke of Athole."

55   At this point the horses of a carriage following the Queen became restive, began to plunge forward, and all but collided with the royal carriage. When an equerry told the Queen that there had been no damage done, she said, "This is a pretty job, certainly," and asked which of the horses had been the culprit. The equerry replied: "It was Wasp." "I thought as much," commented the Queen: "It was like him."

56   The ponies used by the Queen, Prince Albert and the Princess Royal were presented to them by Lord Glenlyon at the end of the visit.

57   Chief Equerry and Clerk Marshal to the Queen.

58   In 1689.

59   John Graham of Claverhouse. Carried to Blair Castle, he died that night.

60   A title belonging to the eldest son of the Sovereign of Scotland and therefore held by the Prince of Wales as eldest son of the Queen, the representative of the ancient kings of Scotland.

61   8th Duke, succeeding his father in 1847. He had married the eldest daughter of the 2nd Duke of Sutherland in 1844.

62   Afterwards 3rd Duke of Sutherland (1828–1892).

63   Afterwards 9th Duke of Argyll. He married in 1871 Princess Louise, fourth daughter of Queen Victoria.

64   King of Scotland (1198–1249). He died at Kerrera while on an expedition to reduce the Western Isles, which were then dependent on Norway.

65   2nd Marquess (1791–1868).

66   February 1692.

67   12th Baron (1802–1875). Lord Lieutenant of Inverness-shire.

68   2nd Marquess and 1st Duke of Abercorn (1811–1815). Groom of the Stole to Prince Albert.

69   Later replaced by an iron bridge.

70   Lord Abercorn had rented a deer forest on a long lease from Cluny Macpherson and the house by Loch Laggan from Lord Henry Bentinck. The influx of guests stretched the accommodation of Ardverikie to the limit, and the four eldest children, two boys and two girls, were moved from their comfortable nursery to cramped quarters in the home farm in order to make room for the royal children. This upset four-year-old Claud considerably. Lady Abercorn took her children to present them to the Queen, the girls dressed in their best frocks and the boys in kilts. The three eldest children behaved impeccably, but Claud, resenting his expulsion from the nursery, refused to bow. Instead, he stood upon his

head, the top half of him being naked. It was a trick of which he was very proud, and only force brought him back to his feet. The Queen was far from amused. He was taken away, lectured, expressed his penitence, and was once more taken to the Queen. Again he stood on his head, and consequently was in disgrace for the remainder of the royal visit. In after years Lord Claud Hamilton became a Member of Parliament and a Lord of the Treasury. From 1887 to 1897 he was ADC to the Queen.

71 In a letter to the Duchess of Kent, Prince Albert wrote of Ardverikie: "The reporters call it an 'un-come-at-able place', because they are quartered on the other side of Loch Laggan, which is only to be crossed on a flying bridge, that belongs exclusively to ourselves."

72 Sir Edwin Landseer was a frequent guest of Lord and Lady Abercorn. Owing to the isolated position of Ardverikie, the interior decoration was simple, the walls being whitewashed. Landseer complained that the glare hurt his eyes. One day he asked for a set of steps and began decorating the dining-room with frescoes in colour. He continued until all the offending walls were covered with his drawings. The originals of "The Monarch of the Glen", "The Challenge" and "The Sanctuary" appeared as mural decoration at Ardverikie. They were lost when the house was destroyed by fire on 17th October 1873.

73 Opened in 1822.

74 Lord Adolphus FitzClarence, Captain of the Royal Yacht. He was a natural son of William IV.

75 Prince Albert's ghillie.

76 Head-keeper, who had been nearly twenty years with Sir Robert Gordon.

77 A groom.

78 1st Earl (1792–1878). Prime Minister 1846–1852.

79 Rear-Admiral Sir W. E. Parry (1790–1855). Arctic explorer, author of *Narrative of the Attempt to reach the North Pole*, etc. The Queen's statement was an exaggeration.

80 Sir Archibald Alison (1792–1867). Author of *History of Europe*.

81 7th Duke (1798–1859). He was living at the time at Mar Lodge.

82 Afterwards 5th Earl Fife (1814–1879). He married in 1846 Lady Agnes Georgina Hay, daughter of the Earl of Erroll and his wife Lady Elizabeth Fitzclarence, daughter of William IV and Mrs Jordan.

83 Afterwards the Hon. Mrs Parnell.

84 Afterwards Duchess of Wellington.

85 The Queen's nephew. Married Marie, Princess of Baden.

86 The history of the Braemar Gathering goes back for a thousand years, and began with Braemar's importance as a gathering point, for it is a centre for drove roads and tracks which lead out through the hills in all directions. It was to the Braes of Mar that Malcolm III (known as *Ceanmor* or *Great Head*), who ascended the throne in 1058 and was killed at Alnwick in 1093, summoned the clans so that he might select, by competition, "his hardiest soldiers and his fleetest messengers". It was at Braemar in September 1715 that John Erskine, 6th Earl of Mar, leader of the adherents of James Edward, the Old Pretender, proclaimed James VIII King of Scotland, England, France and Ireland, an ill-fated venture which ended at the Battle of Sherriffmuir. A century later people gathered at Braemar for a very different purpose. Under the aegis of the Braemar Wrights Friendly Society, meetings were held every quarter for the purpose of collecting subscriptions to help the sick and the old, widows and orphans. It was an early, and very worthy, experiment in social insurance. In 1826 the Society broadened its interests and became

the Braemar Highland Society. Its aims now included the preservation of the kilt and the language and culture of the Highlands, and the promotion of sport. Each year a gathering, known as the "Wrights' Walk", took place. Then a procession, headed by pipers, made its way to a selected spot, and the members enjoyed piping and dancing and joined in athletic competitions. The royal association began in 1848 when Queen Victoria attended the Gathering at Invercauld. Later the Queen bestowed the honour of royal patronage on the Society. She contributed to its funds and retained her keen interest in the Gathering throughout her long life. During her reign the Games were held at Braemar Castle, Balmoral, Invercauld House or Old Mar Lodge. In 1906 the Duke of Fife presented the existing twelve-acre site.

87 Afterwards Sir Charles Forbes, of Castle Newe.

88 After the race the winner, and other contestants, spat blood as a result of their exertions. Duncan, who became a keeper in 1851, never fully recovered from the strain. As a result the up-hill race was discontinued.

89 In 1848 Lord Aberdeen had asked Dr Robertson to make arrangements for the reception of the Queen at Balmoral. Thereafter he undertook the management of the Deeside estates, being appointed Commissioner in Scotland for the Queen, Prince Albert and, later, for the Prince of Wales, a combined post which he held for nearly thirty years.

90 It was at this point in her diary that Queen Victoria introduced to her readers, by means of a footnote, her ghillie, John Brown, whose name was to be written indelibly into the story not only of Balmoral but also of the Queen's life during the period 1864–1883, the year of Brown's death. During these twenty years he rarely left the Queen's side. The footnote was written in 1867. It reads:
*The same who, in 1858, became my regular attendant out of doors everywhere in the Highlands; who commenced as gillie in 1848, and was selected by Albert and me to go in my carriage. In 1851 he entered our service permanently, and began in that year leading my pony, and advanced step by step by his good conduct and intelligence. His attention, care, and faithfulness cannot be exceeded; and the state of my health, which of late years has been sorely tried and weakened, renders such qualifications most valuable, and indeed, most needful in a constant attendant upon all occasions. He has since (in December, 1865), most deservedly, been promoted to be an upper servant, and my permanent personal attendant. He has all the independence and elevated feelings peculiar to the Highland race, and is singularly straightforward, simple-minded [sic], kind-hearted, and disinterested; always ready to oblige; and of a discretion rarely to be met with. He is now in his fortieth year. His father was a small farmer, who lived at the Bush on the opposite side to Balmoral. He is the second of nine brothers,—three of whom have died—two are in Australia and New Zealand, two are living in the neighbourhood of Balmoral; and the youngest, Archie (Archiebald) is valet to our son Leopold, and is an excellent, trustworthy young man.

91 A shooting lodge between Braemar and the Linn of Dee.

92 14th Earl (1799–1869). First Lord of the Treasury, 1852.

93 Afterwards Earl and Countess of Fife.

94 Appointed Queen's Piper in 1843, and considered to be one of the best in Scotland. He went out of his mind in 1854 and died the following year.

95 A keeper, who always led the dogs when Prince Albert went stalking.

96　The Minister of Crathie and his wife. The Rev. Mr Anderson died in 1866. Both he and his dog were well known characters on Deeside. Mrs Patricia Lindsay recounts: "One member of the congregation in those times used to excite much interest and amusement among strangers. This was the Minister's collie, who was a regular attendant at church, following Mr Anderson up the pulpit steps and quietly lying down at the top. He was always a most decorous, though possibly somnolent, listener, but he was also an excellent time keeper, for if the sermon was a few minutes longer than usual Towser got up and stretched himself, yawning audibly. When the Queen first came, Mr Anderson feared she might object to such an unorthodox addition to the congregation, and shut up Towser on Sunday. Her Majesty next day sent an equerry to the Manse to inquire if anything had happened to the dog, as she had a sketch of the interior of the church in which he appeared lying beside the pulpit, and if he were alive and well, she would like to see him in his old place. Greatly to Towser's delight he was thus by royal command restored to Church privileges."

97　Princess Victoria, the Princess Royal.

98　So named as at this spot lay the levers of an old saw-mill which had been demolished some forty years earlier.

99　Dr Norman McLeod returned to preach at Balmoral on a number of occasions. Not only did the Queen turn to him for support after the death of her husband, but she valued his views on religious matters in Scotland. He died in 1872.

100　A Cabinet Minister was always in attendance upon the Queen at Balmoral.

101　Afterwards Crown Prince of Prussia and Emperor Frederick of Germany. Princess Victoria, the Princess Royal, was born on 21st November 1840.

102　Jane Lady Churchill, who became a Lady of the Bedchamber in 1854. Until her sudden death on Christmas Day 1900 Lady Churchill remained in constant attendance upon the Queen.

103　Willie Blair was known as the Queen's fiddler. He was an essential guest at every festive gathering on Deeside, for not only was he unrivalled in playing for the reels but he was also a composer. One of his dance tunes was called "The Brig of Crathie". A wag and a stern critic of the dancers, he lived to be over ninety. Mrs Patricia Lindsay recalled of him: "So much was Willie in social request that over-conviviality was apt to follow. When this occurred he always made his way at once to the Manse to take what is called in Scotland 'the first word o' flytin'', for the minister had often warned Willie against over-indulgence on festive occasions when the whisky bottle circulated too freely. Asking to see the minister, he would say, 'I've been ower to a dance at the Inver, Mr. Anderson, and I jist came on my wye hame tha ye micht see me, in case ye sud hear I wis waur nor I am.' "

104　Princess Helena. Born 1846.

105　On the 14th the Prince Consort had presided over the meeting of the British Association at Aberdeen.

106　"Shiel" means a small shooting lodge.

107　Private Secretary to the Prince Consort.

108　Daughter of Jean, Duchess of Gordon.

109　Princess Alice had become engaged to Prince Louis of Hesse and the Rhine on 30th November 1860.

110　11th Earl, 2nd Baron Panmure (1801–1874). Secretary at War, 1846–1852 and 1855–1858.

111　This originally belonged to the extinct town of Kincardine.

112　Lord Lieutenant of Kincardine.

113　The Duchess of Kent died on 16th March 1861.

114   Prince Louis of Hesse.

115   A felt hat with a broad brim.

116   Lady-in-Waiting.

117   The fording of the Poll Tarff was the subject for a drawing by Carl Haag.

118   The death of the Duchess of Kent.

119   Princess Helena.

120   Prince Albert, the Prince Consort, died at Windsor Castle on 14th December 1861. These sad words were added by the Queen in 1867 as she read her Highland Journal prior to the publication of the first volume, which ended at this point.

Part two

1   Princesses Helena and Louise.

2   Princess Alice and Prince Louis of Hesse and the Rhine were married at Osborne in July 1862.

3   Crown Prince and Princess Frederick William of Prussia were staying at Abergeldie with their children, William (afterwards German Emperor), born 1859, Charlotte (afterwards Duchess of Saxe-Meiningen), born 1860, and Henry, born 1862.

4   Smith was pensioned in 1864 and died two years later, having been thirty-one years in royal service.

5   Details of the accident were kept secret, and when Mr Gladstone, who was at Balmoral, informed Lord Palmerston he was reprimanded by the Queen. He warned against the dangers of such night drives, but she replied that her actions were based on those which had been practised by her husband, and she had no intention of altering them.

6   Princess Beatrice, born 1857.

7   Prince Leopold, born 1853.

8   Jane, Marchioness of Ely. Lady of the Bedchamber.

9   Boundary.

10   Died 16th January 1864.

11   In the eighth century the Culdees owned a monastery at Dunkeld. Four hundred years later David I converted it into a cathedral. It was unroofed during the Reformation, and fell into ruin. (In 1918 it was given to the nation by the Duke of Atholl.) Among its famous bishops was Gavin Douglas (1474–1522), translator of the *Aeneid*. After the Battle of Killiecrankie the Cameronian regiment was stationed at Dunkeld, under command of Colonel William Cleland. Attacked by 5000 Highlanders, Cleland posted his men in the cathedral and in the grounds of the Earl of Atholl's house. The Highlanders were forced to withdraw, but Cleland lost his life when leading a sortie.

12   Sir William Drummond-Stewart (1796–1871).

13   Sir William Napier (1785–1860). Soldier and military historian.

14   Princess Louise, born 1848.

15   This was a favourite view-point of Sir Walter Scott and here he climbed with Washington Irving to look out over Borderland. George Eyre-Todd, in *Byways of the Scottish Border*, wrote in 1886: "The supernatural lore with which the whole countryside is invested has a legend to account for the strange shape of the mountain. It seems that Michael Scott (the wizard) at one time found himself compelled to provide occupation for a certain troublesome fiend. First he set the latter to build a dam across the Tweed. This behest, however, to the wizard's surprise and dismay, was accomplished in a single night. The result is still to be seen near Kelso. A more formidable command seemed to be to 'cleave Eildon Hill in three'. But the too energetic familiar accomplished this second herculean feat likewise in a night; and he was only found in constant employment finally by being set the somewhat unsatisfactory task of manufacturing ropes out of sea-sand."

16   The gardener, Hector Rose, later became head gardener at Windsor.

17 Lord Lieutenant of Selkirkshire; Lord-in-Waiting to the Queen.

18 In 1812 two stone coffins were found in a small aisle south of the chancel. On one of them was a carving of a St John's cross and inside was the skeleton of a man six feet tall. The bones were identified by tradition as those of the wizard of six centuries before.

19 In 1832.

20 Afterwards 7th Duke of Roxburghe.

21 Sister of the above. Married, 1857, Sir James Grant-Suttie.

22 6th Duke of Richmond (1818–1903). Lord Lieutenant of Co. Banff. President of the Board of Trade. Created Duke of Gordon and Earl of Kinrara, 1876.

23 A shooting lodge belonging to the Duke of Richmond.

24 Near Balmoral, not far from Loch Bulig.

25 Extract from the Queen's Journal, 15th October 1839: "At about ½ p. 12 I sent for Albert; he came to the Closet where I was alone, and after a few minutes I said to him, that I thought he must be aware *why* I wished him to come here, — and that it would make me *too happy* if he would consent to what I wished (to marry me). We embraced each other, and he was *so* kind, *so* affectionate . . ."

26 Prince Arthur, born 1850.

27 John Brown's fourth brother.

28 John Brown's eldest brother.

29 Afterwards General Sir Henry Ponsonby. Private Secretary to the Queen.

30 In 1868.

31 Previously known as Drunkie House. The change was made as "Drunkie" was not considered a suitable name for a house where the Queen was to stay.

32 The residence of Mary Queen of Scots for a few months before her departure for France at the age of five.

33 The Queen rode him up to the top of the Rigi (near Lucerne), 5000 feet high, in 1868.

34 A Scottish word for quarrels or "rows", but taken from fights between "collies".

35 John Douglas Sutherland, Marquis of Lorne, was the twenty-five-year-old heir to the 8th Duke of Argyll. He succeeded his father as 9th Duke in 1900, and died in 1914. Not since Mary, youngest daughter of Henry VII, married the Duke of Suffolk in 1515 had a princess married, with the sovereign's official sanction, outside the confines of a reigning house.

36 1st Baron Hatherley (1801–1881).

37 Maid of Honour.

38 Groom-in-Waiting.

39 Governess.

40 Commanding the forces in Scotland.

41 Mr Duncan Anderson, Keeper of the Chapel-Royal and author of *Historical Guide to the Palace and Abbey of Holyrood*.

42 8th Earl (1828–1880).

43 The 4th Earl, the distinguished statesman who had played a part in the purchase of Balmoral, died in 1860. His heir survived him by only four years. The 6th Earl, born in 1841, led a life of romantic adventure and was drowned on a journey from Boston to Melbourne in 1870. He was succeeded by his brother, John Campbell (1847–1934), Governor-General of Canada 1883–1888.

44 King of the Belgians.

45 Beauty, so called from the French "Beau lieu".

46 3rd Duke (1828–1892).

47 Youngest brother of the 3rd Duke. MP for Sutherland.

48 Anna, daughter of John Hay-Mackenzie. Married 1849. Created, 1861, Countess of Cromartie, Viscountess Tarbat, etc., in her own right. Died 1888.

49 The 2nd Duke died in 1861 and his wife, Mistress of the Robes to the Queen, in 1868. Lord Ronald Gower, in *My Reminiscences*, recalls that his parents had prepared rooms in the

expectation of a visit to Dunrobin of the Queen and the Prince Consort.

50 MP for St Germains and the Northern Burghs; Governor of Forth and Clyde Canals; factor at Dunrobin. His youngest son, Henry Brougham, was created first Baron Loch.

51 In *Henry Ponsonby: His Life from his Letters*, Arthur Ponsonby commented: "The Duke of Sutherland had purposely, but without warning, invited H. M. Stanley, the explorer, in order that he might be presented to the Queen. There happened to be at the time a considerable controversy about Stanley's reliability owing to his practice of self-advertisement and sides were hotly taken in public. Lord Granville, who was in attendance, and Ponsonby, and indeed the Queen herself, were greatly annoyed at being trapped into a recognition of and consequently conferring an honour on Stanley. The Duke refused to yield. When it was found there was no way out, it culminated in Stanley being presented and receiving a gold snuff-box with brilliants."

52 Another favourite collie. Noble died on 18th September 1887. His monument is among the memorials to dogs at Balmoral.

53 5th Baronet (1831–1914). MP for Monmouth. Under-Secretary for War, 1857–1858.

54 Richard Ansdell (1818–1885). Popular painter of animal and sporting pictures. An example of his best work is "Stag at Bay" (1846).

55 3rd Baron (1826–1892). Lieutenant-General. Married, 1863, Ella, daughter of Commodore Magruder, US Navy.

56 At the time of the illness of the Prince of Wales in 1871.

57 The seizure of the *Arrow* by Commissioner Yeh in 1856 brought Britain into war with China. Lord Elgin went as special envoy with the resulting expedition.

58 Earl Charles John Canning (1812–1862). Governor-General of India 1856; Viceroy 1858.

59 In August 1746 Prince Charles Edward joined Lochiel and Cluny Macpherson, hiding with them until two French ships arrived at Loch-na-nuagh and he was able to escape to France.

60 In conversation with Lord Macaulay, Queen Victoria referred to "my ancestor, Charles I". Back came the crushing retort: "You mean your Majesty's predecessor." The Queen's claim to the throne was owing to her descent from Elizabeth, daughter of James VI & I.

61 Highland servant of the Queen since 1870, and cousin to Brown.

62 20th Earl (1818–1884).

63 The heroic poet of the Gaels, the son of Fingal, who is said to have lived in the third century.

64 Drinking vessel.

65 *Chrysanthemum leucanthemum*, white ox-eye daisy.

66 *Chrysanthemum segetum*, yellow ox-eye or corn marigold.

67 Second wardrobe maid, a native of Balmoral.

68 7th Earl (1851–1922). Treasurer of the Queen's Household 1880–1885.

69 Princess Louise and the Marquess of Lorne.

70 8th Duke (1823–1900). Married, 1844, Lady Elizabeth Georgiana, daughter of 2nd Duke of Sutherland.

71 The Duke of Argyll was the Keeper. It was at Dunstaffnage that the "Stone of Destiny", now contained in the Coronation Chair at Westminster Abbey, was kept before its removal to Scone. Princess Louise was particularly interested in the historic castle and, after her husband succeeded as 9th Duke, an appeal was opened for its restoration.

72 At Edinburgh in 1661.

73 1721–1795. One-time Commander-in-Chief.

74 Between 1744 and 1761.

75 Elizabeth Gunning, widow of the 6th Duke of Hamilton.

76 1671–1734. In the 1715 rising the famous Highland outlaw sided with the Pretender. Although he took no active part in the Battle of Sheriffmuir he was included in the Act of Attainder. He made submission at Inveraray and, through the influence of the Duke of Argyll, obtained a promise of protection.

77 Elizabeth, Duchess of Argyll, died 1878.

78 When Queen Victoria visited Lucerne in 1868 she stayed at the Villa Wallace, which stood on a hill overlooking the town, with the Rigi to the left and Mont Pilatus, distinguished by its serrated edges, to the right.

79 Prince Arthur, created Duke of Connaught in 1874. At this time he was a major in the 7th Hussars, and living at the Piers Hill Barracks, near Edinburgh, where his regiment was quartered.

80 The Duchess of Kent was staying at Cramond, in a house overlooking the Firth of Forth.

81 Prince Leopold's valet.

82 Afterwards Viscount Cross.

83 Keeper of the Privy Purse.

84 This march was always played for Prince Albert, and was originally composed for his and the Queen's grand-uncle, Field-Marshal Prince Francis Josias of Saxe-Coburg-Saalfeld.

85 The Queen explained: "When we went on board the *Thunderer*, August 12, at Osborne, Brown had fallen through an open place inside the turret, and got a severe hurt on the shin. He afterwards damaged it again, when it was nearly healed, by jumping off the box of the carriage, so that when he came to Balmoral about a fortnight afterwards, it was very bad, and he was obliged to take care of it for some days previous to the fresh journey."

86 Louis Napoleon, only child of Emperor Napoleon III and the Empress Eugenie. Born in 1856.

With the end of the Franco-Prussian War and the fall of France the Prince Imperial joined his parents in exile at Chislehurst, Kent, where the Emperor died in 1873. The Prince Imperial was educated at the Royal Military Academy, Woolwich, from 1872 to 1875. Thereafter his name was coupled romantically with that of Princess Beatrice. In 1879 he volunteered for service in South Africa, where the Zulu war had broken out. He was given permission to accompany the troops in the capacity of spectator and observer, attached to the staff of Lord Chelmsford.

87 Wife of Sir Bartle Frere, Governor of Cape Colony and High Commissioner for South Africa.

88 Field-Marshal Sir Henry Evelyn Wood (1838–1919).

89 Lord-Lieutenant of Kent, Lord Steward to HM Household.

90 Chancellor of the Exchequer; afterwards Earl of Iddesleigh.

91 Wife of the 18th Earl; Lady-in-Waiting.

92 On the night of 28th December 1879, in a violent gale, a portion of the Tay Bridge, together with a train which was crossing it, was blown into the firth. Some seventy-five lives were lost.

93 The coffin of the Prince Imperial, on board HMS *Orontes*, arrived at Spithead on 11th July, full military honours being paid, including a salute of twenty-three guns, one for each year of his age. At the funeral at Chislehurst the Prince of Wales acted as pall-bearer. The coffin was placed in St Mary's Chapel, Chislehurst, beside that of his father. When the Empress moved to Farnborough both coffins were moved in 1888 to the mausoleum which she built there.

94 Duchess of Connaught.

95 The Empress was staying at Abergeldie, to which the Queen had urged her to come for a little quiet and change of air after the shock of her son's death.

96   The lodge of "the clear water burn".
     The Gelder joins the Dee above the
     Castle.

Conclusion notes

1   Princess Alice, Grand Duchess of
    Hesse, died in 1878. Thereafter the
    Queen watched over Princess
    Victoria and her brothers and sisters.
2   Marquess of Carisbrooke, born
    1886, died 1960.
3   Queen Victoria Eugenia of Spain,
    born 1887, died 1969.
4   Lord Leopold Mountbatten, born
    1889, died 1922.
5   Born 1891, killed in action 1914.
6   It was hoped that the Deeside air
    would benefit the throat disease from
    which he was suffering, but only too
    soon afterwards the disease was to be
    confirmed as cancer. He succeeded
    his father as Emperor Frederick III in
    March 1888 and died in June of
    that year.
7   Princess Irene of Hesse. Married,
    1888, Prince Henry of Prussia.
8   Prince Albert Victor, Duke of
    Clarence.
9   Princess Victoria of Wales.
10 The shiel in the Ballochbuie Forest,
    near the Falls of Garbh-allt.
11 Afterwards Sir John Hare.
12 Afterwards Sir J. Forbes-Robertson.
13 Afterwards Sir Squire Bancroft.
14 Afterwards Lady Bancroft.
15 Princess Margaret, afterwards Crown
    Princess of Sweden.
16 Princess Victoria Patricia, afterwards
    Lady Patricia Ramsay.
17 Grand Duchess Olga.
18 Duke and Duchess of York.
19 Duke of Cambridge.
20 Princess Victoria of Schleswig-
    Holstein.
21 Prince Francis Joseph of Battenberg.
22 The previous longest reign had been
    that of George III—25th October
    1760 to 29th January 1820.
23 The royal photographer. The film was
    shown in the Red Drawing-room at
    Windsor on 23rd November.
24 Prince Edward, afterwards Edward
    VIII and Duke of Windsor.
25 Prince Albert ("Bertie"), born 1895.
    Afterwards George VI.
26 Prince and Princess Francis Joseph of
    Battenberg.
27 Countess of Antrim, Lady of the
    Bedchamber.

ACKNOWLEDGEMENTS

The editor and publishers would like to thank the following for their kind permission to reproduce illustrations in this book:

Reproduced by Gracious Permission of Her Majesty the Queen: 10, 21 (centre and bottom), 33, 34, 35, 42, 51, 52, 61 (lower), 62, 69, 73, 75 (upper), 79 (upper), 80, 81 (upper), 83, 84 (left), 85, 86, 95, 96, 97, 99, 103, 104, 108, 111, 116, 119, 125, 128 (lower), 137, 138 (upper), 140, 142, 155, 158, 162, 165, 196, 224

M. J. F. Barnett: 21 (top)

Ernest J. Cooke: 156, 189, 190, 207, 208

David Duff: 7, 14, 20, 29, 41, 64, 79 (lower), 84 (right), 118, 123, 138 (lower), 144, 212, 213, 216, 218

Mary Evans Picture Library: 13, 16, 19, 22, 23 (lower), 26, 28, 32, 36, 39, 40, 43, 46, 47, 48, 49, 50, 54, 56, 57, 58, 65, 66, 67, 93, 113, 115, 127, 129, 133, 135, 146, 161, 181, 184, 201, 210, 211, 214, 221

The Mansell Collection: 23 (upper), 45, 81 (lower), 82, 91, 98, 102, 126, 128 (upper), 131, 152, 160, 169, 176, 183, 199, 205

John Topham Picture Library: 27, 31, 55, 61, 75 (lower), 147, 163, 173, 186

INDEX